DICTIONARY
OF
POPULAR
SLANG

THE JONATHAN DAVID

DICTIONARY OF POPULAR SLANG

by
ANITA PEARL

jD JONATHAN DAVID PUBLISHERS, INC.
MIDDLE VILLAGE, NEW YORK 11379

THE JONATHAN DAVID
DICTIONARY OF POPULAR SLANG
by
Anita Pearl

Copyright © 1980
by Jonathan David Publishers, Inc.

Jonathan David Publishers, Inc.
68-22 Eliot Avenue
Middle Village, New York 11379

This is a reprint edition distributed by Bookthrift, New York. Bookthrift is a registered trademark of Simon & Schuster, Inc.

ISBN-0-671-07107-6

Library of Congress Cataloging in Publication Data
Pearl, Anita May.
    Dictionary of popular slang.
    1. English language—Slang—Dictionaries.
2. Americanisms.   I. Title.
PE2846.P4   427'.9'73   79-21062

PRINTED IN THE UNITED STATES OF AMERICA

Acknowledgments

Special thanks to:
Nicolette Jamesley, R.N., Albert Einstein Medical Center, New York
Brian Wilson, Assistant District Attorney, Bronx County Supreme Court.
  New York
Christina Jamesley, Bucknell University, Lewisburg, Pennsylvania
Marguerite Jamesley, Fashion Institute of Technology, New York
Lewis Leone, Princeton University, Princeton, New Jersey
Richard Jamesley, Stevens Institute, Hoboken, New Jersey
Gladys Farrow Smith
Stuart Oderman, writer and composer
Charles Ludlam, The Ridiculous Theatrical Company
Matthew Inge, Councillor, Actors' Equity Association
and my Mother, who wishes to remain anonymous.

Introduction

slang *n.* informal, non-standard language typically composed of colorful, exaggerated metaphors, newly-coined words, or words and phrases that have taken on new meaning.

Language is only effective when it can express the feelings and ideas of a people with immediacy and precision. To be current, it must always be in a state of transition. As the attitudes of a people change, words once used in a particular sense begin to take on new meaning; new words are created as well. Slang, defined above, helps keep language vital, picturesque, and current.

In the United States, each succeeding group of immigrants has brought a richness of experience to be expressed, as well as a language with which to express it. Over the years, American English has benefited immeasurably from colorful new terms entering the language. During colonial times, for example, the English language borrowed heavily from the Dutch: thus *pape kak*, or soft excrement, became the standard interjection of disdain, "poppycock."

The French influence is felt most in Louisiana today, where great effort has been expended to maintain the linguistic heritage of French Americans. And many words have entered the mainstream of the American tongue. "Lagniappe," a little bit extra added to a portion, for example, is a popular word of French origin. And "poor boy," the large sandwich known also as the hero or submarine, comes from the French *pourboire*, a tip, just the bit of money needed to buy such a sandwich.

Afro-Americans have made considerable contributions to the English language over the years. Many of the words from the Gullah language have been systematically adopted into English. "Yam," for example, meaning sweet potato, was first introduced by the blacks. The "jive talk" of the jazz era, largely the language of black musicians, enriched the English vocabulary. The language of the urban ghetto, largely dominated by blacks, still enriches our vocabulary with phrases that take on fresh meaning: "Get off my case," an admonition to stop annoying, is clearly derived from comments by welfare recipients critical of case workers who investigate each client.

Yiddish, the language of East European Jews, influenced by German,

Russian, Polish, etc., has given American English many vivid words and expressions. These were generally popularized by Jewish performers at first, especially comedians, and have become standard words: "shtik," for example, is now used to describe a performer's characteristic attention-getting movements, grimaces, etc. And note how many Yiddish words are now used to designate a foolish or ineffectual, clumsy person: nebbish, nudnik, schmendrick, schmuck, schlemiel, schmo, shnook, etc.

Newer to the general American vocabularly are the Spanish terms introduced by the large groups of immigrants over the past twenty-five years, but their use is yet to become universal.

The jargon used by members of many professions has also colored the American vocabulary, particularly that used by those in the world of entertainment, journalism, police and crime, sports, etc. The terminology of baseball, football, basketball, and tennis, for example, has infiltrated the American vocabulary. An unsuccessful suitor is said to be unable "to get to first base" [baseball]. When we challenge someone to respond, we often say, "the ball is in your court" [tennis].

The Jonathan David Dictionary of Popular Slang presents the most popular slang words and expressions in use today. These have been gathered from all areas of interest and concern to contemporary man. Parts of speech are indicated in italics. (Because slang is used loosely, however, the reader should not be surprised to find an adjectival word or phrase used as an adverb or nominative, or a nominative used as an adjective or verb, etc.) Where useful to the reader, the area in which the slang term is primarily used today or the language from which it derives is given in parentheses. For example, following the entry **angel,** *n.* indicates that the word is a noun, and [ENTERTAINMENT] indicates that the word is used as a slang expression in the field of entertainment.

Of course, no study of slang is definitive. By its very nature, slang is constantly changing—responding to the needs of a people, and changing with its attitudes and experiences.

ANITA PEARL

A

aboard *adv.* [BASEBALL] on base.

above board *adj.* [GAMBLING] legitimate, proper, honest. From the practice of an honest gambler who shuffles a deck of cards in full view, on the table (board), and therefore does not stack the deck *See* stacked deck.

Acapulco gold *n.* [DRUG CULTURE] a marijuana of superior grade.

accidentally-on-purpose *adv.* deliberately done, but with feigned innocence.

AC/DC *adj.* bisexual. Literally, alternating current/direct current, the two alternate ways of channeling electrical current.

ace *n.* 1. [GAMBLING] the highest ranking playing card in a deck 2. the best in a particular field; an expert 3. [TENNIS] a point won by a single stroke 4. [GOLF] a score of one stroke on a hole.

ace-in-the-hole *n.* 1. [GAMBLING] a decisive surprise element in a strategy 2. an advantage held in reserve until needed.

ace out *v.t.* to better—*v.i.* to do something extraordinarily well.

ace up one's sleeve *n.* [GAMBLING] a decisive surprise element in a strategy.

acid *n.* [DRUG CULTURE] LSD, an hallucinogenic drug.

acid head *n.* [DRUG CULTURE] a frequent or habitual user of LSD.

acid rock *n.* [DRUG CULTURE/MUSIC] unrelenting loud music duplicating audio impressions experienced under the influence of drugs.

ack ack *n.* an antiaircraft gun or its fire.

acoustical perfume *n.* [BUSINESS] a background noise, imitating the sound of a ventilating system, that is played in large open office space to provide a sound screen for private conversation.

across the board *adv.* 1. [GAMBLING] referring to equal bets placed on one horse "to win, to place, and to show" in the same race by the same bettor 2. equally pertaining to all in the same category (particularly in use in labor union negotiations) 3. [BROADCASTING] the scheduling of a show or commercial to appear at the same time each day Monday through Friday.

act drop *n.* [ENTERTAINMENT] the curtain that is closed or lowered between the acts of a play, usually to allow time for change of scenery.

action *n.* 1. gambling activity, usually illegal 2. sexual activity, as in "to get some action."

activate *v.* [SPORTS] to return a player to competition.

activist *n.* one who is deeply involved in political or sociological reform.

Adam's ale *n.* water.

advance man *n.* one who makes all the arrangements for the benefit of a traveling celebrity, business magnate, campaigning candidate, etc., in all places to be visited.

advertising *adj.* [TRUCKERS' CB] of a police car, driving with flashing lights.

African dominoes *n.* dice. Derived from the game of craps, popular among black Americans after it was introduced in New Orleans from France in the mid-nineteenth century. *See* craps.

afro *n.* a hairstyle characterized by tight curls arranged evenly around the head. Originally an adjective, now com-

1

monly used as a noun.

afternoon drive *n*. [BROADCASTING] the evening rush hour when people drive home from work and listen to radio broadcasts.

-aholic *suffix* addicted to. Used loosely in such constructions as workaholic, foodaholic, etc.

air, the *n*. a dismissal—*v*. "to get (or to give someone) the air": 1. to be dismissed (or to dismiss someone) from employment 2. to be rejected (or to reject someone) from friendship.

air ball *n*. [BASKETBALL] a ball that misses the basket and does not even touch the backboard or the rim of the basket.

air head *n*. a fool.

air mail *n*. [STUDENT CULTURE] no letters received in one's mail box, i.e., it is "full of air."

aisles, in the *adv*. [ENTERTAINMENT] referring to the expression of approval by an audience. Generally used as "to have them (the audience) in the aisles."

alligator clips *n*. fastener clips resembling an alligator's jaws, used to attach wire cable to battery poles to carry electrical charge.

all-night jock *n*. [BROADCASTING] the radio broadcaster who works on an all-night show, often the newest or the least experienced member of the staff.

all-out *adj*. total, vigorous, zealous.

all-out war *n*. [MILITARY] warfare involving total mobilization of weapons and troops.

all right *adj*. acceptable; admirable.

all wet *adj*. completely mistaken.

also-ran *n*. a contestant who loses. Often used in horse racing and politics.

amateur night *n*. an expression of scorn indicating a lack of professionalism in any sphere. Actually, an evening of entertainment provided by nonprofessional performers.

ambulance chaser *n*. a dishonest lawyer; one who seeks out the victim of an accident to offer his legal services whether needed or not.

ammo *n*. [MILITARY] abbreviation for ammunition.

anchorman *n*. [SPORTS] the best batter on a baseball team. Originally, the key player on a team in tug o' war. *See* anchorperson.

anchorperson *n*. [BROADCASTING] the principle member of a team of news broadcasters who serves as narrator/moderator and whose functions include introducing the reporters "in the field" and presenting synopses of their stories.

angel *n*. [ENTERTAINMENT] one who invests money in a show.

angel dust *n*. [DRUG CULTURE] an hallucinogenic drug that has been used as a sedative in veterinary medicine.

angle *n*. ulterior motive.

Annie Oakley *n*. a free ticket; a pass.

answer print *n*. [PHOTOGRAPHY] the first picture printed from a negative, which is used to check density, color reproduction, etc.

ante *n*. [GAMBLING] 1. the initial bet in a game of poker 2. any bet 3. a contribution—*v*. 1. to place a bet in poker 2. to make a financial contribution, i.e., "to ante up."

antifreeze *n*. [DRUG CULTURE] heroin.

ants in one's pants, have *v*. to be nervous; particularly, to await something impatiently.

A-number-one *See* A-1.

any old *adj*. a coy or derogatory form of "any," as in "Any old gift will do" or "Serve the in-laws any old thing for dinner" or "Any old thing will be good enough."

A-OK All is fine; in excellent order. A term popularized by the astronaut Alan Shepard, who was supposed to have broadcast it from the first suborbital flight around the Earth on May 5, 1961. Actually National Aeronautics and Space Administration (NASA) public relations man Colonel Powers misunderstood Shepard, who said only "OK," and so it is Powers who really coined the expression and gave it out to news reporters.

A-1 *adj.* [NAUTICAL] the best. In Lloyd's ship register, vessels are rated both by letter and number: "A" is the best grade of hull, "1" is accorded to the equipment in top shape.

ape *n.* an ugly or menacing person.

ape, go *v.* to revert to apelike behavior, i.e., to become inordinately excited.

apple *n.* [SPORTS] a baseball.

apple of someone's eye *n.* a favorite; one especially dear. Originally, the expression meant literally the pupil of the eye, hence the idea of dearness to one's well being.

apple polish *v.* to curry favor through flattery.

apple polisher *n.* one who seeks to ingratiate himself through flattery.

applesauce *n.* nonsense.

apron *n.* [ENTERTAINMENT] that part of a stage which juts out past the proscenium arch and is nearest the audience.

arm, put the arm on *v.* to arrest or restrain.

armchair expert *n.* one who freely offers opinions and advice on subjects he is not qualified to deal with. SYNONYMS: armchair quarterback, armchair strategist, armchair general. *See* Monday morning quarterback *and* sidewalk superintendent.

around the bend *adv.* 1. having completed the major part of a task 2. getting old 3. [DRUG CULTURE] high on drugs.

artillery *n.* [DRUG CULTURE] the equipment used for the injection of narcotics.

artsy-craftsy *adj.* given to dabbling in the arts, especially the visual arts, usually in the sense of a minimally talented dilettante.

ashcan *n.* [MILITARY] a depth charge.

ask for it *v.* to provoke trouble consciously or unconsciously.

ass *n.* 1. a fool 2. the buttocks.

ass backwards *adv.* 1. in reverse order 2. in a confused manner. Often used as "bass ackwards."

asshole *n.* 1. the anus 2. an extremely stupid person.

ass kiss *v.* to fawn; to court favor by flattery. Often used in acronym form, AK.

ass kisser *n.* one who courts favor in a self-debasing manner.

asswipe *n.* toilet paper.

attaboy *interj.* abbreviation for "that's the boy," an exclamation of approval and support. Also, attagirl.

audience flow *n.* [BROADCASTING] the regular listeners to a show, whose tastes partially determine the format.

aunt *n.* 1. the female head of a brothel 2. an elderly homosexual.

Aussie *n.* abbreviation for Australian.

avalanche *n.* [POLITICS] an unusually large number of votes cast in an election.

away *adj.* [SPORTS] of a sports competition held in an opponent's home town. *See also* blow away; get away with; put away; *and* put it away.

AWOL [MILITARY] acronym for absent without leave. Now commonly used in any situation where one absents oneself without permission.

axe, the *n.* termination—*v.* "to get (or give someone) the axe": to be dismissed (or to dismiss someone) from employment or friendship.

B

B *n*. [DRUG CULTURE] benzedrine.

Babbitt *n*. a conformist. From the title character in the Sinclair Lewis novel.

babbling brook *n*. a gossip, an incessant talker.

babe *n*. an attractive and appealing woman.

babe-in-the-woods *n*. a naive person.

baby *n*. 1. a sweetheart 2. a favorite project that has been nurtured with special care—*v*. to treat like an infant; to pamper.

baby doll *n*. a coy, attractive girl.

baby dolls *n*. feminine sleepwear consisting of a short, generally loose, top and panties.

baby kisser *n*. a politician who seeks to please the public by showing exaggerated interest in it.

baby spot *n*. [ENTERTAINMENT] a small portable spotlight.

bach *n*. abbreviation for bachelor—*v*. to live like an unmarried man.

back *n*. [SPORTS] a player positioned toward the rear of the team line-up—*v*. 1. to subsidize financially 2. [GAMBLING] to bet on a contestant in a sports competition.

back *See* get off someone's back.

back alley *n*. a slum area, usually associated with clandestine, illegal activities.

Back Bay *n*. and *adj*. an exclusive section of Boston; hence, elite, wealthy.

backbencher *n*. [POLITICS] a congressperson lacking seniority.

backbone *n*. courage.

backburner, put something on the *v*. to delay tending to something, either to take care of more pressing business or to allow the situation to progress to another stage. Derived from the back-burner on a stove, which is traditionally smaller and often conducts less heat than a front burner, and where things are therefore placed to warm or simmer.

backdoor play *n*. [BASKETBALL] a maneuver in which a player avoids the defense of the opposing team and attains a position under the basket to receive the ball and make a shot.

back down *v*. 1. to concede a loss in an argument 2. to recoil from a problem or confrontation.

backer *n*. 1. [ENTERTAINMENT] one who invests money in a show 2. [POLITICS] one who supports a particular candidate, issue, or party.

backing *n*. a musical accompaniment.

backlash *n*. [POLITICS] extreme popular reaction against and resistance to certain policies.

back loaded *adj*. [LABOR] describing a labor contract covering several years with the major gains to be awarded in the last year.

back off *v*. 1. to recoil 2. to concede a loss in an argument 3. to cease bothering someone.

back nine *n*. [SPORTS] the last nine holes to be played in an eighteen-hole golf course.

backroom *n*. [POLITICS] the internal workings of a political party, used often in a derogatory sense, implying secret dealings that may be unethical—*adj*. used in the expression "backroom politics."

4

back seat driver *n.* an automobile passenger who gives unwanted advice to the driver, hence anyone who offers advice in a field in which he is not qualified.

backstop *n.* [SPORTS] the catcher in a game of baseball.

back talk *n.* a disrespectful response directed to a person in a position of authority; impertinence—*v.* to talk back disrespectfully.

back-to-back *adv.* in uninterrupted sequence.

back to the drawing board an expression indicating the necessity for a revision of plans, as a draftsman returns "to the drawing board" to improve a mechanical or architectural design.

back-up *n.* 1. a supporting member or several supporting members of a group or team 2. [ENTERTAINMENT] an understudy—*v.i.* to recoil—*v.t.* 1. to support 2. [PRINTING] to print the second or reverse side of a printed sheet.

back up, have one's *v.* to be angry or defensive. An animal, especially a cat, automatically raises its back in periods of anger or fear, hence a person is said to have that same reaction, at least figuratively.

back yard, one's own *n.* used figuratively to denote familiar territory, a field or domain in which one feels comfortable.

bad *adj.* [BLACK CULTURE] very good.

bad checks *n.* 1. checks written for more money than is actually in the bank account 2. [TRUCKERS' CB] police patrolling in unmarked cars.

baddie *n.* a villain. Usually used humorously or affectionately when pertaining to a naughty child or pet.

bad egg *n.* a dishonest and wicked person.

bad mouth *v.* to speak badly and falsely about someone or something.

bad news *n.* an unfortunate or unpleasant person, thing, or situation.

bad time *n.* 1. A disagreeable situation 2. difficulties.

bafflegab *n.* [POLITICS] language which serves to obscure and confuse.

bag *n.* 1. an ugly woman, often used in the expression "old bag" 2. a specialty or interest: "Photography is her bag" 3. [DRUG CULTURE] a quantity of drugs sold in plastic or paper wrap 4. [BASEBALL] a base—*v.* [HUNTING] to kill.

bagged *adj.* [CRIME] with predetermined results, of a race or game of chance.

bag, go in the *v.* [CRIME] to accept a bribe.

bag, in the *adv.* 1. an assured success 2. drunk.

bag it *interj.* a command to stop talking, to stop annoying.

bag, left holding the *See* holding the bag.

bag limit *n.* [HUNTING] a government restriction placed on each licensed hunter or fisher dictating the maximum amount of game or fish which may be killed during a particular period of time.

bagman *n.* 1. [CRIME] a subordinate who serves as intermediary to deliver the money involved in the payment of graft 2. [DRUG CULTURE] one who deals in illegal drugs; a pusher.

bail out *v.* 1. to parachute from an airplane 2. to abandon any project in the face of danger 3. [BASEBALL] to recoil quickly from one's normal batting position to avoid being hit by a ball 4. [SURFING] to jump from a surfboard to avoid being swept off by a wave.

baker's dozen *n.* thirteen. Perhaps from the fifteenth-century practice of fining bakers who short-weighted orders, thus forcing them to give thirteen loaves on an order of twelve to be sure to avoid the fine.

balderdash *n.* nonsense. Also used as an interjection. In the late sixteenth century, balderdash was the name of a frothy drink. Later, Ben Jonson defined it as a mixture of buttermilk and beer—a strange mixture—leading to the idea of something preposterous.

ball *n.* a good time—*v.* to coit.

ball and chain *n.* a spouse. Used figuratively as something which imposes restrictions and is a burden, like the steel ball and chain attached to a prisoner.

ball bounces, that's the way the an expression of resignation to fate.

ball, have it on the *v.* to be clever and industrious.

ball hawk *n.* [SPORTS] an excellent defensive player.

ball is in someone's court, the a response must be forthcoming from the person in question before further action can be taken. From tennis, in which the players hit the ball into each other's court until one misses and the other wins a point or the serve.

ball of fire *n.* a gifted, eager, ambitious person.

ball, on the *adj.* eager and capable.

balloon freight *n.* [TRUCKERS' CB] a light cargo.

ball rolling, keep the *See* keep the ball rolling.

balls *n.* 1. testicles 2. courage, determination.

ball up *v.* to confuse or complicate.

ballyhoo *n.* loud, enthusiastic publicity.

balmy *adj.* [BRITISH SLANG] crazy or foolish.

baloney *n.* 1. nonsense 2. [TRUCKERS' CB] an automobile or truck tire, most often used in the plural.

baloney bender *n.* one who exaggerates.

banana *n.* [ENTERTAINMENT] a comedian, the best being the "top banana."

banana ball *n.* [GOLF] a ball propelled to the side by a slice stroke.

banana oil *n.* insincere, foolish talk.

banana race *n.* [CRIME] a racing competition with an illicitly predetermined outcome.

banana republic *n.* any small tropical country of which the chief export may be bananas; used in a derogatory way to indicate a backward, underdeveloped, generally illiterate country with an unstable government.

bananas *adj.* crazy—*v.* to go bananas.

B and E *n.* [CRIME] the crime of breaking into and entering a place.

bandwagon, jump on the *v.* to show active and enthusiastic support; to join when the end result is assured. From the practice of local politicians lending support to a candidate by riding on the wagon carrying the band in a parade.

bang *n.* 1. a blow 2. [DRUG CULTURE] an injection of drugs 3. coitus—*v.* 1. to hit 2. to coit.

bang out of something, get a *v.* to derive pleasure or excitement from something.

bangtail *n.* [HORSE RACING] originally, a horse with a cropped tail; now, any race horse.

bang-up *n.* a collision—*adj.* excellent—*v.* to do physical harm.

banjo hitter *n.* [SPORTS] a baseball player who hits weakly, as if wielding a banjo instead of a bat, or as if using only enough energy to pick a banjo string, not to hit a ball.

bankroll *v.* to finance an endeavor.

banzai *interj.* a cry of determination and challenge. This was a Japanese war cry meaning "may you live ten thousand years," shouted by pilots on suicide missions.

barbecue *n.* [CRIME] the electric chair.

barf *v.* to regurgitate. On airlines, passengers are supplied with small sacks to use in the event of air sickness: these are commonly referred to as "barf bags."

barfly *n.* one who frequents bars; a drunkard.

bargaining chip *n.* an advantage.

barge *n.* [SPORTS] a large unmaneuverable boat.

barge in *v.* 1. to interrupt 2. to enter without permission.

bar girl *n.* a woman, frequently a prostitute, used to entice customers to buy drinks at a bar. Often used in the abbreviated form, B-girl.

bark *v.* [ENTERTAINMENT] to advertise a show.

bark up the wrong tree *v.* to mistake

one's goal. From a hunting dog that barks at prey hiding in a tree.

barley wagon *n*. [TRUCKERS' CB] a truck carrying beer.

barmaid *n*. [BOWLING] a pin that remains standing behind another after the first ball of a frame has been played.

barmy *adj*. [BRITISH SLANG] silly; idiotic.

barnburner *n*. an exciting competition, often used for a sporting event.

barndoor *n*. [ENTERTAINMENT] hinged flaps on a spotlight which permit focusing the beam of light.

barnstorm *v*. [ENTERTAINMENT] 1. to travel through the country entertaining in barns, usually indicating a second-rate performer playing to a naive audience 2. [POLITICS] to make campaign speeches around the country—*n*. barnstormer.

barnyard golf *n*. the game of horseshoes.

barrel, over a *adv*. in a situation in which one is at a distinct disadvantage.

barrelhouse *n*. 1. a sleazy bar 2. a brothel 3. [MUSIC] a style of jazz music originating in bars and brothels.

base *adj*. taking a position that is unsound.

Baseball Annie *n*. a woman or girl who seeks association with baseball players.

base play *n*. [SPORTS] an inept play in baseball.

bash *n*. a party. Originally, used by jazz musicians to refer to a gathering where impromptu jazz is played. *See* jam session—*v*. to hit hard.

bass ackwards *See* ass backwards.

bat *n*. an ill-tempered or ugly woman. Often, "old bat."

bat down on blacks *v*. [BROADCASTING] to adjust the dark tones of a televised image electronically to make an even, uniform black, usually used as a background for white letter captions.

bath *v*. to suffer a loss.

bathtub *n*. a small ship.

bat one's gums *v*. to prattle.

bats *adj*. crazy.

bats in one's belfry, have to be crazy.

battery acid *n*. coffee.

bat the breeze *v*. to talk casually; to chat.

battle axe *n*. an aggressive, tough woman.

battle wagon *n*. a battleship.

batty *adj*. mildly insane.

bawl *v*. to scold angrily.

bay window *n*. a fat belly which makes a rounded protrusion similar to that of the window.

bazoo *n*. the mouth, particularly as an organ of speech, as in "shut your bazoo and listen."

bazoom *n*. the bosom.

bear bait *n*. [TRUCKERS' CB] a driver without a Citizens' Band radio, hence one likely to be caught speeding by police who set up a speed trap.

bearcat *n*. an aggressive person.

bear cave, bear den *n*. [TRUCKERS' CB] a police station.

bear in the air *n*. [TRUCKERS' CB] a police helicopter.

bear taking pictures *n*. [TRUCKERS' CB] police using radar to monitor the speed of vehicles.

beat *n*. [MUSIC] rhythm—*adj*. exhausted.

beat a dead horse *v*. to engage in futile effort. The expression is often used as advice: "Don't beat a dead horse."

beat around the bush *v*. to approach a subject obliquely, rather than to the point. In the fifteenth century, "batfowling" was a common form of hunting in which a hunter would rouse sleeping birds by beating around the bush, then killing them with a bat.

beak *n*. the nose.

beam, on the *adv*. [AVIATION] accurate. Pilots flying on a correct course hear directional radio signals at their loudest when they are right in the center of the beam guiding the flight.

bean *n*. the head.

beanball *n*. [BASEBALL] a ball pitched directly at the batter's head.

beanpole *n*. a tall, thin person.

beans *n*. 1. nonsense 2. something of little value. Often used in the expres sion "it doesn't amount to a hill of beans," meaning something is of no value 3. dollars. Five dollars can be expressed as "five beans."

beans, know one's v. to be expert in one's field.

beans, spill the *See* spill the beans.

bean wagon n. a cheap restaurant.

bear n. 1. a stubborn and disagreeable person 2. [TRUCKERS' CB] a policeman. From Smokey the Bear.

beat it v. to leave rapidly.

beatnik n. an idealistic social rebel of the 1950s, a member of the Beat Generation.

beat one's brains out v. to expend great personal energy or mental effort on an endeavor.

beat out v. to surpass.

beat out something v. to typewrite. Also, to "beat out a tune": to play a piece on the piano.

beat someone's time v. to divert the attention of someone's lover.

beat someone to the punch v. to accomplish something before someone else does.

beat something into the ground v. to discuss something to excess.

beat the band, to adv. vigorously; to the point of excess. Literally, from the desire to arrive on time to see the whole parade; the spectators must arrive before the band of musicians leading the parade begins to play.

beat the rap v. to be found innocent of a crime; often used to imply actual guilt of it.

beat up v. to thrash—adj. dilapidated.

beaut n. abbreviation of beauty, used in the sense of something outstanding, but not necessarily beautiful. "That 'shiner' (*see* shiner) is a real beaut."

beauty adj. the best.

beaver n. 1. a diligent worker. Often used as "eager beaver." 2. a woman.

bed n. [BROADCASTING] the instrumental background to spoken words.

bed bug hauler n. [TRUCKERS' CB] a moving van.

bed, go to or put to bed [PRINTING] ready to be printed, of a publication.

bedpost n. [BOWLING] a split leaving the two rear corner pins—the 7 and 10—standing.

bedroom community or **bedroom suburb** n. a suburban area whose population, for the most part, works in the city and comes home just to sleep.

bed with someone, go to v. to coit.

beef n. 1. a complaint; 2. muscle—v. to complain.

beefcake n. a suggestive photograph of an attractive, scantily-clad man. *See* cheesecake.

beefeater n. an Englishman.

beef up v. to improve; to make more vigorous.

bee in one's bonnet, have a to be slightly, not unpleasantly, insane.

beer belly n. a fat abdomen.

beer joint n. a tavern.

beeswax n. a humorous substitute word for "business," as in the expression "none of your beeswax."

beezer n. the nose.

be had, to v. to be duped.

behind n. the buttocks.

behind the eight ball adv. unfortunate; jinxed; in a difficult situation. In the game of Kelly pool, the billiard balls must be played in numerical order, except for the ball bearing an eight, which is played last. If a player touches or hits this ball sooner, he is penalized; if, however, it lays between the cue ball and the one to be hit, the player is at a distinct disadvantage.

be into someone v. to owe someone money.

be into something v. to be interested or involved in a project, field, or endeavor.

bejabbers interj. an expression of fear. Also, "bejesus."

bells on, with adv. promptly and eagerly.

bell, that rings a *See* that rings a bell.

bellyache n. a complaint—v. to complain.

belly button *n.* the navel.

belly flop or **belly whop** *n.* an aborted dive in which the diver strikes the water flat on his belly—*v.* to dive and land on the water flat on one's belly.

bellyful *n.* a great quantity, usually in a negative sense, of all that one can tolerate.

belly laugh *n.* a hearty laugh, one that causes the belly to shake.

belly up *v.* to approach something boldly.

belong *v.t.* to be the owner.

below the belt *adv.* unfairly done. In boxing, opponents are not permitted to hit each other below the belt.

belt *n.* 1. a slap 2. a gulp of liquor—*v.* 1. to hit, as with a belt 2. "to belt down": to drink in one gulp.

belting *n.* a hard blow; a drink.

belt out *v.* 1. to sing vigorously and loudly 2. to belt. *See* belt.

belt song *n.* [MUSIC] a song requiring a dynamic singing style.

bench jockey *n.* a player on a bench who taunts other players.

bench warmer *n.* [SPORTS] a participant seldom called upon to join the action.

bender *n.* a drinking spree.

bend one's elbow *v.* to imbibe.

bend someone's ear *v.* to importune someone with persistent talk.

bends, the *n.* pain caused by rapid depressurization. A term often used in deep sea diving and space travel.

bend the law *v.* to seek means to achieve one's goals through basically unethical, although not blatantly illegal, means.

benny, bennie *n.* [DRUG CULTURE] abbreviation for Benzedrine, an amphetamine.

bent *adj.* drunk.

Betsy *n.* a gun.

better half *n.* one's spouse. A humorously gallant expression from the idea that in marriage two people are made one and that one's spouse is superior to oneself.

betwixt and between *adv.* undecided.

BG *n.* [BROADCASTING] acronym for background, either visual or audio.

bibful *n.* 1. a surfeit 2. gossip, in the sense that it dribbles from the mouth, much like food on a baby's bib.

Bible belt *n.* that part of the southern and midwestern United States where many people practice a fundamentalist Christianity based on the Word of God in the Holy Bible. The term was coined by H. L. Mencken.

biddy *n.* a petty, ill-willed old woman.

biff *n.* a blow; a strike—*v.t.* to hit; to strike.

Big Brother *n.* the spying forces of totalitarian governments that keep a close watch on the population. From the novel *Brave New World*, by Aldous Huxley.

big bucks *n.* a lot of money.

big C *n.* cancer.

big cheese *n.* a person of importance.

Big Daddy *n.* [TRUCKERS' CB] the Federal Communications Commission, which regulates all broadcasting in the United States.

big deal *n.* an expression of disdain, often an interjection, used to underscore the idea that someone or something has been accorded exaggerated importance.

big game *n.* a goal of major significance.

biggie *n.* a person or thing of great importance.

big Harry, big H., Harry *n.* [DRUG CULTURE] heroin.

big house *n.* the penitentiary.

big one *n.* one-thousand dollars. "Five big ones," five-thousand dollars.

big mouth *n.* a person who talks too much.

big shot *n.* a person of importance, or one who mistakenly believes he is a person of importance.

big stink *n.* a persistent, loud objection; an uproar.

big talk *n.* exaggerated claims.

big time, the *n.* the most remunerative

and important level of accomplishment in any given field.

big time operator *n.* one who uses his wits to manipulate people and situations to achieve great profit.

big timer *n.* one who participates in big time activity, such as a Broadway actor, a major league baseball player, etc.

big wheel *n.* a person of importance.

bigwig *n.* 1. a person of importance 2. a political party leader. From the British magistrates who wear large wigs; the more important the magistrate, the bigger the wig.

bike *n.* 1. abbreviation for bicycle 2. a motorcycle—*v.* to ride a bicycle or motorcycle.

bilge *n.* meaningless verbiage.

bill *n.* 1. the nose 2. a one-hundred dollar bill.

billboard *n.* [BROADCASTING] the list of credits that appears at the beginning or the end of a television show or movie.

billy club *n.* a policeman's wooden club.

bimbo *n.* a girl. Abbreviation for *bambino*, baby in Italian.

bind, in a *adj.* in a difficult situation.

bindle *n.* a bundle of bedding.

bindlestiff *n.* a migratory worker.

bingo *interj.* an exclamation of triumph. From the game of the same name in which the first to cover an entire row of numbers vertically, horizontally, or diagonally cries out "Bingo!" to indicate having won.

bippy, you can bet your (sweet) *interj.* a vigorous affirmation.

Bircher *n.* [POLITICS] a member of the John Birch Society; a virulent anti-communist.

bird *n.* [BRITISH SLANG] a girl.

bird, the *n.* heckling—*v.* "to get (or give) someone the bird": to heckle.

bird brain *n.* a silly person.

bird cage *n.* 1. a prison cell 2. [SPORTS] a protective face mask worn in football.

bird dog *n.* [POLITICS] one who works aggressively and creatively for an official, particularly at hunting down valuable information.

birdie *n.* [GOLF] a score of one stroke under par on a particular hole—*v.* to score a birdie.

bird legs *n.* extremely thin legs.

birds and bees, the *n.* a euphemism for the facts of human sexuality.

birdseed *n.* a paltry amount of money.

birds, for the *adj.* ridiculous.

birthday suit *n.* a humorous term for the naked body.

biscuit *n.* [CRIME] a gun.

bit *n.* 1. a prison sentence 2. [ENTERTAINMENT] a small acting role.

bitch *n.* 1. a nasty woman 2. a difficult task—*v.* to complain.

bite *v.* to accept gullibly. From the fishing term: a fish will bite the bait with no forethought of danger.

bite the bullet *v.* to anticipate and accept dire consequences. In the Old West, people undergoing an operation without the benefit of anesthetics were given a bullet to bite when the pain became unbearable.

bite the dust *v.* to die.

biz *n.* abbreviation for business; often used in the expression "show biz."

blab *v.* 1. to speak irresponsibly 2. to disclose a secret.

blabbermouth *n.* an excessive talker, particularly one who divulges secrets.

black *adj.* without cream or sugar, referring to coffee or tea.

black, in the *adv.* operating with a profit. A bookkeeper traditionally records a company's profits in his ledger in black ink.

black and white *n.* an ice cream soda made with vanilla ice cream and chocolate syrup.

black and white, in *adv.* 1. in writing, black ink on white paper 2. clearly; distinctly.

black bag job *n.* [POLITICS] illegal entry by the FBI into a foreign embassy, etc., to gather intelligence. From the black bag used to carry payoffs.

blackball *v.* to ostracize. From the ancient Greek practice of voting by casting a small round white stone to accept or a small black stone to reject.

black book or **little black book** *n*. 1. a bachelor's address book purportedly filled with the names and addresses of available young women 2. a book of essential private information, which, if disclosed, might compromise the owner.

black box *n*. electronic equipment.

black cow *n*. an ice cream soda made with root beer and vanilla ice cream.

black eye *n*. a stigma.

black ice *n*. 1. a thin coat of ice on a body of fresh or salt water allowing the darkness of the water to show through 2. ice with dirt embedded in it.

blacklist *n*. a record of people in disfavor—*v*. to ostracize. From the seventeenth century in England: under Charles II, the names of those who participated in the condemnation and execution of his father, Charles I, were inscribed on a blacklist for punishment.

black Maria *n*. a police van used to transport prisoners. Originally, a term used in London.

blackout *n*. 1. loss of consciousness 2. loss of electric power 3. a voluntary shutting off of all lights at night to avoid possible bombing attacks during a war 4. [SPORTS] the absence of television broadcasting of a sporting event in the immediate area surrounding the stadium where it is being held—*v*. 1. to lose consciousness 2. to lose electric power 3. to shut off all lights at night to avoid possible bombing attacks during a war 4. [SPORTS] to refuse broadcast rights to the immediate area surrounding a stadium in order to insure the sale of tickets.

black strap *n*. coffee.

black stuff *n*. [DRUG CULTURE] opium.

blah *adj*. bland, boring.

blah-blah-blah *n*. excessive, meaningless talk.

blahs, the *n*. a feeling of general depression, lassitude.

blanket *n*. 1. a pancake 2. a thin covering, as in "a blanket of snow."

blast *n*. 1. an exciting time 2. a verbal attack—*v*. to excoriate.

blasted *adj*. [BRITISH SLANG] as an expletive, the equivalent of "damned."

bleed *n*. or *adj*. [PRINTING] an illustration which covers one or more edges of a page—*v*. to extort money from someone.

bleeding heart *n*. one who plays on another's sympathies, particularly concerning social injustices. Often used in politics in the expression "bleeding heart liberal."

bleep *n*. [BROADCASTING] an excision of recorded words in a broadcast—*v*. to delete an offensive word or phrase in a broadcast and substitute an electronic sound that is best described as "bleep."

blimp *n*. a fat person.

blind *adj*. drunk. From the possible disastrous effects of drinking homemade or substitute liquor that on occasion can cause blindness.

blind alley *n*. 1. literally, a small narrow street blocked by buildings on three sides 2. figuratively, a deception or a fruitless endeavor.

blind date *n*. a social engagement arranged for two people who have never met.

blind pig *n*. a place where illegal liquor is sold and consumed; a speakeasy.

blind tiger *n*. cheap or inferior whiskey.

blink, on the *adv*. inoperative.

blinkers *n*. the eyes.

blitz *n*. a sudden and violent attack. In German, *blitz* means lightning. *Blitzkrieg*: lightning war.

bloat *n*. a drunkard.

block *n*. the head, as in "I'll knock your block off"—*v*. [ENTERTAINMENT] to plan each move that every actor will make for the staging of a play. The actual, finished staging is called "blocking."

block, on the *adv.* [SPORTS] available for trading to another sports team, of a professional athlete. From the block on which items are displayed for auction sale.

block and tackle *n.* [SPORTS] one's superior or anyone who limits one's activities. From football terminology, to block: to prevent a player from advancing; to tackle: to grab and knock down a player.

blockhead *n.* a stupid person.

bloke *n.* 1. [BRITISH SLANG] a man 2. [DRUG CULTURE] cocaine.

blood box *n.* an ambulance.

blood money *n.* 1. money earned with great effort and by enduring hardship 2. [CRIME] money paid to an assassin 3. money gained at someone's death 4. money gained by an informant instrumental in another's capture.

bloody *adj.* [BRITISH SLANG] cursed.

bloody murder, cry, scream, or **yell** *v.* to vent one's anger or fear by screaming.

blooey, blooie *adj.* not in working condition.

bloom *n.* [BROADCASTING] glare resulting from light reflected on white objects— *v.* to reflect light to such a degree that it becomes a glare.

bloomer *n.* a mistake.

bloomers *n.* loose-fitting pants for women; sometimes applied to long, loose undergarments. Introduced by Amelia Bloomer, an early suffragist who sought to adapt trousers for women.

bloop *v.* [BASEBALL] to bat a ball to the area between infield and outfield.

blooper *n.* 1. an embarrassing verbal error 2. [BASEBALL] a ball batted between infield and outfield.

blotter *n.* the daily record of arrests at a police station.

blotto *adj.* drunk.

blow *v.* 1. to miss an opportunity 2. to spend money recklessly 3. to brag 4. [DRUG CULTURE] to smoke dope 5. to perform fellatio.

blow a fuse *v.* to become angry.

blow away *v.i.* to depart—*v.t.* to kill.

blow coke *v.* [DRUG CULTURE] to inhale cocaine.

blowed *v.* to damn.

blower *n.* 1. a handkerchief 2. [BRITISH SLANG] the telephone.

blowhard *n.* a braggart.

blow in *v.* to arrive casually and unexpectedly.

blow it *v.* to miss an opportunity.

blow it out your barracks bag *interj.* a command to stop boastful talk or lies.

blow off *n.* a boaster.

blow off steam *v.* to express one's anger verbally, thus reducing its force.

blow one's cool *v.* to lose one's self-control.

blow one's cork, lid, stack, or **top** *v.* to become very angry.

blow one's cover *v.* to reveal one's identity, intentions, etc., inadvertently. Originally, of a spy.

blow one's mind *v.* [DRUG CULTURE] to be astonished or overwhelmed by something. Originally, to feel the effects of an hallucinogenic drug.

blowout *n.* the explosion of a tire on a moving vehicle.

blow smoke *v.* to speak nonsense; to exaggerate.

blow someone's doors in *v.* [TRUCKERS' CB] to speed past another driver.

blow the lid off *v.* to expose a secret, generally a scandal or an illegal scheme.

blow the whistle *v.* to inform; to call attention to a disreputable deed.

blowup *n.* 1. a violent expression of anger 2. a photographic enlargement.

blow up a storm *v.* 1. [MUSIC] to play jazz with great expertise 2. to become enraged 3. to create great excitement or fear.

BLT *n.* a bacon-lettuce-tomato sandwich.

blubberhead *n.* a stupid person.

blue *n.* the sky—*adj.* 1. sad 2. obscene.

blue book *n.* a listing of the elite in the

United States; the social register.

blue chip stocks *n*. [GAMBLING] stocks bringing the highest returns. From gambling chips, the most valuable being the blue ones, which are worth ten times the value of the red.

blue collar *adj*. pertaining to the working class.

blue devils *n*. [DRUG CULTURE] barbiturates contained in blue capsules; hence, also a state of depression.

blue funk *n*. a depressed mood.

bluegrass *n*. a style of country music, particularly that originating in Kentucky, the "Bluegrass State."

blue moon, once in a *adv*. rarely.

bluenosed *adj*. puritanical.

blurb *n*. 1. a news item 2. a publicity story 3. a quote from a critic. Coined by the humorist Gelett Burgess.

bo, 'bo-boes *n*. a hobo.

BO *n*. acronym for body odor.

bob *n*. [BRITISH SLANG] money.

bod *n*. an abbreviation for body.

body count *n*. the tabulation of the number of dead in a war or major disaster.

body English *n*. physical gestures used to communicate one's thoughts.

body snatcher *n*. a mortician.

boff *n*. 1. a laugh 2. a punch—*v*. 1. to laugh 2. to punch.

boffin *n*. [BRITISH SLANG] a research scientist.

boffo *adj*. [BRITISH SLANG] excellent.

boffola *n*. a successful joke, one that provokes much laughter. *See* boff.

bogey *n*. [GOLF] a score of one stroke over par on a particular hole—*v*. to score a bogey.

boggle *v*. to confuse, as in "it boggles the mind."

bogue *adj*. [DRUG CULTURE] desperately needing a dose of narcotics.

bogus *adj*. not genuine; fake.

bohunk *n*. a derogatory term for a Hungarian or any person of Eastern European heritage. Also, hunkie.

boiled *adj*. drunk.

bollix *v.t.* to bungle.

boll weevil *n*. [LABOR] a non-union worker. Literally, an insect that bores into and destroys the cotton crop, hence a spoiler in the organization of labor.

bolt *n*. [POLITICS] the leaving of one's party. From horse racing, a wild uncontrolled jump—*v*. 1. to leave one's political party 2. to flee.

bomb *n*. 1. a failure 2. a shocking statement—*v*. to fail, particularly in a public situation. Often said of a performance that receives bad notices.

bomb, drop a *v*. to make a shocking statement.

bombed *adj*. drunk.

bombshell *n*. a beautiful and sexually attractive woman. The term has a connotation of danger to the admirer.

bomb squad *n*. [SPORTS] the group of football players on a team used in the most dangerous plays.

bonehead *n*. a slow-witted person.

bone *v.i.* to study.

boner *n*. a blunder—*v*. "to pull a boner" to err embarrassingly.

bone to pick, a *n*. a source of contention. From the fact that dogs fight over the ownership of a bone.

bones *n*. 1. a thin person 2. [GAMBLING] dice. Originally, dice were made of bone.

bone up (on something) *v*. to review information in a specific field; to study.

bone yard *n*. a cemetery.

bonkers *adj*. crazy.

boob, booby *n*. 1. a stupid person 2. the female breast.

boob *v.i.* [BRITISH SLANG] to make a silly mistake.

boo *v*. to jeer.

boo boo *n*. a stupid mistake.

boo-boo *n*. [BABY TALK] 1. an injury 2. an embarrassing error.

boob tube *n*. a television set.

booby hatch *n*. a mental institution.

booby trap *n*. [MILITARY] any situation planned to catch a victim unawares. From booby, a fool.

boodle *n*. [CRIME] graft; by extension,

any ill-gotten gain.

book, book flat *n.* [ENTERTAINMENT] a construction of two flats (*see* flat) hinged together so that they can stand alone and be stored closed one upon the other like a book.

bookie *n.* [GAMBLING] abbreviation for bookmaker, a bet-taker in illegal gambling.

books, hit the *v.* to study, especially "to cram." *See* cram.

boom *n.* 1. a great increase 2. [POLITICS] a period of affluence, usually followed by recession (*see* bust) 3. [BROADCASTING] a metal beam used to suspend a microphone above a speaker and out of view of the broadcasting cameras—*v.* to thrive. Often in reference to the economy.

boondocks, boonies *n.* back country; isolated terrain. From the Philippine language Tagalog, *bandok,* meaning mountain, heard by the American troops during World War II and taken to mean back country.

boondoggle *v.* 1. [POLITICS] to stimulate the economy by creating government jobs 2. to waste time at trivial occupations.

booster *n.* [CRIME] a professional shoplifter.

boot *v.* [DRUG CULTURE] to inject a narcotic into a vein.

boot, the *n.* a dismissal—*v.* "to get (or give someone) the boot": to be dismissed (or to dismiss someone) summarily, as if kicked.

boot, to *adv.* in addition to.

boot camp *n.* a military training center for recruits.

bootleg *n.* or *adj.* illegally-made or supplied liquor—*v.* to deal in illegally-made liquor. From the practice of carrying illicit merchandise in the top of high boots.

bootlegger *n.* one who makes or supplies illegal liquor.

booze *n.* hard liquor; by extension, any alcoholic beverage.

booze it up *v.* to indulge in drinking hard liquor, usually to the point of drunkenness.

bop *n.* [STUDENT SLANG] to date many different people, as opposed to having one special love interest.

bop *n.* 1. [MUSIC] a style of music popular in the 1940s, also called be-bop 2. [DRUG CULTURE] a pill 3. a hit—*v.* 1. to dance to be-bop music 2. to hit.

borscht belt, borscht circuit *n.* the Catskill mountains resort area in New York State, so called because of the preponderance of hotels catering to a clientele of Eastern European Jewish origin among whom borscht, a beet or cabbage soup, is a favorite dish. This term is a humorous designation coined in imitation of other well-known American "belts"—the Bible belt, corn belt, sun belt, etc.

bosh *n.* nonsense.

boss *adj.* excellent; fine.

bossism *n.* [POLITICS] control of a political party particularly by a non-elected leader.

botch up *v.* to bungle.

bottle baby *n.* a drunk.

bottle, hit the *v.* to drink liquor, usually in great quantity; to get drunk.

bottom *n.* 1. the buttocks 2. [SPORTS] the last half of an inning in baseball.

bottom line *n.* the final result. From the tallies in an accountant's book; the final sums appear at the bottom of each page.

bottom man (on the totem pole) *n.* one with the least authority, seniority, or experience, as in "a private in the army is the bottom man on the totem pole."

bottom out *v.* to level off at a low point, e.g., prices.

bounce *n.* 1. vitality 2. ejection from a place by force 3. [TRUCKERS' CB] the return drive—*v.t.* 1. to eject forcibly from a place, usually because of disruptive behavior 2. to bounce a check: (a) to write a check for more money than that in one's checking account, or (b) for a bank to refuse payment on such a check.

bouncer *n.* one who is employed to eject obnoxious or obstreperous people from a gathering place, such as a party, a night-club, a restaurant, etc.

bow-wow *n.* [BABY TALK] a dog.

box cars *n.* [GAMBLING] a throw of the dice showing two sixes.

box, put someone in a *v.* to kill someone.

boy *interj.* an exclamation, as in "oh boy!"

boy scout *n.* [POLITICS] an idealistic and naive politician.

boys, the *n.* a man's companions, sometimes for gambling, drinking, camaraderie.

boys in the backroom *n.* [POLITICS] those controlling the machinations of a political party.

boys uptown, the *See* boys in the backroom.

bozo *n.* a fool.

brace *v.t.* to ask a loan.

bracelets *n.* handcuffs.

bracer *n.* a drink of alcoholic liquor.

brain *v.* to hit hard on the head.

brain child *n.* an idea or creation; the "offspring" of one's imagination or intelligence.

brain drain *n.* losing the services of the best trained and most creative workers in any sphere to another country or corporation, etc., in a systematic way, usually because one employer has more financial gain to offer than the other.

brain picker *n.* one who adapts the ideas and inventions of others to his own advantage.

brain storm *n.* a sudden brilliant idea.

brain trust *n.* [POLITICS] a group of advisers to a candidate; also, by extension, a group of policy-makers. The expression gained popularity under the Franklin D. Roosevelt administration.

brains fried, get one's *v.* [DRUG CULTURE] to be high on drugs.

brainwash *v.* to alter someone's outlook by constant insidious pressure or indoc-trination.

brass *n.* [MILITARY] high ranking officials. From the braid decorating the hats of military officers.

brass hat *n.* a high official.

brass knuckles *n.* a metal device, often links of chain, worn over the knuckles in order to give greater force to one's punch.

brass tacks *n.* the essentials. Often used in the expression "getting down to brass tacks."

brawl *v.i.* a noisy party.

bread and butter *n.* livelihood; means of support—*adj.* [POLITICS] a designation for an issue involving the economic well-being of the average citizen.

break cover *v.* to emerge from hiding.

breakdown *n.* 1. a cessation 2. a malfunction 3. an emotional collapse.

break down *v.* 1. to cease 2. to malfunction 3. to be overcome with emotion.

break even *v.* to suffer no financial losses in a transaction, but to make no financial gain either.

break-in *n.* a burglary.

break in *v.i.* to force entry—*v.t.* 1. to train (a worker) 2. to tame (an animal) 3. to shape to the proper fit by wearing (apparel).

break it up *v.* to stop. Usually as a command in reference to a fight.

break someone up *v.* to cause in someone an extreme emotional reaction, usually expressed by either laughter or tears.

break the ice *v.* to initiate (a relationship).

break the news *v.* 1. to beat up 2. to be the first to advise.

breakthrough *n.* a key advance in knowledge or technology that will precipitate further advances.

break up *v.* 1. to cause a rift (between people) 2. to end (a relationship, meeting, fight, etc.).

break wind *v.* to eruct.

breathe easy *v.* to relax, in the sense that quickened breath indicates stress.

breather *n.* a rest period; a time to catch

one's breath.

breeches, too big for one's *adv.* convinced of one's own exaggerated importance.

breeze *n.* an easy task.

breeze in *v.* to arrive casually or unexpectedly.

breeze off *v.* to depart casually or unexpectedly, as if caught up in the wind.

breezy *adj.* lively; sprightly.

brick *n.* 1. a stolid, trustworthy person 2. [DRUG CULTURE] a kilogram of marijuana compressed into the shape of a brick.

bricks, hit the *See* hit the bricks.

bricks and mortar *n.* school books and notes, as the structural foundation of an education.

bricktop *n.* a person with "red" hair.

bridge *n.* [BROADCASTING] an element serving to link two scenes, often music.

brig *n.* [NAUTICAL] prison.

bright *n.* daytime.

brig rat *n.* [NAUTICAL] a prisoner.

bring down the house *v.* [ENTERTAINMENT] to achieve a great theatrical success, usually marked by loud applause or standing ovation.

bring home the bacon *v.* to earn a living. Possibly from the tradition that the winner of the greased pig event at country fairs brought home the pig as his prize.

bring home the groceries *v.* to earn a living.

bring someone down *v.* [DRUG CULTURE] to depress someone. Contrary to the feeling of exhilaration of a drug-induced state.

briny *n.* the sea.

bro', brother *n.* [BLACK SLANG] abbreviated form of "soul brother," a term of address indicating comradeship; usually used between men.

broad *n.* a woman.

broke *adj.* without money.

bromide *n.* an old joke or folk saying. Coined by humorist Gelett Burgess.

bronc, bronco *n.* a high-spirited, un-trained horse.

bronco buster *n.* a cowboy who rides and tames wild horses.

Bronx cheer *n.* a sound of derision made by sticking the tongue out and blowing air.

broom *n.* a thin person.

broom up one's ass, have a to be excessively diligent.

brown *adj.* angry; disgusted.

brown bag it *v.* to carry one's lunch to work in a brown paper bag.

browned off *adj.* angry.

brown nose *n.* one who attempts to gain favor by flattery—*v.* to attempt to gain favor by flattery.

brown off *v.* to make an error.

bruiser *n.* a large, pugnacious male.

brunch *n.* a leisurely repast taken in the late morning or early afternoon, combining breakfast and lunch.

brush, the *n.* a rejection—*v.* "to get (or give someone) the brush": to be rejected (or reject someone) from friendship. Also, the brush-off.

brushback *n.* [BASEBALL] a ball thrown by the pitcher that causes the batter to back off from his normal batting position for fear of being hit.

brush up *v.* to review and clarify knowledge.

bub *n.* a term of address for a man whose name is not known.

bubaleh *n.* [YIDDISH] literally, "little grandmother." An affectionate term, the equivalent of dear, honey, etc.

bubble dancer *n.* a dishwasher.

bubble gum music *n.* [BROADCASTING] music appealing to young teenagers.

bubblehead *n.* a fool.

bubble queen *n.* a laundress.

bubbly *n.* champagne.

bubie *n.* [YIDDISH] *See* bubaleh.

buck *n.* 1. a dollar 2. a man, usually used to indicate youth and virility—*v.* to resist.

buckeroo *n.* a cowboy.

bucket *n.* 1. a big, old automobile 2. the buttocks 3. [BASKETBALL] the basket; a basket. Often in the construction "to score a basket."

bucket, kick the See kick the bucket.

bucket head n. a fool.

bucket of bolts n. a humorous term for an old car.

buck general n. [MILITARY] a brigadier-general.

buckle down v. to begin a serious effort, usually after some vague attempts at a task.

buck, pass the v. [GAMBLING] to shirk responsibility. In the Early West, the buck was a marker, often a silver dollar, set before the next person to deal the cards in a game of poker. It served as a reminder of the duty. To pass it to the next player meant that one's responsibility for the deal was over.

buck naked adj. completely nude.

buck private n. [MILITARY] a new recruit in the army.

bucks, in the adv. having money.

buck up v. to overcome discouragement.

bud n. a term of address for a man whose name is not known.

buddy n. a close friend—v. "to buddy up": (a) to seek companionship (b) to act as partners.

buddy-buddy adj. or adv. overly friendly.

Buddy poppy n. an artificial poppy made by disabled veterans and sold for a donation during the weeks preceding Memorial Day.

buff n. a devotee, a fan, an enthusiast.

buffalo v. to deceive.

buffalo head n. a nickel.

buff, in the adv. naked.

bug n. 1. a devotee; an enthusiast 2. a recording device used for eavesdropping 3. a Volkswagen—v. 1. to annoy 2. to place hidden eavesdropping devices.

bugaboo n. an obstacle.

bug doctor n. a psychiatrist.

bug-eyed adj. 1. with slightly protruding eyes; hence 2. astonished.

bugger n. 1. a sodomite 2. a fellow 3. a child who is cute and naughty—v. to sodomize.

buggy n. 1. an old car 2. a baby carriage—adj. crazy.

bughouse n. an insane asylum.

bug in someone's ear, put a v. to excite someone's thoughts or suspicions.

bugs adj. crazy.

build-up n. 1. an increment 2. publicity preceding an event to excite interest—v. 1. to fortify 2. to extol.

bull n. 1. a policeman 2. exaggeration; lies. From the French boule, originally meaning "lie"—v. to bluff.

bulldog n. a tenacious person.

bulldoze v. 1. to pressure someone 2. to deceive, fool, mislead. Originally, "bulldose," a beating in the proper dose for a bull.

bullet n. 1. [GAMBLING] the ace in a deck of cards 2. [PRINTING] a large black dot placed before a phrase, sentence, etc., to draw attention to it 3. [BASEBALL] a fast ball.

bullet bait n. [MILITARY] a member of the armed services in an area of combat.

bullet biter n. a painful, embarrassing situation. From the frontier custom of giving a person about to undergo surgery without anesthesia a bullet to bite on when the pain becomes unbearable.

bull fiddle n. [MUSIC] the double bass viol.

bull fighter n. an empty railroad freight car.

bull headed adj. stubborn.

bull in a china shop, to act or **behave like a** v. to behave awkwardly, clumsily.

bull of the woods n. an important person. Originally, the term applied to the boss of a logging camp.

bull pen n. 1. any confined waiting area 2. [SPORTS] the area where players sit and pitchers warm up during a game of baseball 3. the sleeping quarters in a logging camp.

bull rack n. [TRUCKERS' CB] a truck carrying livestock.

bull session n. a discussion, usually an earnest attempt at problem solving, but also can be idle conversation.

bull's eyes, hit the *See* hit the bull's eye.

bull shit *n.* lies; pretentious nonsense. Also used as an interjection.

bully *adj.* excellent. Also used as an interjection.

bully pulpit *n.* [POLITICS] the authority and dignity of public office exploited to advance personal opinion. Coined by Theodore Roosevelt, who used the Presidency as such.

bum *n.* 1. a derelict 2. [POST OFFICE] an empty mail sack—*v.* to ask for something for free. Often in the construction "to bum something off of someone."

bum *n.* [BRITISH SLANG] the buttocks.

bum, on the *adv.* 1. wandering about aimlessly like a derelict, of a person 2. inoperative, of a thing.

bum around *v.* to spend one's time in a leisurely and aimless manner.

bumbershoot *n.* an umbrella.

bumf, bumph *n.* [BRITISH SLANG] official documents.

bumhole *n.* 1. the anus 2. a stupid, despicable person.

bummer *n.* [DRUG CULTURE] anything that causes a state of depression. Originally, a bad experience with drugs, particularly LSD.

bump *v.* to remove from rightful consecutive place or from competition.

bump off *v.* to kill.

bum's rush *n.* a forcible ejection.

bum steer *n.* false or misleading information.

bun, buns *n.* the buttocks.

bunco *n.* [CRIME] swindling; a confidence racket. *See* con game.

bunco artist *n.* a professional swindler.

bundle *n.* 1. a large amount of money 2. [DRUG CULTURE] a quantity of five-dollar bags of marijuana.

bung *v.* [BRITISH SLANG] to toss; to bruise or damage.

bunk *n.* nonsense.

bunkie *n.* a roommate.

bun on, have a *v.* to be drunk.

bupkes *n.* [YIDDISH] nothing.

buried *adj.* in prison with a long sentence.

burn *v.* 1. to be angry 2. [CRIME] to kill by shooting 3. to electrocute as punishment 4. [SPORTS] to achieve victory over an opponent—*n.* "slow burn": increasing anger.

burn one *v.* [BASEBALL] to pitch a fast ball.

burn the road *v.* to drive at a great speed.

burn up *v.* to anger.

burn with a low flame *v.* to be as drunk as possible.

burned *adj.* 1. cheated 2. humiliated 3. [JOURNALISM] beaten by another reporter to the exclusive or first coverage of a news story.

burned out *adj.* exhausted.

burp gun *n.* [MILITARY] a machine gun. The sound made by its action resembles a series of burps.

burrole *n.* 1. the ear 2. an eavesdropper 3. an informer.

bury *v.* to betray.

bury the hatchet *v.* [AMERICAN INDIAN] to effect a reconciliation.

bus *v.* to clear tables in a restaurant, as employment—*n.* "busboy": one who has such employment.

bush *n.* 1. a beard 2. [DRUG CULTURE] marijuana.

bushes *n.* rural or small town districts.

bush league *n.* [SPORTS] minor league; hence, of little importance. Also used as an adjective.

bushwah, booshwah *n.* nonsense.

business *n.* [ENTERTAINMENT] the physical activity of an actor in a scene. Often, the characteristic gestures associated with familiar entertainers.

business end of something *n.* 1. the most important or dangerous aspect of something. The business end of a gun: the muzzle 2. the financial aspect of an endeavor or pursuit.

business, know one's *v.* to be knowledgeable.

business, the *n.* a deliberately harsh treatment, as in "he gave him the business."

bust *n.* 1. a woman's bosom 2. a failure 3. a police raid 4. a punch 5. [POLITICS] a period of economic recession or depression—*v.* 1. to break 2. to arrest 3. to punch.

bust a cap *v.* [DRUG CULTURE] to take narcotics in capsule form.

bust a gut *v.* to exert oneself extraordinarily.

busted *adv.* arrested.

buster *n.* 1. something large 2. nickname for a boy.

busthead *n.* a drunkard.

bust out *n.* 1. [CRIME] an escape from prison 2. a bankruptcy—*v.* 1. to escape from prison 2. to render bankrupt.

but *adv.* absolutely.

butch *adj.* excessively or ostentatiously masculine. Often used to describe masculine women.

butcher shop *n.* a hospital.

butcher wagon *n.* an ambulance.

butt *n.* 1. the buttocks 2. an object of derision or scorn 3. a cigarette—*v.t.* to mix into another's business.

butter-and-egg man *n.* a rich farmer or small-town businessman who attempts the role of playboy while in a big city.

butterball *n.* a plump person.

buttercup *n.* a pretty young girl.

butterfingers *n.* 1. [SPORTS] one who fumbles 2. one who drops things easily.

butterflies in one's stomach, have to be nervous.

butter up *v.* to curry favor by flattery.

butt in *v.* to interfere in someone's affairs.

buttinski *n.* one who usually interferes in the affairs of others.

button *n.* [BROADCASTING] the finalizing bit of music or sound effects on a commercial.

button, on the *adj.* exactly, precisely.

buttonhole *v.* to detain someone insistently, usually to converse or argue. Originally, "buttonhold."

buttonman *n.* [CRIME] a gunman who uses his weapon in the service of his superiors in a mob.

button one's lip *v.* to be silent.

buttons missing, have some to be insane.

butt out *v.* to refrain from giving unwanted advice.

buy *v.* to accept as truth; to believe.

buy the farm *v.* to die.

buy time *v.* to delay.

buzz *n.* a telephone call—*v.* "to give someone a buzz": to telephone someone.

buzz along *v.* to depart.

buzzard *n.* an ill-disposed old man.

buzz-buzz *n.* noise.

buzz off *v.* to leave. Often used in the imperative.

BVDs *n.* a brand name of men's undergarments, now used popularly to mean men's undershorts of any brand.

by hook or by crook *adv.* attainment of a goal by any means. Possibly from the Old English law forbidding entry to the king's forest lands except to remove dead branches on the ground or still hanging in the trees. These could be removed with ordinary equipment, such as a hook used to harvest grain or a crook used by a shepherd.

C

C *n.* [DRUG CULTURE] cocaine.

Ca *n.* [HOSPITAL JARGON] Cancer.

cab *n.* [AVIATION] the cockpit of an airplane.

cabbage *n.* money.

cabbage head *n.* a stupid person.

cabbage leaves *n.* paper money.

cabbie, cabby *n.* a driver of a taxi cab.

cabin girl *n.* a maid in a hotel, motel, etc.

caboodle *n.* a group of things in its entirety. Often used in the expression "the whole kit and caboodle."

cackleberries and grunts *n.* eggs and bacon.

cackle broad *n.* 1. a woman who talks incessantly 2. a society woman.

cactus league *n.* [SPORTS] major league baseball teams that train in the Southwest, generally in Arizona.

cadet *n.* [OLD SLANG] a pimp.

cadillac *n.* 1. a hand truck used to carry garments from the factory to a store or showroom 2. [DRUG CULTURE] an amount of heroin, usually an ounce.

cage *n.* a prison cell—*v.* to imprison.

cager *n.* 1. a drunkard 2. [BASKETBALL] a basketball player, from "cage," the original name for the game of basketball.

cagey *adj.* wily; deceitfully clever.

cahoots *n.* partnership.

cain *n.* a commotion. *See* raise cain.

cake, take the *See* take the cake.

cake eater *n.* a man known for his success with women.

calaboose *n.* a jail. From the Spanish *calabozo*.

calf love *n.* innocent and immature love.

call *n.* 1. the urge to urinate, usually in the expression "nature's call" 2. [SPORTS] an official decision of a referee or umpire.

call a spade a spade *v.* to speak forthrightly. From an old Greek proverb.

call down *v.t.* to chastise.

call girl *n.* a prostitute, especially one who makes appointments over the telephone.

call house *n.* a brothel.

call it quits *v.* to terminate.

call joint *n.* a brothel.

call someone's bluff *v.* [GAMBLING] to expose someone's pretense. From the card game, poker: a player may bet heavily on a mediocre hand of cards, but eventually another player may insist to see the hand, thus "calling the bluff."

call the shots *v.* [SPORTS] to direct a situation. From a game of billiards, in which a player must indicate which ball will be hit in which hole before attempting a shot.

call the turn *v.* [GAMBLING] to predict. From the card game of faro, in which a player tries to predict the order of the last three cards to be turned over.

camp *adj.* flamboyantly humorous—*v.* to behave flamboyantly, as in "camp it up."

campus *v.* to punish a student by withdrawing some privilege or restricting activites.

campus butcher *n.* a college student known as a ladies' man. *See* ladies' man.

can *n.* 1. the buttocks 2. a toilet 3. a jail—*v.* 1. to dismiss from employment 2.

20

"can it": keep silent.

can, in the adv. [ENTERTAINMENT] said of a film which has been successfully completed and is placed in a round flat protective can for storage until it is to be shown; hence, completed.

canary n. 1. a female singer 2. an informer. See sing.

cancer stick n. a cigarette.

candy n. [DRUG CULTURE] 1. cocaine 2. a cube of sugar soaked in LSD.

candy man n. [DRUG CULTURE] one who sells drugs to addicts; a pusher.

cane corn n. homemade liquor.

canhouse n. a brothel.

can it interj. a command to stop talking, to stop annoying.

canned adj. 1. drunk 2. abandoned, as in "the project was canned."

canned goods n. a virgin.

canned laughter n. [BROADCASTING] prerecorded laughter which is often added to a sound track to accentuate comedic moments. See sweeten.

cannery n. a jail.

cannibalize v. [MILITARY] 1. to obtain personnel from other units to build up the strength and efficiency of one's own unit 2. to remove working parts from an inoperative machine for use in repairing other machines.

cannon n. a gun.

cannonball n. 1. a speedy train or truck 2. [WATER SPORTS] in swimming, a plunge into water with knees tucked against the chin. Also used as an adjective—v. 1. to move swiftly 2. to execute a cannonball dive.

cannon fodder n. a member of the armed services.

canoodle v. to fondle.

can of worms n. a potentially embarrassing, complex, or messy situation with unpleasant implications.

can on, get a v. to get drunk.

can opener n. a burglar's tool used to open a safe.

cant n. [SPORTS] the secret slang of beggars.

cantaloupe n. [SPORTS] a baseball.

canto n. [SPORTS] the period, section, or division of any sports contest or game.

canvasback n. [SPORTS] a prize fighter who is repeatedly knocked down or out and who spends most of his time on his back on the canvas.

cap n. [DRUG CULTURE] a capsule containing a narcotic—v.t. 1. to improve on another's performance in a contest, etc. 2. "cap off": to finish.

Cape Cod turkey n. codfish.

caper n. [CRIME] a criminal activity.

capon n. 1. an effeminate man 2. a homosexual.

card n. 1. an amusing or eccentric person 2. [DRUG CULTURE] an amount of narcotic used by an addict.

card-carrying adj. dedicated to a specific cause, as if carrying a membership card.

card shark n. a dishonest gambler who cheats at cards. From the predatory nature of the shark.

cards, in the adj. predictable, as in the cards of a fortune teller; inevitable.

car hop n. one who waits on patrons seated in their cars at a drive-in restaurant.

carny n. 1. one who works in a carnival 2. a carnival.

carpetbagger n. [POLITICS] a political interloper who seeks office in a district which is not his own. During the period of Reconstruction after the Civil War, unscrupulous Northerners packed a few belongings in bags made of carpet and left for the South to prey on the inexperience of newly enfranchised blacks to gain political power.

carpet, on the adv. being reprimanded by one's superior.

carrot-top n. a person with "red" hair.

carry v. [SPORTS] 1. of a player, to be the major force leading to a team's victory 2. of a ball, to move powerfully and accurately 3. [BOXING] to fight in such a way as to make a weaker opponent seem better and fight for a longer period of time.

carry a heavy load *v.* to be drunk.

carry a lot of weight *v.* to be of importance.

carry off *v.t.* to accomplish, usually indicating a difficult or delicate task.

carry the ball *v.* [FOOTBALL] to advance on the field against opposition toward scoring a touchdown; hence, to lead one's associates courageously through adversity.

carry the difference *v.* to have a gun on one's person.

carry the load *v.* to be the most responsible or diligent person involved in a group effort.

carry the mail *v.* to bring a project to a successful conclusion.

carry the torch for someone *v.* to love without hope of reciprocity.

cartwheel *n.* large coin; silver dollar.

casanova *n.* a man reputed to be a great lover. From the eighteenth-century adventurer who published his *Memoirs*, in which his romantic escapades are recounted.

case *n.* one who is difficult to deal with, as in "he is a case"—*v.* to observe; to scrutinize for a purpose; as in, "he cased the joint in search of drug dealings."

case-dough *n.* an insignificant amount of money.

case note *n.* a dollar.

cash in one's chips *v.* [GAMBLING] to die, as if withdrawing from a game of chance.

cash in on something *v.* to take full advantage of something.

castles in the air *n.* fanciful plans; aspirations.

cast-off *n.* [PRINTING] an estimate of the number of pages a manuscript will make in final book form.

cat *n.* 1. an ill-tempered woman 2. a malicious gossip 3. [JAZZ MUSICIANS' SLANG] a fellow 4. a Cadillac.

catch *n.* 1. a particularly desirable prize (person or thing) 2. an obstacle to a plan—*v.* to see or hear, of a spectacle or entertainment.

catch flies *v.* to be bored.

catch hell *v.* to be castigated.

catch it *v.* to be reprimanded.

catch off-guard *v.* to surprise at a moment of unpreparedness.

catch on *v.* to understand.

catch phrase *See* catchword.

catch up *v.* to overtake.

catchword *n.* a single word that expresses a concept with great clarity. Also, "catch phrase," a succinct expression that captures the essence of a situation.

catfit *n.* an expression of great anger.

cathaul *v.* to interrogate at great length.

cathouse *n.* a brothel.

catman *n.* [CRIME] a burglar who gains entrance to premises by climbing through the window. From the agile and silent aspects of a cat's movements.

cat out of the bag, let the *v.* to reveal a secret.

cat and dogs, raining *See* rain cats and dogs.

cat's eye *n.* a clear glass marble with a streak of color in the middle, resembling the eye of a cat with its oblong pupil.

cat's meow, cat's pajamas, or **cat's whiskers, the** *n.* something wonderful. Expressions popular in the 1920s.

cat's paw *n.* one easily duped. From the Aesop fable in which a monkey persuades a cat to pull chestnuts out of the fire with his paw.

cattle drive *n.* [TRUCKERS' CB] congested traffic.

caught red-handed *adv.* surprised in a compromising position with irrefutable evidence of guilt, as a murderer may be discovered with hands tainted with his victim's blood.

caught with one's pants down *adv.* surprised in an embarrassing situation or at a moment of unpreparedness.

cauliflower ear *n.* [BOXING] an ear misshapen from repeated blows.

cave *n.* any dark room.

caveman *n.* a strong, rough, sometimes brutal man.

CB *n.* the acronym for Citizens Band radio, the network of privately owned and operated low-power radio broadcasting units used primarily for communication between truck drivers or hobbyists.

ceiling, hit the *See* hit the ceiling.

celeb *n.* abbreviation for celebrity.

century *n.* one-hundred dollars.

chaff *n.* exaggerated or nonsensical talk.

chaingang *n.* a group of prisoners attached to each other by chain and shackles and made to work outdoors.

chain lightning *n.* illicitly manufactured liquor.

chain smoke *v.* to smoke cigarettes one after the other compulsively. As the links of a chain are attached, so the cigarettes seem to be as well.

chair, the *n.* 1. [CRIME] the electric chair 2. [BUSINESS] (a) the authority conveyed by the position of leadership in a meeting (b) the position of chairperson itself. The phrase "the chair" is used when policy statements are made in order to indicate that the ruling is official. From the Latin *ex cathedra*, "from the chair"—*v.* to take leadership of a meeting.

chair warmer *n.* a useless or lazy person; one who occupies a seat and does no work.

chalk *n.* a favorite to win in horse racing.

chalk talk *n.* a lecture given with diagrams, etc., drawn on a chalkboard, usually to plan a strategy for a football team. Often used in business.

champ *n.* a champion.

change livery *v.* [SPORTS] to play for a different team.

change the channel *v.* to change the topic in a discussion, as if changing the channel on a television set.

chank *n.* syphilis.

channel *n.* [DRUG CULTURE] the vein into which an addict injects a narcotic.

chappie *n.* [BRITISH SLANG] a fellow; a little fellow.

chapter and verse *n.* a precise knowledge of one's moral code which can be expressed at any time to substantiate one's acts. From the numbered subdivisions in the text of the Bible, which many people call upon to justify their actions and opinions. Often in the expression "to quote chapter and verse."

character *n.* an unusual or eccentric person.

character assassin *n.* one who attempts to destroy another's reputation by calumny.

charge *n.* excitement; pleasure—*v.* "to get a charge (out of something)": to be excited and pleased (by something). From an electric charge, a sudden revitalizing burst of electricity.

charger *n.* a driver.

chariot *n.* a humorous term to indicate an automobile.

charisma *n.* an intangible quality of attraction and vitality possessed by those with leadership qualities.

Charley coke *n.* [DRUG CULTURE] cocaine.

charleyhorse *n.* a muscular cramp usually felt after strenuous exercise.

chart *n.* [GAMBLING] detailed information published about a horse race after the fact.

charts *n.* [MUSIC] the list of currently popular recordings.

chase *v.* to court aggressively.

chase oneself *v.* to be occupied foolishly, wastefully, and futilely. Often used as a command, as in "go chase yourself": leave me alone, occupy yourself elsewhere.

chaser *n.* a non-alcoholic or mild alcoholic beverage taken after a drink of hard liquor.

chassis *n.* the body, particularly used by men to indicate a well-shaped woman. Often in the expression "classy chassis."

chaw *n.* a portion of chewing tobacco or other substance chewed but not swallowed—*v.* 1. to chew without ingesting, usually chewing tobacco 2. to talk idly; to ruminate.

cheap adj. 1. miserly 2. unworthy 3. tawdry.

cheap high n. [DRUG CULTURE] amilnitrate, a drug producing a brief but intense feeling of euphoria, often used as an aphrodisiac.

cheap shot n. [SPORTS] an easy attack on a weakened opponent.

cheap shot artist n. one adept at taking advantage of a weakened opponent.

cheapskate n. a miserly person. Originally "cheapskite"; "skite" means fellow.

cheat v. to commit adultery. Often in the construction "to cheat on one's spouse."

cheat sheet n. written information containing probable answers to examination questions illegally concealed and consulted by students during a test.

check interj. understood; OK. Originally from shortwave radio terminology.

check crew n. [LABOR] work teams with both black and white members.

checkerboard n. a demographic area with both white and black inhabitants.

checkeroo n. any article displaying a checkered pattern.

cheerio interj. [BRITISH SLANG] a parting greeting; goodbye.

cheese n. 1. a person of importance, often in the expression "big cheese" 2. money—v. of a baby, to regurgitate. From the smell of curdled milk in a baby's regurgitation. Often, "to cheese up."

cheesecake n. a suggestive photograph of an attractive and scantily-clad woman. See beefcake.

cheesed off adj. frustrated; angry.

cheesehead n. a fool.

cheese it v. to leave quickly.

cheesy adj. of inferior quality; in poor taste.

cherry n. the hymen; virginity.

cherry picker n. elevator tower.

cherry pie n. an easy task; an easily won prize.

chest hardware n. [MILITARY] medals pinned on the chest of a uniform.

chestnut n. an old joke.

chew a lone something v. to do something without company, usually implying loneliness.

chewed up adj. depressed.

chewing gum n. 1. confused speech 2. confused information.

chew one's tobacco v. to express one's opinion with finality. "Never to chew one's tobacco twice": to refuse to reconsider an opinion.

chew out v. to castigate; to reprimand.

chew over v. 1. to discuss something carefully 2. to consider all possibilities before taking action.

chew someone's ear off v. 1. to expostulate lengthily 2. to reprimand in a tirade.

chew the fat v. to converse idly.

chew the rag v. to argue or debate.

chew the scenery v. [ENTERTAINMENT] to act or perform with such misplaced energy that one appears to be capable of chewing the scenery in a burst of emotion: to overact.

chichi adj. [FRENCH SLANG] pretentiously stylish.

chick n. a girl or woman.

chicken n. 1. a coward 2. a young boy viewed as prey of an older homosexual.

chicken colonel n. [MILITARY] a full colonel.

chicken coming home to roost, one's the results of one's past actions affecting the present.

chicken feed n. an insubstantial amount of money.

chicken fight n. a water game in which two adversary players, each mounted on a partner's shoulders, try to knock each other into the water.

chickenhawk n. an older homosexual who preys on young boys.

chickenheart, chickenliver n. a coward.

chickenhearted, chickenlivered adj. cowardly.

chicken out v. to withdraw in fear.

chicken shit *n.* 1. a meager amount 2. a weak or inconsequential person 3. a lie.

chicken tracks *n.* illegible handwriting.

chickie *n.* [CRIME] a lookout.

chief *n.* a familiar and casual term of address to one's superior.

Chief Itch and Rub *n.* a leader; the most important person in any system, often one with an exaggerated idea of his own importance.

chill *v.* to lose interest.

chill, put on the *v.* to treat with disdain or coldness.

chiller-diller *n.* a work of popular literature or cinema that strives to frighten and keep the reader or spectator in suspense.

chill on someone, put the *v.* [CRIME] to murder someone.

chime in *v.* to voice one's opinions, interrupting a discussion between other individuals.

chin *v.* to talk idly.

chin, take it on the *v.* 1. to undergo a severe setback 2. to accept reverses gracefully.

china *n.* teeth.

Chinaman's chance *n.* little or no opportunity to succeed. From the days of the Chinese immigration to the West Coast of the United States, when Chinese prospectors were only allowed to search for gold in areas that others had tried and left as worthless.

Chinese tobacco *n.* [DRUG CULTURE] opium.

chin fest *n.* a lively gossip session.

chink *n.* 1. a derogatory term for a Chinese person 2. [OLD SLANG] coin or cash.

chinks *n.* 1. Chinese food 2. a Chinese restaurant 3. a Chinese laundry.

chin music *n.* idle speech.

chintzy *adj.* 1. gaudy; cheap looking; inferior 2. miserly; stingy. From chintz, a cheap brightly-colored glazed cotton fabric.

chip *n.* a french-fried potato—*v.* to rob.

chip in *v.* to contribute one's share of money, effort, time, etc., to a group fund or project.

chip on one's shoulder, have a *v.* to be resentful. From the practice of daring an adversary to knock an actual chip of wood off one's shoulder to provoke a fight.

chippie, chippy *n.* 1. a promiscuous woman 2. [BASKETBALL] an unblocked shot.

chippie joint *n.* a brothel.

chips, in the *adv.* 1. having money 2. having good luck.

chips are down, the [GAMBLING] an expression indicating misfortune, as in "I've lost all my money. The chips are down." From the pile of betting chips a gambler uses: during a strain of bad luck the size of the pile diminishes.

chirp *v.* 1. to sing 2. [CRIME] to reveal information to the police 3. to inform.

chisel *v.* 1. to swindle 2. to bargain down.

chiseler *n.* one who cheats, swindles, or attempts to get a better deal for himself.

chitchat *n.* idle talk; gossip. Also a verb.

chocolate *adj.* pertaining to the black race.

choke up *v.* 1. to be overcome with emotion or nervousness to the point of being unable to function properly 2. [BASEBALL] to hold the bat higher up than normal in order to have more control.

chop *n.* an unpleasant or critical remark.

chop-chop *interj.* a command to move more quickly. Originally, a military term from the Hindustani word *chop*, a stamp of approval placed on official documents.

chop one's teeth *v.* to speak idly.

chopper *n.* 1. a helicopter 2. the mouth.

choppers *n.* false teeth.

chops *n.* the mouth.

chotchke *n.* [YIDDISH] 1. a thing of little value 2. a toy 3. an ornamentation 4. a pretty young woman.

chow *n.* food. From the Chinese *ch'ao*, to cook.

chowderhead *n.* a stupid person.

chow down *interj.* [MILITARY] a call to

table in the army.

chow hall *n.* an eating place.

chow hound *n.* an avid, indiscriminate eater.

chow line *n.* a queue of people waiting to be served food.

chow time *n.* the hour when food is served.

Christmas card *n.* [TRUCKERS' CB] a traffic ticket.

chuck *n.* food—*v.* 1. to throw 2. "chuck it": cease; desist.

chucklehead *n.* a fool.

chuck wagon *n.* a small roadside restaurant.

chugalug *v.* to drink; swill; guzzle.

chum *n.* a friend.

chump *n.* a person easily deceived.

chump, off one's *adj.* crazy.

church key *n.* a can opener.

chutzpa *n.* [YIDDISH] nerve; impudence; guts.

cig *n.* abbreviation for cigarette.

cinch *n.* an easy task—*v.* to make certain; to assure success.

circuit slugger *n.* [SPORTS] a baseball player known for consistently hitting home runs.

circular file *n.* [BUSINESS] a wastebasket. A humorous term indicating where many so-called important letters are filed.

circus *n.* a disordered or tumultuous situation.

circus catch *n.* [SPORTS] a catch of the ball calling for a remarkable play by a team member.

city slicker *n.* a shrewd city dweller, usually indicating one who dupes innocent country dwellers.

civvies *n.* [MILITARY] civilian apparel, as opposed to military uniform.

clam *n.* a dollar.

clambake *n.* a party. Originally, a party on the beach at which the main dish served is baked clams.

clamp down *v.* to become more rigorous in enforcing rules.

clamps on, put the *v.* to rob.

clam up *v.* to refuse to talk; to become tense. From the tightly-closed shell of a clam resembling closed lips.

clanks, the *n.* delirium tremens.

clap *n.* gonorrhea.

claptrap *n.* nonsensical speech. Originally, a theatrical term for improvised crowd-pleasing lines used by an actor to get (trap) applause (clap).

class *n.* style, elegance—*adj.* classy.

claw on someone, put the *v.* of the police, to arrest someone.

clay pigeon *n.* 1. an easy target 2. a person easily duped. From the targets used in practicing marksmanship.

clean *adj.* [CRIME] not carrying a gun—*v.* *See* wash.

cleaners, go to the *v.* to lose one's financial assets, usually through the duplicity of others.

clean out *v.* to take away all of someone's money.

clean sweep *n.* [POLITICS] an election victory in which many candidates from one political party win office.

clear sailing *adv.* easily accomplished, of a task or project, often after exerting a considerable effort to start the project.

clem *n.* 1. a naive country dweller 2. [CIRCUS SLANG] a fight.

click *v.* 1. to succeed 2. to fit into a pattern or integrate easily into a situation 3. to fall into place.

cliff dweller *n.* one who lives in a high-rise apartment building.

cliffhanger *n.* 1. an exciting and suspenseful piece of literature or cinema 2. a situation where the outcome is not known until the very end. Originally pertaining to nineteenth-century serialized novels in which segments often concluded with the protagonist hanging off a cliff to excite interest in the next episode.

clinch *n.* [BOXING] entangling one's opponent—*v.* 1. to entangle and hold an opponent in order to gain time and regain strength 2. to finalize.

clincher *n.* a finalizing element.

clink *n.* a jail.

clinker *n.* an embarrassing mistake.

clip *n.* a strike—*v.* 1. to strike 2. to cheat out of money.

clip artist *n.* one adept at swindling.

clip joint *n.* a business establishment in which customers are cheated, usually by excessively high prices charged for inferior merchandise.

clobber *v.* 1. to strike 2. to defeat conclusively.

clock *v.* to time.

clock watcher *n.* a lazy worker, one who eagerly awaits the end of the working day and looks repeatedly to see the time.

clodhopper *n.* 1. an ungainly person 2. a clumsy garment.

clonk *v.* to strike.

closed shop *n.* [LABOR] a place of employment where only union members are permitted to work.

closer *n.* [SPORTS] 1. the ninth inning in a game of baseball 2. the seond game of a double-header. *See* double-header.

close ranks *v.* [POLITICS] to restructure loyalties within a political party after the invectives of a primary campaign. Originally, a military maneuver.

close shave *n.* a narrow escape. From narrowly missing cutting one's skin with a razor while shaving.

closet *adj.* secret, as in "she is a closet conservative."

closet liberal *n.* [POLITICS] a politician declared conservative but with liberal leanings.

closet queen *n.* a homosexual who has not made his preference public.

close-up *n.* a view at close range.

clot *n.* [BRITISH SLANG] stupid person.

clotheshorse *n.* a person who shows great interest in and habitually wears the latest fashions.

clothes tree *n.* a free-standing pole with hooks used for the purpose of hanging clothing.

cloud, on a *adv.* in a blissful state.

cloud nine, on *adv.* in a blissful state. From the United States Weather Bu-reau practice of giving a number code to different types of cloud formations, type nine being *cumulonimbus,* a very thin high cloud. Popularized by the Johnny Dollar radio show of the 1950s.

clout *n.* influence; strength—*v.* to strike.

clover, in *adv.* 1. fortunate 2. happy.

clover-kicker *n.* a person from the country.

clown *n.* an habitual joker—*v.* "clown around": to behave foolishly or frivolously.

cluck *n.* a fool. Often in the expression "dumb cluck."

clue in *v.* to inform; to explain.

clunk *n.* a stupid person—*v.* to strike.

clunkhead *n.* a stupid person.

clunker *n.* old machine in poor condition.

clutch *n.* 1. a handshake 2. a hug.

clutches *n.* grasp.

clutch up *v.* to become nervous, tense.

Clyde *n.* a clumsy, stupid person.

C-note *n.* a one-hundred dollar bill. The Roman numeral C means one-hundred.

coast *v.* 1. to achieve success with little effort 2. to maintain past patterns of behavior in the present.

coat-tails, hanging on someone's *adv.* [POLITICS] reaping benefits by association with an influential politician.

cob *n.* an unsophisticated country dweller. From corn cob.

cobber *n.* [AUSTRALIAN SLANG] close companion.

cobbler *n.* [CRIME] a forger, particularly one specializing in passports or bonds.

cock *n.* the penis.

cockamamy, cockamamie *adj.* ridiculous.

cock-and-bull story *n.* an improbable explanation, usually told by one desiring to hide the facts.

cockeyed *adj.* 1. with crossed eyes 2. crazy.

cock-of-the-walk *n.* a conceited man. From the barnyard hierarchy, where the strong rooster dominates and struts proudly on the walk.

cock tease *n.* a female flirt who entices a man and then refuses to give sexual favors.

coconut *n.* the head.

codswallop *n.* [BRITISH SLANG] nonsense.

coed *n.* a female student in an institution of higher learning with both male and female students. Abbreviated form of coeducational.

coffee and cake *n.* a minimal salary. Also used as an adjective.

coffee klatsch *n.* a lively meeting over a cup of coffee. From the German *kaffeeklatsch*.

coffee pot *n.* [BROADCASTING] a small commercial radio broadcasting station that reaches an equally small audience.

coffin *n.* any vehicle that seems unsafe.

coffin corner *n.* [SPORTS] a corner of a football field delineated by the goal line and the side line.

coffin nail, tack *n.* a cigarette. From the widely-held belief that heavy cigarette smoking can lead to death.

coffin varnish *n.* liquor.

coke *n.* [DRUG CULTURE] cocaine.

coke head, cokie *n.* an habitual user of cocaine.

cold *adj.* completely unconscious; naive; ignorant.

cold biscuit *n.* a frigid or unattractive woman.

cold cock *v.* to strike and make unconscious.

cold feet *n.* cowardice. Usually in the expression "to get (or to have) cold feet": to be timorous.

cold fish *n.* one lacking vitality or emotion.

cold meat *n.* a corpse.

cold meat box *n.* a coffin.

cold pack *n.* [BOXING] a knockout.

cold shoulder *n.* a disdainful treatment; a snub. Usually in the expression "to give someone the cold shoulder." From the practice during the Middle Ages of offering a traveling knight a hot dinner, and a cold one to a traveling com-

moner.

cold storage *n.* a grave.

cold turkey *n.* a complete and abrupt withdrawal from any addictive element—*v.* "to go cold turkey": to withdraw suddenly from an addiction.

cold war *n.* ideological conflict. *See* all-out war.

collar *v.* to apprehend.

color man *n.* [BROADCASTING] a reporter who supplies background information, statistics, and anecdotes to enliven sports commentating.

combo *n.* [MUSIC] a small group of musicians who play together.

come *v.* to achieve orgasm.

come across *v.* 1. to provide an expected service, often in reference to sexual favors or money 2. to make an impression.

come again *v.* to repeat one's words, usually at the request of a listener for added clarity, as in the expression "Please, come again!"

come apart at the seams *v.* 1. to disintegrate 2. to lose one's emotional self-control or physical well-being.

come around *v.* to accede eventually to another's opinions or wishes.

comeback *n.* [ENTERTAINMENT] a return to fame, success, or popularity, usually after a period of retirement.

come down *n.* an abasement; a reversal of fortune.

come down with *v.* to become ill with.

come hell or high water *interj.* no matter what happens. An expression of determination.

come off it *interj.* a command to face reality or to stop acting foolishly.

come off one's perch *v.* to behave in a less pretentious manner than usual.

come-on *n.* an enticement.

come on like gangbusters *v.* to make a forceful and energetic entrance. From the 1940s radio program *Gangbusters*, which always began with the sound of wailing sirens and machine gun fire.

come on strong *v.* to exert an overly

aggressive and dynamic personality.

come out *v.* to be introduced into society for the first time.

come out of the closet *v.* to declare openly one's homosexuality.

come out with *v.* 1. to present a new item to the public 2. to say something startling.

comer *n.* one destined for success. *See* up and coming.

come through *v.* 1. to survive a trying period or experience 2. to produce an expected result.

come to school *v.* to conform to rules. From the demands placed on students to observe certain requirements.

comeuppance *n.* a suitable recompense for one's behavior, usually referring to a minor punishment.

come up with *v.* 1. to invent 2. to say something startling.

comfortable *adj.* 1. in good financial position 2. drunk.

commie *n.* or *adj.* abbreviation for Communist.

commit *v.* to confine to a mental institution.

comp *n.* [ENTERTAINMENT] a free ticket of admission; the abbreviation for complimentary.

company man *n.* a worker who conforms to the procedures of his place of employment.

con *n.* 1. abbreviation for convict 2. a swindle—*v.* to swindle. From the abbreviation for confidence, the feeling induced in a victim before the swindler can extort money or valuables—*adj.* pertaining to dishonest behavior.

con artist *n.* one adept at winning favor in a deceitful manner. This term is sometimes used affectionately when applied to an appealing child.

conchy, conchie *n.* a conscientious objector.

Coney Island *n.* a frankfurter served with ketchup, relish, onion, etc. The term reflects the popularity of frankfurters in Coney Island, a beach and amusement area in Brooklyn, New York, but it is only used outside of New York. In Coney Island itself, frankfurters are usually called "hot dogs."

confab *n.* a business meeting.

con game *n.* [CRIME] a swindle involving gaining the confidence of victims in order to dupe them of their valuables.

con job *n.* exaggerated promises to dupe the listener.

conk *n.* the head—*v.* to hit on the head.

conk-buster *n.* a problem involving much thought to solve.

conk out *v.* 1. to fall quickly into a deep sleep 2. to become inoperative, of a machine.

conman *n.* [CRIME] a criminal who establishes a feeling of confidence in victims in order to induce them to turn over valuables and money.

connect *v.* 1. to succeed in an enterprise 2. to fit into a pattern 3. to be understood 4. to establish a mutual feeling between persons.

connected *adj.* under the protection of a powerful or influential person. Often used in criminal circles.

connection *n.* 1. an acquaintance in a position of importance 2. one who sells illegal drugs to addicts; a pusher.

conniption *n.* an hysterical, angry harangue.

constructed *adj.* with an attractive physique.

contact *n.* one who serves as a link between someone and his goal.

contact high *n.* [DRUG CULTURE] euphoria felt by a person who has taken no drugs but is with a group of friends who have and who are experiencing a drug-induced state, or by one who does not smoke a narcotic but inhales the smoke of another's pipe or cigarette.

contacts *n.* abbreviation for contact lenses.

contact sheet *n.* [PHOTOGRAPHY] a page of small positives developed from 35mm film, usually used to choose photographs to be printed in larger size.

contract *n.* 1. [CRIME] an assignment to murder someone (*see* put out a contract) 2. [POLITICS] a promise.

control bench *n.* [PRISON] a prison tribunal that hears the case of prisoners accused of infractions of the prison code.

convict *n.* [CIRCUS SLANG] a zebra.

cooch *n.* a suggestive dance.

coo coo *adj.* crazy.

cook *v.* 1. to function smoothly 2. of a creative artist, to produce excellent work during a given period 3. [PRISON] to die in the electric chair.

cooked *adj.* defeated. *See* cook someone's goose.

cookie *n.* 1. a shrewd person 2. a cute child 3. an attractive woman 4. [MILITARY] a nickname for the cook or the cook's assistant.

cookie pusher *n.* 1. an effeminate man 2. [POLITICS] a diplomat more concerned with the observance of traditional form than with action.

cook someone's goose *v.* 1. to frustrate someone's attempts 2. to punish 3. to harm.

cook up *v.* to invent; to devise.

cook with gas *v.* to function stylishly and well. Originally, to typify modernity, when gas ranges were first introduced for popular use in the 1920s.

cool *adj.* 1. unemotional 2. sophisticated 3. wonderful—*v.* to lose interest.

cooler *n.* [CRIME] 1. a prison 2. a deck of cards prearranged in order to assure a dishonest gambler of winning, i.e., a stacked deck.

cooling-off period *n.* [LABOR] a time allowed to both management and labor to negotiate a contract, during which time neither side may instigate retaliatory action.

cool it *interj.* a command to relax, to be silent, or to stop an activity.

cool off *v.* to become less excited or angry.

cool off man *n.* [GAMBLING] an accomplice in a dishonest gambling scheme, whose function is to calm a victim after a heavy loss.

cool one's heels *v.* to be kept waiting.

coon *n.* a derogatory term for a black person.

coop *n.* a jail.

cooping *n.* [POLICE] shirking one's duties and napping during a work shift.

coot *n.* an eccentric or ill-tempered old man.

cootie *n.* [BRITISH WORLD WAR I SLANG] a louse.

cop *n.* a policeman. Also, copper—*v.* to steal; to take what is not deserved.

copacetic *adj.* excellent.

cop a plea *v.* [CRIME] to plead guilty.

cop out *n.* 1. a cowardly retreat 2. a feeble excuse 3. one who perpetually disappoints—*v.* 1. to withdraw in a cowardly manner from a project, agreement, etc. 2. to abandon one's principles.

copper *n.* a policeman—*v.* to bet against another's bet.

copy *v.* [SHORTWAVE BROADCASTING] to understand.

copy cat *n.* an habitual imitator. A term often used by children.

copy the mail *v.* [TRUCKERS' CB] to listen to one's CB radio and to talk very little.

corazon *n.* [SPANISH] heart; courage. A term indicating solidarity.

cork *v.* to lose one's temper; to become enraged.

corker *n.* something excellent or remarkable.

corking *adj.* exciting.

corn *n.* liquor.

cornball *n.* one given to sentimentality—*adj.* old-fashioned; sentimental; odd.

corn belt *n.* that area of the Midwest where corn is the major crop.

cornfed *adj.* rural, unsophisticated.

corn rows *n.* a hairstyle popular among blacks, characterized by many small tight braids forming interesting patterns on the scalp and often decorated with beads or shells.

corny *adj.* trite, sentimental.

corral *v.* to take possession of; to take hold of.

cosh *n.* [BRITISH SLANG] a stick; a skewer—*v.* to strike with a cosh.

cosmic *adj.* huge; significant.

cotton-picking *adj.* 1. a euphemism for "damned." 2. lowdown.

couch doctor *n.* a psychiatrist.

cough up *v.* to produce something that is expected.

count *n.* [PRISON] a roll call.

count, off the *adv.* [PRISON] missing, escaped, or dead. Literally, to be absent from the roll call.

count, on the *adv.* [PRISON] present.

counterculture *n.* [SOCIOLOGY] a general term grouping American social dissidents, particularly in use in the late-1960s to mid-1970s.

counter, under the *adv.* surreptitiously—*adj.* secret.

country bumpkin *n.* a naive rural dweller.

country club *n.* [PRISON] a prison where the inmates are treated well.

county mounty *n.* [TRUCKERS' CB] a county police officer.

cousin *n.* [BASEBALL] a pitcher whose pitches are so easy to hit that one assumes him to be the batter's cousin.

cove *n.* [BRITISH SLANG] a boy; a man, chap, or fellow.

cover *n.* 1. a person with a weapon who protects someone 2. one who takes over another's responsibilities 3. [ENTERTAINMENT] an understudy 4. one who provides an alibi 5. a disguise—*v.* 1. to protect someone, usually with a weapon 2. to take over someone's duties and responsibilities 3. [ENTERTAINMENT] to understudy 4. to alibi for someone 5. to disguise, obscure.

cover up *n.* an obfuscation—*v.* to obscure, confuse.

cow *n.* 1. milk 2. beef 3. a slow-witted, sloppy woman.

cowabunga *interj.* an exclamation of surprise or triumph. The shibboleth of Chief Thunderthud, a character on the *Howdy Doody* television show of the 1950s.

cow college *n.* a school of agriculture.

cowhide *n.* [SPORTS] a baseball.

cow juice *n.* milk.

cowpoke, cowpuncher *n.* 1. a cowboy 2. a ranch employee hired to look after cattle. From the practice of driving herds of cattle with "prod poles," poking them to make them move.

cozy *adj.* cautious so as to avoid risk.

cozy up *v.* to become physically close to someone, as in "I'd like to cozy up to her."

crab *n.* an ill-tempered person—*v.* to complain.

crabs *n.* 1. body lice 2. syphilis.

crack *v.* 1. to suffer a mental breakdown 2. [CRIME] to open a safe by illegal means 3. to break silence under extreme stress and reveal a secret 4. to decipher (a code) 5. to open.

crack a smile *v.* to grudgingly accede to an impulse to smile after displaying an unemotional countenance.

crack down *v.* to enforce strict control.

cracked *adj.* crazy.

cracker *n.* a derogatory term for a poor white southerner.

crackerbarrel *n.* a gathering place for informal discussion and philosophizing. From the actual barrel of crackers in every general store, the central meeting place in rural areas—*adj.* rustic.

cracker jack *n.* a dynamic person—*adj.* excellent.

crackers *adj.* crazy.

cracking, get *v.* to begin a project or undertaking with great energy.

cracksman *n.* a burglar; a safecracker.

crack up *n.* 1. an automobile accident 2. a mental breakdown—*v.i.* 1. to wreck a vehicle in an accident 2. to suffer a mental breakdown 3. to laugh—*v.t.* to cause someone to laugh.

cradle snatcher *n.* one who marries someone much younger.

cram *v.* to study intensively, usually just before an examination.

cramp someone's style *v.* to have a deleterious effect on someone's performance.

crank *n.* an ill-tempered person—*adj.* bothersome or rude.

crank in *v.t.* to initiate the use of.

crank out *v.* to produce work in an automatic way. Often used in reference to a writer who produces a steady stream of mediocre pieces purely for financial gain.

crap *n.* 1. excrement 2. nonsense—*v.* "to take a crap": to defecate.

crape- (or **crepe-**) **hanger** *n.* 1. an undertaker 2. one who engulfs in gloom. From the practice of draping black fabric, usually crape (crepe) in a home where a death has recently taken place.

crap out *v.* to avoid responsibility.

craps *n.* [GAMBLING] a dice game.

crash *n.* a sudden, devastating economic or emotional depression—*v.* 1. to suffer a sudden and devastating economic or emotional depression 2. to enter a social gathering without an invitation 3. [DRUG CULTURE] to emerge from the effects of a narcotic 4. to sleep—*adj.* 1. extreme and sudden, as in crash diet, crash program, etc. 2. pertaining to sleep.

crash car *n.* [CRIME] a vehicle escorting a car in which a criminal is making an escape and which, in case of police interference, is used to block the road.

crash house *n.* [TRUCKERS' CB] a hospital.

crash pad *n.* a place to sleep, particularly when no other lodging is available.

crash program *n.* a drastic and speedy change from past policy.

crate *n.* a dilapidated old car.

craw *n.* the throat.

crawl *v.* [BRITISH SLANG] to go from one pub to another (pub crawl).

crazy *adj.* excellent; wild; fantastic. Also used as an interjection.

crazy about or **for** *adv.* extremely fond of.

cream *v.* 1. to defeat completely 2. to batter.

creampuff *n.* a weakling.

credibility gap *n.* [POLITICS] the public's disbelief in information from an official source.

credible deterrent *n.* [MILITARY] a show of military strength, real or imaginary, sufficient to convince an enemy not to attack.

creek, up the *adv.* in trouble, as in "I made a big mistake, and I'm up the creek."

creep *n.* 1. a stodgy, sanctimonious, generally unpleasant person 2. [CRIME] a sex offender.

creeping socialism *n.* [POLITICS] the government's encroachment into economic and social fields beyond its traditional jurisdiction. Used primarily by those who fear the effect on private enterprise.

creeps, the *n.* a feeling of discomfort or fear, as in "I've got the creeps."

creepy *adj.* 1. eerie 2. odd.

crib *v.* to cheat on an examination.

crib sheet *n.* written information containing answers to probable examination questions, illegally concealed and consulted by students during a test.

croak *v.i.* to die—*v.t.* to kill.

crock *n.* 1. anything or anyone worthless 2. a medical patient who complains chronically about his minor or imaginary illnesses.

crocked *adj.* drunk.

crocker *n.* a doctor.

crocodile tears *n.* hypocritical grief. The ancient Greeks and Romans believed that a crocodile wept while devouring its prey.

crony *n.* [BRITISH UNIVERSITY SLANG] friend of longstanding.

crook *v.* to steal.

cross *n.* 1. a dishonest action 2. a fixed contest.

cross one's heart and hope to die *v.* a child's shibboleth attesting to the veracity of a statement.

cross shot *n.* [BROADCASTING] a picture taken by a camera positioned at an oblique angle to the scene.

cross someone's palm *v.* to pay for services rendered; to bribe or tip. From the supposed shibboleth of gypsy fortune tellers who will predict the future for a fee.

cross-up or **cross up** *n.* 1. confusion 2. a betrayal—*v.* 1. to confound 2. to betray.

crown *v.* to hit on the head.

crud *n.* 1. a deposit of dirt, filth 2. a dishonorable person 3. anything disgusting or contemptible.

cruddy *adj.* 1. dirty 2. mean 3. inferior.

cruise *v.* to go leisurely in search of a sexual partner, usually in bars or in a particular area of a town known for such activity. Usually for homosexual activity.

crumb *n.* a contemptible person. Also, crumb bun.

crummie *n.* manager of the bunkhouse in a lumber camp.

crummy *adj.* 1. inferior 2. contemptible.

crunch *n.* intense political or economic pressure.

crush *n.* a strong romantic attachment. Adolescent girls often "have a crush" on a boy.

crush out *v.* [BROADCASTING] to reduce color contrast in a televised image by merging similar tones electronically.

crust *n.* nerve.

crusty *adj.* 1. hardened 2. audacious.

cry baby *n.* 1. a weakling 2. a complainer.

crying towel *n.* false commiseration offered to an habitual complainer.

cry uncle *v.* to admit defeat.

CT *See* cock tease.

CU *n.* [BROADCASTING] acronym for close-up, a view at close range.

cubbyhole *n.* a small closet or hiding place.

cube *n.* 1. an excessively old-fashioned or stodgy person, more prim than a square (*see* square) 2. [DRUG CULTURE] a sugar cube soaked in LSD.

cuckoo *adj.* crazy. Also used as a noun, as in "he is a cuckoo."

cuff, off the *adv.* unrehearsed. A humorous expression from the masculine practice of the nineteenth century of writing memoranda on highly-starched shirtsleeve cuffs to have the information available at a moment's notice.

cuff, on the *adv.* on credit, of a purchase. From the practice of jotting notes on one's shirt cuffs.

cuke *n.* abbreviation for cucumber.

cully *n.* [OLD SLANG] 1. a dupe 2. a companion; a mate—*v.* to deceive; to cheat.

culture mavin *See* culture vulture.

culture vulture *n.* a humorous evaluation of one with little real appreciation for the arts who remains abreast of all cultural activities in a frenetic and predatory way in order to appear refined, intellectual, etc. "Culture mavin" is a less sarcastic term indicating a real interest in artistic activities.

cunt *n.* 1. the female pudendum 2. a stupid and unpleasant woman.

cup of coffee *n.* [SPORTS] a short stay in the major leagues, just enough time for a cup of coffee. Often used to designate a minor league baseball player.

cup of tea *n.* a special interest, as in "that's my cup of tea."

cups, in one's *adv.* drunk.

cure, take the *v.* to refrain from drinking alcoholic beverages.

currents *n.* [BROADCASTING] currently popular recordings.

curry favor *v.* to seek advancement by flattery. From the mediaeval French allegory *Le Roman de Fauvel,* in which a horse, Fauvel, is the symbol of cunning and deception. Fauvel was eventually changed to the more familiar English word "favor," but kept its original meaning.

curse, the *n.* menstruation.

curtain raiser *n.* 1. [BASEBALL] the first inning in a game 2. [BASEBALL] the first game of a double-header (*see* double-header) 3. [ENTERTAINMENT] the first act in a variety show.

curtains *n.* [ENTERTAINMENT] death, as in "the play's a flop—call it curtains!"

From the practice of closing the curtain at the end of a play.

cushion n. [BROADCASTING] a section of a pre-recorded program that can be shown in full, or partially cut, without loss of continuity in order to fit the show perfectly into a time slot.

cushiony See cushy.

cushy adj. easy; secure. From "cushiony": shielding from harshness.

cuss n. 1. a tough man 2. a curse word—v. to use curse words.

customer n. a person with whom one has dealings. Often in the sense of one hard to please.

cut n. 1. a share; a portion 2. an insult 3. [ENTERTAINMENT] a deletion of dialogue or action from a show 4. an absence from class—v. 1. to stop action 2. to excise 3. to edit a show 4. to be absent from class without justification.

cut and dried adj. straightforward; without ramifications; unchanging. As a flower is preserved by cutting and drying it.

cut a rug v. to dance. "Cut a mean rug": to dance very well. From the movement of feet wearing out a rug.

cutie n. one who is either 1. attractive 2. coy 3. impudent.

cut in v. to interrupt a dancing couple in order to dance with one of the partners oneself.

cut it out v. to eliminate. Also used as an interjection as a command to desist.

cut out v. 1. to eliminate 2. to leave.

cut-plug n. a worthless horse.

cut-rate adj. offering a discount in price, as in a "cut-rate drug store."

cut some Z's v. [TRUCKERS' CB] to rest; to nap. The sound made by pronouncing a series of Z's approximates the sound of snoring.

cut the mustard v. to fulfill expectations.

cut to something v. [BROADCASTING] to change abruptly from an initial image to another one, or from a topic of discussion to a new subject in a show.

cut up or **cut-up** n. one given to levity—v. to behave disruptively in a humorous manner.

D

DA *n*. 1. acronym for district attorney, the public prosecutor 2. a hairstyle popular among teenage boys in the 1950s, characterized by longish hair brushed back from the face and toward the base of the skull, curling up to resemble a duck's tail feathers, thus the name "duck's ass," abbreviated to DA.

daddy *n*. a lover, usually an older man, who bestows extravagant gifts or who supports his mistress. Often in the term "sugar daddy."

daddy-o *n*. originally, a term of disrespect or familiarity to any older man. Then, a general form of address to any male who was part of the contemporary scene in the late 1950s. From Evan Hunter's novel, *Blackboard Jungle*, a movie extemely popular at the time.

daffodil *n*. a folk saying.

daffy *adj*. crazy.

dagged *adj*. drunk.

dag-nabbed *adj*. a euphemism for "damned."

dago *n*. a derogatory term for an Italian.

dago red *n*. any cheap red wine.

dagwood *n*. a huge sandwich made with many ingredients. From the character Dagwood Bumstead in Chic Young's comic strip *Blondie*, who prepares himself immense sandwiches as snacks.

daily double, win the *v*. [GAMBLING] to be successful in two areas at the same time. In order to win a daily double, a bettor must accurately pick the winner in two races or competitions.

daisies, push up the *v*. to be dead and buried, as in "he's pushing up the daisies."

daisy *n*. anything of excellence.

damaged *adj*. drunk.

damaged goods *n*. a non-virgin girl.

dame *n*. a woman; a girl.

damper *n*. anything that depresses high spirits—*v*. "put a damper on something": to negate joy.

dance *v*. to perform in a servile fashion before authority.

dance, go into one's *v*. to tell a lie, usually one which is long and complicated. Often used with song, as in "he's going into a whole big song and dance."

dance on air *v*. to die by means of hanging. From the death throes of a hanged person.

dancer *n*. 1. a coward 2. [PRIZEFIGHTING] one who avoids punches and never lands a forceful blow himself.

dance the carpet *v*. to be reprimanded by one's superior.

dander up, get one's *v*. to become angry.

darb *n*. a person or thing regarded as remarkable or excellent.

darby *n*. money.

dark *adj*. [ENTERTAINMENT] closed for business. Usually used in reference to a theater, as in "on Monday most theaters are dark."

dark, in the *adv*. without information, as in "I'm in the dark about the entire matter."

dark horse *n*. [POLITICS] a candidate chosen to run only when other preferred ones default. The expression was taken from a novel by Benjamin Disraeli, *The Young Duke*, in which a previously unnoticed dark horse won a surprise victory in a race. *See* front runner.

darn *adv.* very. A euphemism for "damn."

darn it *interj.* an expression of frustration.

daylights *n.* consciousness—*v.* "beat the living daylights out of someone": to thrash someone soundly.

daylight, see *v.* 1. to understand, usually after a long struggle with a problem 2. to approach the finish of a project that has required much effort.

deacon *v.* 1. to pack fruit so that only the best shows 2. to practice trickery.

dead *adj.* 1. exhausted 2. boring 3. [SPORTS] a ball which is out of play 4. [SPORTS] a ball which is played weakly—*adv.* very; completely, as in "she's dead tired."

dead air *n.* [BROADCASTING] an unwanted period of silence during a radio broadcast.

dead as a dodo *adj.* 1. abandoned and forgotten, of a project 2. dead [literally] and forgotten, of a person. From the dodo bird, now extinct.

dead as a doornail *adj.* completely dead. From the stud placed under the knocker on a door to make a sharp sound each time someone knocks. Such a nail suffers constant heavy blows on its head, and had it once been alive would certainly be dead.

dead beat *n.* one who does not repay incurred debts.

dead broke *adj.* completely out of money.

dead duck *n.* one doomed to failure.

dead eye *n.* an accurate marksman.

deadfall *n.* a restaurant that remains open all night.

deadhead *n.* a stupid or unimaginative person.

dead heat *n.* [SPORTS] a tied score in a contest. Also used as a verb.

dead hour *n.* an unoccupied hour in a college student's schedule that falls between two other hours of scheduled classes, as in "two to three o'clock is a dead hour for me."

deadlights *n.* the eyes.

dead man's hand *n.* [gambling] in poker, a pair of aces and a pair of eights. Wild Bill Hickok held these cards when he was shot in the back (1896); hence, bad luck.

deadneck *n.* a slow-witted person.

deadpan *adj.* without visible emotion; expressionless. Also used as a noun.

dead pigeon *n.* one doomed either to failure or death.

dead proof *n.* [PRINTING] a preliminary printing of copy that is no longer the working copy because it has been revised and a new proof is being used.

dead ringer *n.* a duplicate of something or someone, startling by its exact resemblance.

dead to rights *adv.* 1. sure, certain 2. in an unassailable position.

dead to the world *adv.* sleeping very deeply.

deadwood *n.* 1. a hindrance 2. [BOWLING] pins which have been knocked down during a first frame of play and have not been removed for the second frame.

deal *v.* 1. to sell illegal drugs 2. to distribute playing cards—*n.* dealer.

deal, make a big *v.* to create a fuss, usually over an insignificant element.

deal someone in (or out) *v.* [GAMBLING] to include (or exclude) someone in (or from) an activity or business venture. A term used in poker to indicate whether or not a specific player will be playing the next hand of cards.

deal them off the arm *v.* to work as a waiter, referring to the manner in which a waiter often carries several dishes precariously balanced on his arm.

Dear John *n.* a letter cutting off a relationship. Originally, a term used during World War II indicating a letter sent to a serviceman by his wife requesting a divorce.

death wish *n.* [DRUG CULTURE] an hallucinogenic drug, originally used in veterinary medicine as a tranquilizer.

deb *n.* abbreviation for debutante, the daughter of a socially prominent family who is being introduced into society.

debug *v.* to find and remove hidden electronic equipment.

debunk *v.* to expose a fraud.

deck *n.* [DRUG CULTURE] five dollars worth of heroin—*v.* to knock down.

deck, hit the *See* hit the deck.

deck, on *adv.* 1. ready to begin a task 2. present 3. [BASEBALL] waiting to be next at bat.

decks awash *adj.* drunk.

decode *v.* to make more clear, of speech, the written word, etc.

deduck *n.* a tax deduction.

deejay *n.* [BROADCASTING] a disc jockey, i.e., one who introduces recorded music on a radio broadcast.

deep freeze *n.* [POLITICS] a disdainful treatment; ostracism, particularly of a former ally.

deep-sea chef *n.* a dishwasher.

deep six *n.* [NAUTICAL] a burial; a grave—*v.* 1. to bury 2. to hide. Originally, burial at sea, which is normally accomplished at an area six fathoms deep.

dehorn *n.* a drunk.

deli *n.* a delicatessen.

delish *adj.* a humorous variation of delicious, as in "the dish was delish."

deliver *v.* 1. to live up to expectations 2. to fulfill a promise 3. to accord sexual favors. Often used in the expression "deliver the goods."

demo *n.* [BROADCASTING] a demonstration copy of a recording, a commercial, etc., made to test its marketability and to make any necessary changes before the actual copy is produced.

demolition derby *n.* a competitive game in which drivers in delapidated cars crash into one another until only one car remains operable.

derrick *n.* [CRIME] a clever and successful shoplifter.

derriere *n.* [FRENCH] the buttocks.

desert rat *n.* one who enjoys life on the desert, specifically a prospector.

Desi *n.* [SPORTS] in baseball, the designated hitter, i.e., the player who goes to bat for the pitcher but plays no position in the field.

desk jockey *n.* an office worker.

desperado *n.* one whose standard of living is higher than income warrants.

Detroit *n.* a masculine hairstyle popular in the 1950s, characterized by a brush-cut on top with long sides combed back.

deuce *n.* 1. two dollars 2. two puffs on a cigarette 3. [CRIME] a two-year prison sentence.

deuce of clubs *n.* one's two fists.

deucer *n.* 1. [CRIME] a person in jail with a two-year sentence 2. [BASEBALL] the second game of a double header 3. [BASEBALL] a hit permitting the runner to gain two bases 4. [HORSE RACING] the horse that finishes second 5. [ENTERTAINMENT] the second act on the program of a variety show or a circus.

deuce spot *n.* the position after first place in a game or competition.

deuce, what the *interj.* an expression of surprise, indignation, or resignation.

devil-may-care *adj.* daring, as in "he has a devil-may-care attitude."

dex, dexie *n.* [DRUG CULTURE] Dexedrine.

DI *n.* [MILITARY] an army drill instructor.

diamonds *n.* the testicles.

diary *n.* [BROADCASTING] an analysis of daily listening habits over a week compiled and submitted by randomly chosen broadcast audience members for a survey.

dibs *n.* 1. money 2. a share of profits. From divvy, to divide.

dibs on something, have *v.* to have claim to something.

dice *n.* [AUTOMOBILE RACING] a situation in which drivers maneuver to overtake the leading car in a race. Also used as a verb.

dick *n.* 1. a detective 2. the penis.

diddie bag *n.* a small bag for personal

effects.

diddle v. 1. to fidget nervously 2. to cheat.

diddly adj. of little value.

didie n. [BABY TALK] an infant's diaper.

dido n. an objection or complaint.

diehard n. [POLITICS] one who espouses a losing cause.

die standing up v. [ENTERTAINMENT] to fail.

die with one's boots on v. [COWBOY SLANG] to die courageously; to die fighting as opposed to dying in bed.

diff n. abbreviation for difference, as in "what's the diff!"

dig n. an unpleasantly critical remark— v. 1. to understand 2. to appreciate. The use as a verb was most popular in the 1960s.

digger n. an Australian or New Zealander.

diggings n. a gold miner's camp.

dig something the most v. to take extreme pleasure in something. An expression popular in the 1960s.

dig up v. to find.

dig up some dirt v. to gossip.

dilbert n. a fool.

dilly n. anything remarkable or excellent.

dilly-dally v. to proscrastinate; to waste time.

dim n. night—adj. slow-witted.

dim bulb n. a slow-witted person.

dime n. 1. ten percent of a sum 2. [CRIME] a prison sentence of ten years.

dime a dozen adj. easily obtainable; plentiful, as in "college graduates are a dime a dozen."

dime bag n. [DRUG CULTURE] a ten-dollar package of marijuana.

dime on someone v. to inform on someone.

dime store n. a department store carrying relatively inexpensive merchandise. Originally, most items cost only a dime in stores of this type.

dim view of, take a v. to regard with suspicion or disapproval.

dimwit n. a fool.

dinero n. [SPANISH] money.

ding n. [SURFING] an imperfection or damaged spot on a surfboard.

ding-a-ling n. an eccentric or foolish person.

dingbat n. a fool. Popularized by the Archie Bunker character of the *All in the Family* television show.

ding-dong n. [BABY TALK] a bell—adj. enthusiastic.

dinger n. 1. a surprise element decisive in victory 2. [BASEBALL] a home run 3. a tramp.

ding ho interj. OK. A Chinese expression in American use during and after World War II.

dingus n. an object for which the proper name is unknown.

dinkum adj. [AUSTRALIAN SLANG] genuine, true, real—n. the truth.

dinky adj. puny; inferior.

dinosaur wing n. [POLITICS] the archconservative members of a political party. First used by Adlai Stevenson in 1952 to describe certain Republicans.

dip n. 1. a fool 2. [CRIME] a pickpocket— v. 1. to steal by picking pockets and purses 2. [BROADCASTING] to dye cloth, usually to achieve the best tones for color broadcasting.

dip one's bill v. to drink. From the action of a bird dipping its bill to drink.

dippiness n. eccentricity.

dippy adj. crazy.

dipshit n. a despicable, stupid person.

dipso, dypso n. abbreviation for dipsomaniac, a drunk.

dipsy-do n. [CRIME] a prize fight in which the two combatants have illegally agreed to pre-determine the outcome.

dipsydoodle n. trickery; deceit.

dirt n. malicious gossip.

dirt, do someone v. to harm someone deliberately.

dirt, hit the dirt v. drop to the ground.

dirty adj. 1. lascivious 2. dishonest 3. mean.

dirty dog n. a dishonorable person.

dirty linen or **wash** *n.* one's personal problems—*v.* "wash one's dirty linen in public": to make public one's private problems.

dirty pool *adj.* unfair or dishonest tactics.

dirty work *n.* an illegal or unpleasant task.

dirty shame *n.* an unfortunate circumstance.

disappear *v.* [CRIME] to be murdered.

disc *n.* a phonograph record.

disc jockey *n.* [BROADCASTING] a radio announcer who introduces recorded music.

disco(theque) *n.* a gathering place where people dance to loudly playing recorded music in an exotic atmosphere created by lighting and special effects. This phenomenon is closely related to the drug culture.

discomania *n.* a violent adherence to dancing in a disco(theque), as in "adolescents have been overcome by discomania."

discombobulate *v.* to confuse.

discouraged *adj.* drunk.

disguised *adj.* drunk.

dish *n.* 1. an attractive woman 2. one's specialty.

dish back *v.* to retaliate.

dish it *v.* to give verbal abuse.

dish it out *v.* 1. to give, usually with a connotation of aggression 2. to argue forcefully.

dish out *v.* to distribute.

dish rag *n.* 1. a weak-willed person 2. an overworked, tired housewife.

dish of tea *See* cup of tea.

dish the dirty *v.* to gossip.

dishwater *n.* any liquid food that looks or tastes unappetizing.

dissolve *n.* [BROADCASTING] one image fading as another appears. Also used as a verb.

dissy *adj.* distracted; illogical.

ditch *v.* to abandon, as in "I ditched the project."

dive *n.* 1. a dilapidated, dirty, low-class public establishment 2. [BOXING] an illegally prearranged knockdown—*v.* "take a dive": to feign greater injury than is real and fall to the ground during a prize fight.

divvy *n.* a portion; a share—*v.* to divide. Often "divvy up."

Dixieland *n.* a style of jazz music.

DOA *adj.* acronym for dead on arrival (at the hospital).

do a barber *v.* to talk excessively. (Barbers are reputed to be extremely loquacious.)

do a number *v.* 1. to connive, usually with flattery 2. to convince someone that something valueless is of great worth.

do a number on *v.* to spread false information about someone.

doc *n.* 1. abbreviation for doctor 2. a term of address for one whose name is unknown.

dock *v.* to withhold a portion of a worker's salary, usually in punishment for infractions against the company code.

dock rat *n.* a derelict.

doctor *n.* 1. [CRIME] one who illegally administers drugs to a horse before a race to increase the horse's speed—*v.* 1. [ENTERTAINMENT] to rewrite parts of a script in order to improve it before the official opening of a play 2. to alter the taste or appearance of something.

dodo *n.* a stupid person.

do, do up *v.* [DRUG CULTURE] to take drugs.

dog *n.* 1. abbreviation for hot dog, a frankfurter 2. an ugly person 3. determination—*v.* to follow, pursue.

dog and pony show *n.* [CIRCUS SLANG] a small circus.

dogbiscuit *n.* an army field ration biscuit.

dog days *n.* the hottest and most oppressive days of the summer. From Sirius, the dog star, which rises about July 3, and remains until mid-August, thought by the ancient Romans to add its heat to that of the sun.

dog face *n.* an enlisted man in the army·

dog food *n.* any food that is made up of small bits difficult to identify; specifically, corned beef hash.

doggone *adj.* accursed. Probably from the seventeenth-century British oath "a dog on it."

doghouse, be in the *v.* to be in disfavor.

dog it *v.* to shirk responsibility.

dognapper *n.* one who steals dogs. Often, one who returns an animal after a reward has been offered.

do-gooder *n.* a reformer, usually used in a derogatory sense 2. one who does good deeds ostentatiously.

dog, put on the *v.* to flaunt one's possessions.

dog robber *n.* [MILITARY] an officer's orderly.

dog tags *n.* [MILITARY] the identification tags worn by members of the armed services.

dohinky *n.* anything for which the proper name is unknown.

do in *v.* to kill.

dolce vita *n.* [ITALIAN] literally, sweet life. A hedonistic lifestyle.

doll *n.* 1. a beautiful girl or woman 2. any kind, agreeable, generous person 3. [DRUG CULTURE] a capsule of narcotics.

dollar diplomacy *n.* [POLITICS] exerting economic or political pressure on other countries to assure their acceptance of the American position in world politics.

dollface *n.* 1. an affectionate term of address 2. one with an attractive face. Often a term of admiration or of derision for a young man with an attractive face.

doll up *v.* to take special care with dress or make-up so as to appear attractive.

dolly *n.* a platform on wheels used to facilitate the moving of heavy objects.

dome *n.* the head.

dominoes *n.* the human teeth.

don *n.* the head of an Italian crime family.

done in *adj.* 1. exhausted 2. killed.

done up *adj.* attractively arrayed.

donkey act *n.* a foolish deed.

donkey's years *n.* a very long period of time. A humorous play on the words "donkey's ears," which are quite long.

donnicker *n.* a toilet.

donnybrook *n.* a noisy, violent scuffle. From the annual fair held in Donnybrook, a suburb of Dublin, until 1885, when it was forbidden because of all the violence that became associated with it and synonymous with its name.

doobie *n.* [DRUG CULTURE] a marijuana cigarette.

doodad *n.* any object for which the proper name is unknown, usually a small item.

doodle *n.* a simple drawing—*v.* to draw aimlessly.

doodlysquat *n.* [BLACK SLANG] 1. anything, nothing: "They don't know doodlysquat" 2. money. Also used as an interjection as an expression of disbelief or disparagement.

doofus *n.* a fool.

doohickey *n.* a humorous name for any object or small item,

doojigger *n.* any object for which the proper name is unknown.

doolie *n.* [MILITARY] a freshman cadet at the United States Air Force Academy.

do one's own thing *v.* to pursue one's interests.

do one's stuff *v.* to perform with mastery in one's area of achievement.

doozie *n.* anything surprising or excellent.

dope *n.* 1. narcotics 2. information, usually from a privileged source—*v.* "dope up": to drug.

dope fiend *n.* [OLD SLANG] a drug addict.

dope sheet *n.* 1. [GAMBLING] a collection of information on contestants in a sporting event 2. [BROADCASTING] detailed written instructions for filming an animated sequence.

dopey, dopy *adj.* 1. under the influence of a narcotic 2. mentally slow 3. confused.

do-re-mi *n.* money.

dork *n.* a fool.

dorm *n.* abbreviation for dormitory.

Dorothy bag *n.* a small carrying bag for personal effects. A 1920s expression.

dose *n.* a case of venereal disease.

doss *n.* [BRITISH SLANG] a bed or bunk—*v.* [BRITISH SLANG] to sleep.

doss house *n.* a place where a night's lodging can be had cheaply.

do time *v.* to serve a prison sentence.

dot, on the *adv.* precisely on time.

double back *v.* to return to a place one has just left; to repeat a traveled path.

double-bang *v.* [CRIME] to burglarize the same place twice.

doublecross *n.* a betrayal—*v.* to betray.

double-dealing *adj.* deceitful.

double decker *n.* 1. a bus with upper and lower levels for passenger seating 2. a sandwich made with any filling placed between three slices of bread.

double dipper *n.* a person receiving a pension who also receives a salary at another job.

double-domed *adj.* intelligent. Literally, having two heads.

double Dutch *n.* 1. deceitful speech 2. a game of jump rope in which two ropes are turned—one clockwise, one counterclockwise—simultaneously for one jumper who skips from foot to foot quickly.

double-gaited *adj.* bisexual.

double-header *n.* [SPORTS] two complete baseball games played by the same adversary teams on the same day.

double in brass *adj.* expert in more than one area.

double nickels *n.* [TRUCKERS' CB] the current national speed limit on highways, 55 miles per hour.

double-o *n.* close scrutiny—*v.* to scrutinize.

double, on the *adv.* quickly.

double-saw *n.* a twenty-dollar bill. *See* sawbuck.

double shuffle *n.* 1. ambiguous or evasive speech 2. an evasive rejection.

double take *n.* one glance followed quickly by a second startled look at the same thing—*v.* "do a double take": to look twice at the same thing, the second time in disbelief. Comedians often do double takes.

double talk *n.* misleading verbiage.

double trouble *n.* anything that causes disruption and difficulty.

double up *v.* 1. of two people, to occupy a place together 2. of one person, to bend at the waist, usually in pain or laughter.

double wood *n.* [BOWLING] one pin left standing directly behind another.

dough *n.* money.

doughboy *n.* an American soldier. First used during the Civil War; in wide use during World War I.

dough-head *n.* a stupid person.

doughnut factory *n.* an inferior restaurant.

doughnuts *n.* [TRUCKERS' CB] tires.

do up brown *v.* to accomplish in the best or most complete way. From baking, in which the best breads have an even brown crust.

dove *n.* a pacifist, one opposed to war. From the symbol of the dove of peace.

dovetail *v.* to fit perfectly, to fall into place; as in carpentry, to fit corresponding mortises and tenons to form a strong corner joint.

down *n.* a state of depression, or that which causes such a state—*v.* to swallow—*adj.* 1. depressed 2. fine, excellent 3. willing.

down and out *adj.* completely defeated; impoverished.

downer *n.* 1. that which depresses 2. [DRUG CULTURE] a narcotic that slows down the metabolism.

down, get *v.* to make a bet.

downhill *adj.* 1. in decline 2. of a task, easy to accomplish.

down-home *adj.* in a southern manner.

down in the dumps *adj.* depressed.

down in the mouth *adj.* unhappy. From the facial expression of an unhappy person.

downstage *n.* [ENTERTAINMENT] the area of a stage nearest the audience. In the past, stages were built on a slant and the area toward the front was actually down compared to the area toward the rear. *See* upstage *and* raked.

down the hatch *interj.* [NAUTICAL] a call to drink one's drink. The hatch is the opening to the hold, or storage area, of a ship.

down the line *adv.* pertaining to all related elements in any sphere. "They all denied it down the line." "There's not a broken one among them down the line."

Down Under *n.* Australia.

down yonder *n.* the southern part of the United States.

dozens, the *n.* a rhyming game of clever insults, usually beginning with imprecations about someone's parents. Originally, a contest of wit among black men.

DPT *n.* [DRUG CULTURE] Dipropylphyotamine, an hallucinogen.

Dr. Feelgood *n.* any medical doctor who freely dispenses amphetamines or other drugs to patients who may be, or then become, addicts.

drag *n.* 1. a street 2. a bore 3. a puff on a cigarette—*v.* 1. to race automobiles, often on city streets 2. to puff on a cigarette—*adj.* pertaining to travesty.

drag, in *adv.* dressed in the garb of the opposite sex; in travesty.

drag ass *v.* 1. to procrastinate 2. to appear sad.

draggin' wagon *n.* a tow truck.

drag in *v.* to arrive finally.

drag one's tail *v.* to be depressed.

drag out *v.* to extend beyond normal time limits.

drag party *n.* a social gathering attended by transvestites.

drag queen *n.* a male homosexual transvestite.

drag race *n.* an automobile race.

dragster *n.* an automobile appropriate for drag racing.

drag strip *n.* a road appropriate for drag racing.

drag tail *v.* to move slowly.

draw *n.* a contest ending without a victory for any competitor.

draw a blank *v.* to forget suddenly and completely.

drawdown *n.* [PRINTING] determining exact color of an ink by putting a small glob on paper and spreading it by drawing down with a spatula to get a thin film of ink on paper.

dreamboat *n.* a person for whom one feels a romantic attraction.

dream up *v.* to invent; to devise.

dreamy *adj.* 1. excellent 2. wonderful. A term of approval.

dreck *n.* [YIDDISH] literally, excrement; hence 1. anything of inferior quality 2. junk. Also used as an interjection.

dress *v.* [ENTERTAINMENT] to distribute free tickets to a theatrical performance in order to have a full theater. Often in the expression "dress the house"—*n.* abbreviation for dress rehearsal.

dress down *v.* to reprimand harshly, as in "I really dressed him down for his poor behavior."

dressing down *n.* a severe reprimand.

drifter *n.* a homeless person, usually by choice.

drift, get the *v.* to understand.

drift, on the *adv.* [COWBOY SLANG] unemployed; drifting from place to place.

drill *v.* to move rapidly and powerfully.

drink *n.* the ocean.

drink one's beer *v.* to cease talking.

drip *n.* an unappealing, boring person.

drive *n.* great energy, dynamism.

drive-in *adj.* pertaining to a business establishment where clients are served while they remain seated in their cars, such as a drive-in movie, bank, restaurant, etc. Also used as a noun.

drive someone up a wall *v.* to annoy, infuriate, or frustrate someone.

drool *v.* 1. to be excited to the point of salivating in anticipation 2. to envy.

drop *v.* 1. to spend (money) quickly 2. to lose (money) at gambling, in extravagant purchases, etc. 3. [DRUG CULTURE] to take a narcotic.

drop a brick *v.* to commit an embarrassing social blunder.

drop, backdrop *n.* [ENTERTAINMENT] a painted cloth used for background scenery in a play.

drop dead *v.* to expire suddenly—*interj.* a command to stop annoying.

drop dead list *n.* a list of people in one's disfavor.

drop in *v.* to visit, often unexpectedly.

drop on (get the) *v.* 1. to draw and aim at one 2. to get any advantage over.

drop out *n.* one who leaves before completion of a task or commitment. Specifically, a student leaving school before graduation—*v.* 1. to leave before completion 2. to reject current social values, a concept popular in the 1960s and early 1970s—*adj.* pertaining to leaving or to deliberate rejection.

drop the hammer *v.* [TRUCKERS' CB] to increase driving speed.

drop the other shoe, wait for someone to *v.* 1. to anticipate a logical or seemingly inevitable conclusion 2. to wait in suspense.

drown one's troubles *v.* to seek solace in drinking alcoholic beverages.

druggie *n.* a habitual drug user; an addict.

drugstore cowboy *n.* one who aspires to be a cowboy or to play the role of cowboy in films, but who spends his time at the local drugstore, looking handsome and strong to impress the local girls.

drum beater *n.* an enthusiastic supporter.

drum up *v.* to bring to the surface.

drum up some business *v.* to create one's own market for a service or goods.

drummer *n.* an energetic salesperson.

druthers, have one's *v.* to have one's preference.

drunk *n.* a drunken person—*v.* to go on a drinking spree.

drygulch *v.* 1. to deceive 2. to thrash.

dry out *v.* to refrain from drinking alcoholic beverages; to become sober.

dry run *n.* 1. a rehearsal 2. [BROADCASTING] the rehearsal of a show or part of a show without the camera.

dry up *interj.* a command to stop annoying. Literally, "wither and die."

DTs *n.* delirium tremens. A nervous reaction to withdrawal from an addictive substance.

dub *v.* [BROADCASTING] to substitute the voice of one actor for that of another in a recorded scene.

ducat *n.* a dollar.

duchess *n.* an attractive but haughty woman.

duck *v.* to bend or squat quickly, usually to avoid something. Used both literally and figuratively.

duck bumps *n.* the appearance of roughness on the skin caused by the erection of the papillae in reaction to fear or cold. *See* goose bumps.

duck egg *n.* a swelling caused by a bump on the head.

duck fit *n.* a noisy expression of anger.

ducks *n.* white summer slacks.

duck soup *n.* anything easy to accomplish.

duck tail *n.* a euphemism for duck's ass. *See* DA.

ducky *n.* [BRITISH SLANG] an affectionate term of address, often "ducks"—*adj.* excellent.

dud *n.* 1. an inoperative explosive 2. anything faulty.

dude *n.* 1. a city man viewed by a country dweller, hence 2. any man who is well dressed.

dude ranch *n.* a resort ranch designed for vacationing city dwellers.

dude up *v.* to dress in one's best clothing.

Dudley Dooright *n.* a proper, overly solicitous person.

duds *n.* garments.

due(s), pay one's *v.* to earn certain rights, privileges, etc., as by having suffered in struggle.

duff *n.* the buttocks.

duffer *n.* 1. a weekend player with minimal skill at a game 2. an old man, often an eccentric.

duji *n.* [DRUG CULTURE] heroin.

duke it out *v.* to have a fist fight.

dukes *n.* the fists.

dukes, put up your *interj.* a command to prepare to fight.

dullsville *adj.* tedious, boring.

dumbbell *n.* a fool.

dumb bunny, cluck, or **ox** *n.* a stupid person.

dumb Dora *n.* a stupid or naive woman. An expression popular in the 1920s.

dumb John *n.* a dupe; one easily deceived.

dumdum *n.* 1. a fool 2. [MILITARY] a bullet with a hollow tip that explodes upon entry into flesh.

dummy *n.* 1. a fool 2. [PRINTING] a complete paste-up of all the proofs of a book, article, etc., showing the print type chosen, page size, trim size, and instructions concerning illustrations.

dummy up *v.* to keep silent.

dump *n.* a dilapidated or shabby place— *v.* 1. to get rid of 2. [SPORTS] to lose a competition purposely.

dump on someone *v.* 1. to criticize someone unfairly 2. to blame someone.

dumps, in the *adj.* sad; depressed. An Elizabethan song or dance with a slow rhythm and soulful sound was called "a dump."

dunk *v.* to dip into a liquid.

dupe *n.* abbreviation for duplicate.

dust *n.* [DRUG CULTURE] cocaine.

dust, bit the *See* bite the dust.

dust, hit the *See* hit the dust.

dust, lick the *v.* to be servile; to grovel.

dustup *n.* a commotion, quarrel, or fight.

dutch (beat the) [OLD GERMAN SLANG] to be very unusual or extraordinary.

dutch, go *v.* to pay only one's own way on a social outing.

dutchman *n.* [ENTERTAINMENT] a strip of cloth glued to hide the crack between two flats of scenery (*see* flat). From the legend of Peter Brinker, a Dutch boy who plugged a hole in the dike with his finger, thus heroically preventing a flood.

dutch oven *n.* a large covered cooking pot.

dutch treat *n.* a social outing during which the participants each pay their own way.

dutch uncle *n.* one in authority who reprimands severely—*v.* "treat like a dutch uncle": to scold harshly.

DX *v.* to listen to commercial or CB radio.

dyed-in-the-wool *adj.* 1. genuine 2. of a long-time adherent to a cause. From the process of dying wool before it is to be woven so that the color is more deeply ingrained and the texture stronger.

dying to *adv.* extremely desirous of doing something.

dynamite *adj.* and *interj.* excellent. Particularly popular in the mid-1970s, the shibboleth of the character J.J. on the television comedy series *Good Times*.

E

eager beaver n. a diligent and energetic worker.

eagle n. 1. [GOLF] a score of two strokes under par on a hole 2. [AVIATION] an experienced and expert fighter pilot.

eagle day n. [MILITARY] payday. From the picture of the American eagle on a soldier's pay envelope. Also called "the day the eagle shits."

eagle eye n. a careful observer, one not easily deceived. Also used as an adjective.

ear, on one's adj. surprised.

ear bender n. an excessive talker.

earful n. 1. gossip 2. talk. "I've heard an earful."

ear hanger n. a braggart.

earn one's wings n. [AVIATION] to prove one's merit and ability. A new pilot earns wings when at last able to fly an airplane.

ears on, have one's v. [TRUCKERS' CB] to listen to one's Citizen Band radio.

easy, take it v. to relax. Often used as a command to calm someone down.

easy as pie adj. extremely easy.

easy digging n. anything easily accomplished.

easy make n. a gullible person. Often used with the connotation of one easily persuaded to engage in sexual activity, as in "she's an easy make."

easy mark n. 1. a gullible person 2. one prey to any fraud.

easy street n. financial security.

eat v. to perform fellatio or cunnilingus.

eat crow v. to be humiliated.

eat dirt v. to be humiliated.

eat one's heart out v. to be exceedingly jealous.

eat out v.i. to eat in a restaurant—v.t. to reprimand or criticize severely.

eat shit v. to be humiliated.

eat the ball v. [SPORTS] of a football quarter back, to avoid throwing an unsuccessful pass and thus be tackled carrying the ball.

eat up v. 1. to accent wholeheartedly 2. to take delight in.

edge, have on an v. to be slightly intoxicated.

edge on, have an v. to have an advantage over someone.

egg n. 1. the head 2. a person. See bad egg and good egg.

egg, lay an v. to fail completely.

eggbeater n. 1. an outboard motor on a boat 2. a helicopter.

eggcrate n. the grillwork in front of an automobile radiator.

egghead n. an intellectual.

egg on v. to incite.

egg sucker n. one who seeks to gain favor by flattery.

ego trip n. any act that gratifies one's sense of self-esteem.

eight adv. in an unfavorable position. See also behind the eight ball.

88 n. a piano. From the eighty-eight notes on the keyboard.

87½ [RESTAURANT] a pretty girl is there.

86 1. [RESTAURANT] there is no more of a particular item that has been ordered 2. [BAR] serve a particular customer no more liquor.

82 n. [RESTAURANT] a glass of water.

elbow grease n. 1. energy 2. diligence 3. work.

45

elbow in v. to intrude.

elder statesman n. [POLITICS] 1. a respected older politician 2. a former president.

electioneer v. [POLITICS] to work hard to win votes for a particular candidate or party.

elevated adj. drunk.

Elmer n. a country dweller.

embalmed adj. drunk.

embalming fluid n. liquor.

emcee n. a master of ceremonies, actually from the pronunciation of the acronym, MC—v. to serve as master of ceremonies and introduce speakers or entertainers, present awards, etc.

emmy n. any of the statuettes awarded annually for special achievement in television.

end, the n. the most excellent. Often in the expression "the living end," which is a superlative meaning better than the best.

end of one's rope, at the adv. pressed to the limit of one's patience or endurance. From the practice of chaining an animal that will strain at the rope or chain but can go no farther than a certain point.

enforcer n. [CRIME] a criminal who upholds underworld rule with violence.

equal time n. [BROADCASTING] broadcast time available to opposing candidates or to "responsible spokespersons" with views differing from those expressed by the management of a television or radio station in an editorial report.

erase v. to kill.

Ethel n. an effeminate man.

euchred adj. outwitted. From the card game, euchre.

even money n. [GAMBLING] money won on a bet, identical with the sum originally bet.

even-Steven adv. in equal portions; equally divided.

even with, get v. to retaliate.

evil adj. 1. excellent 2. sarcastic.

evil eye n. bad luck, as in "I gave him the evil eye."

excess baggage n. anything superfluous.

extra n. [ENTERTAINMENT] an actor who plays in crowd scenes and has no lines of dialogue; a background player.

evil adj. annoyed; angry.

exacta n. [GAMBLING] a form of betting in which the gambler must pick the first and second winners of a race, in the correct order to win.

extracurricular activity n. an illegal or immoral pastime.

eye n. 1. a television set 2. a private detective. From the symbol of the watchful eye adopted by the Pinkerton detective agency in 1850.

eye, give someone the v. to flirt.

eye, in a pig's v. never; under no circumstance.

eye, my interj. an exclamation of contradiction or astonishment.

eyeball v. to scan, look over quickly.

eyeball-to-eyeball adj. in direct confrontation, as in "the matter was discussed eyeball-to-eyeball."

eyeful n. a person or thing that looks striking or unusual.

eyes for someone, have v. to feel a romantic attraction for someone. Often used in a limiting sense, i.e., to have eyes only for one person.

eyewash n. nonsense.

F

face the music *v.* to accept the consequences of one's acts.

fade *n.* [BROADCASTING] a camera shot that disappears slowly—*v.* 1. to go away 2. [BROADCASTING] to make a camera shot disappear slowly. When one image fades and another appears slowly, the terms applied are "fade out" and "fade in."

fade away *v.* 1. to leave 2. to die.

fag *n.* 1. a male homosexual 2. a cigarette (no longer in common use)—*adj.* pertaining to homosexuals.

faggot *n.* a male homosexual. Also used as an adjective, although the adjectival form more commonly used is "faggoty."

faggoty *adj.* *See* faggot.

fagin *n.* an old thief, especially one who teaches the craft to youngsters. From the character Fagin, who trained and masterminded a band of pickpockets in Charles Dickens' *Oliver Twist*.

fair-haired boy *n.* a promising young protégé who can seemingly do no wrong, usually in politics or business. From the young heroes in nineteenth-century novels who, by dint of hard work, virtue, and luck, overcome all obstacles and succeed.

fair shake *n.* just treatment, as in "I got a fair shake."

fair weather friend *n.* one who abandons a friend at a moment of crisis or difficulty.

fairy *n.* a male homosexual.

fake *v.* to simulate reality convincingly.

fake it *v.* to simulate comprehension of, or ability to perform, a specific task.

fall, take a *v.* 1. [CRIME] to be convicted of a crime 2. [BOXING] to feign being knocked down.

fall apart *v.* 1. to lose one's emotional composure; to become upset 2. to be in very poor physical health.

fall apart at the seams *v.* 1. of a person, to become emotionally and physically unstable 2. of an object, to become dilapidated.

fall for *v.t.* 1. to be deceived by 2. to become enamored of.

fall guy *n.* a dupe, specifically, one who is blamed or takes the blame for another's misdeeds.

fall in *v.* to assume one's place discreetly.

fall in line *v.* [MILITARY] to conform to established standards or procedure.

fall in love *v.* to feel sudden and great romantic attraction.

fallout *n.* 1. a disagreement 2. negative side effects to a strategy, policy, or event, as from the by-products of nuclear warfare—*v.* "fall out" or "have a falling out": to have a disagreement.

fall short *v.* to disappoint; to fail to meet expectations.

falsie *n.* that which is artificial, specifically, padding added to a brassiere to make the breast appear larger.

family jewels *n.* the testicles.

fan *n.* an enthusiast; a devotee.

fancy *adj.* [BLACK SLANG] sophisticated.

fancy Dan *n.* a man who is stylishly dressed.

fancy pants *n.* a prissy or effeminate man.

fandangle *n.* a trinket or ornamentation.

fan it *interj.* a command to relax, to slow

47

down, to keep silent.

fanny *n.* the buttocks.

fanny dipper *n.* a surfer's term for a wader or swimmer who does not surf.

fan the breeze *v.* to talk.

fantabulous *adj.* remarkably good.

farblonjet *adj.* [YIDDISH] lost; confused.

far gone *adj.* losing one's mind; crazy.

farm *n.* [BASEBALL] a minor league team in which a major league team trains new players.

farm out *v.* [BASEBALL] to send a player to train in the minor leagues.

far out *adj.* excellent; unusual. Also used as an interjection.

fart *n.* 1. an emission of intestinal gas 2. an obnoxious, complaining person—*v.* to eruct.

fart around *v.* 1. to waste time 2. to annoy.

farthole *n.* an obnoxious or foolish person.

fashion plate *n.* one who is always attractively dressed in the most stylish clothing. From the illustration plates in nineteenth-century fashion magazines.

fast *adj.* lascivious, as in "he's a fast one with the girls."

fast buck *n.* money quickly earned with little effort, usually unethically or illegally.

fast food *n.* quickly-prepared standard fare such as hot dogs, hamburgers, etc., sold in restaurants specializing in quick meals.

fast one *n.* trickery; deception—*v.* "pull a fast one": to trick.

fast shuffle *n.* 1. ambiguous or evasive language 2. an evasive and abrupt rejection.

fast talk *n.* deception—*v.* "give someone fast talk": to deceive.

fat, chew the *v.* to talk together; chat.

fat cat *n.* [POLITICS] a person of importance and influence.

fat chance *n.* an unlikely possibility.

fat farm *n.* a resort for overweight adults in which supervised diet and exercise fosters weight loss.

fathead *n.* an egotistical fool.

fat lot *adj.* very little or nothing.

featherbed *v.* [LABOR] to coerce an employer to hire more workers than is necessary for a job.

feather in one's cap *See* feather in one's ear.

feather in one's ear *n.* a mark of achievement. In the fourteenth century, a warrior was awarded a token feather to wear for valorous service in battle.

feather merchant *n.* one who does little work.

feather one's nest *v.* to accumulate wealth, usually to provide for future needs. From the practice of many birds who pluck their own soft down to line the nest for eventual egg laying.

feature *v.* to understand.

fed *n.* 1. an employee of the federal government 2. an agent of the Federal Bureau of Investigation.

federal case *n.* exaggerating the importance of a trifling element—*v.* "make a federal case of something": to exaggerate the importance of something.

fed up *adj.* annoyed.

feeb *n.* a fool. Abbreviation for feeble-minded.

feed *n.* a meal.

feed, off one's *adj.* upset, physically or mentally.

feedback *n.* reaction, usually tabulated response to a policy in politics or business that will be used in formulating future plans of action.

feedbag *n.* a meal—*v.* "put on the feedbag": to eat.

feedbox information *n.* privileged information that can help to predict an outcome. *See* horse's mouth, straight from the.

feed one's face *v.* to eat, usually greedily or automatically.

feed the bears *v.* [TRUCKERS' CB] 1. receive a police summons 2. to pay a fine.

feed the kitty *v.* [GAMBLING] 1. to add a sum to the prize money in a game from a player's own funds in the form of a penalty or a bet 2. to contribute to any general fund.

feel a draft *v.* to detect racial prejudice, as in an icy cold attitude.

feel no pain *v.* 1. to be drunk 2. to be dead.

feel one's oats *v.* to feel strong, energetic, happy and aggressive, like a well-nourished horse.

feel out *v.* to gain information subtly.

feel up *v.* to grope at someone's body for pleasure.

fem, femme *n.* [FRENCH] 1. a woman 2. the feminine partner in a lesbian couple.

fence *n.* [CRIME] a dealer in stolen goods—*v.* to deal in stolen goods.

fence, on the *adv.* weighing alternatives; undecided.

fence buster *n.* [BASEBALL] a powerful hitter, capable of batting a ball hard enough to break the fence.

fence hanger *n.* one who vacillates.

fence mending *n.* 1. [POLITICS] assuring political support in one's district by meeting with and tending to the needs of one's constituents 2. problem solving.

fetching *adj.* attractive.

fiddle *v.* to swindle in a petty way.

fiddle faddle *n.* aimless behavior; nonsense.

field *v.* 1. [SPORTS] to introduce into competition 2. to launch a new project.

field, in the *adv.* [BROADCASTING] of a reporter, covering stories outside of the studio.

-fiend *suffix* an addict, as in "drug-fiend," "nork-fiend," etc.

fifth column *n.* [POLITICS] traitors undermining a system from within.

fifth wheel (on a wagon) *n.* a hindrance; a useless commodity. Usually in the expression "to feel like (or to be) the fifth wheel": to feel useless and unwanted, a single among couples.

fifty-fifty *adv.* in two equal parts, fifty percent each of the whole.

file *n.* 1. a pickpocket 2. [BRITISH SLANG] a crafty rascal.

filler *n.* extraneous unimportant elements added to make the original work more lengthy. Often used in reference to excess verbiage in a written piece or in a commentator's broadcasted reports.

fill in *v.t.* to provide someone with necessary information.

filly *n.* a young woman. Literally, a young female horse.

filthy *adj.* wealthy. Often used as an adverb in the expression "filthy rich."

fin *n.* a five-dollar bill.

finagle *v.* to scheme; to use unethical means to achieve a goal.

finger *v.* [CRIME] 1. to inform on 2. to mark for assassination.

finger, the *n.* an insulting gesture made with an erect middle finger and other fingers folded, indicating disdain and meaning "fuck you" or "up yours." Often used in the construction "give him the finger."

finger on, put one's *v.t.* 1. to specify 2. to recall 3. to recognize.

fink *n.* 1. [LABOR] an informer 2. a fool—*v.* to inform.

fire *v.t.* to dismiss from employment.

fireball *n.* 1. an energetic and enthusiastic worker 2. [BASEBALL] a fast ball.

fireballer *n.* [BASEBALL] a pitcher noted for throwing fast balls.

firebug *n.* a pyromaniac.

fired up *adj.* angry.

fire eater *n.* one who faces danger bravely.

fireman *n.* [BASEBALL] a reliable pitcher sent in to relieve the starting pitcher during a game.

fire up *v.* to start a motor.

firewater *n.* hard liquor.

fireworks *n.* anything characterized by a profound emotional reaction, specifically (a) a noisy fight (b) falling in love.

first base *n.* [SPORTS] a successful overture. From baseball, in which a successful batter runs to first base as the initial move in scoring a home run for the team—*v.* "get to first base": to achieve an initial success. Also used in the negative form "can't get to first base": can't accomplish any part of a goal.

first off *adv.* first.

first-of-May *adj.* 1. young 2. inexperienced 3. new.

first-rate *adj.* excellent.

first water, of the *adv.* of the finest quality. From the designation given by seventeenth-century gem merchants to the most perfect diamonds or pearls. Lesser gems were of the second or third water.

fish *n.* 1. a dollar 2. an unemotional person, i.e., a "cold fish" 3. a weak-willed or foolish person, i.e., "a poor fish"—*v.* to seek information indirectly and subtly.

fisheye *n.* an unresponsive look.

fish hooks *n.* the fingers.

fishing expedition *n.* [POLITICS] looking into the affairs of an opposing group to see whatever information might be available to undermine their efforts or reputation.

fish lips *n.* thick protrusive lips.

fish story *n.* a great exaggeration. From the propensity of sports fishermen to exaggerate the size of the fish caught and to describe dramatically "the one that got away."

fishtail *v.* to lose traction and swerve the rear of an automobile from side to side.

fishy *adj.* questionable; suspicious.

fistful *n.* a substantial amount, as in "a fistful of dollars."

five-and-dime, five-and-ten cent store *n.* a department store that specializes in selling inexpensive items. Originally, all items sold in such a store actually did cost five and ten cents.

five-finger *n.* a thief.

fiver, five spot *n.* a five-dollar bill.

fix *n.* 1. [DRUG CULTURE] a supply of narcotics 2. [CRIME] an illegal arrangement to influence the outcome of a competition—*v.* 1. to predetermine il-legally the outcome of a competition 2. of an animal, to neuter.

fixed *adj.* 1. with a predetermined outcome, of a competition 2. of an animal, neutered 3. wealthy.

fixer *n.* a person who sells narcotics illegally to addicts.

fix someone's wagon *v.* to retaliate.

fix up *v.t.* to arrange—*v.* "fix someone up with someone": to arrange a social engagement for two people who have not yet met.

fizz *n.* effervescence.

fizzle, fizzle out *v.* to fail, usually progressively after a propitious beginning.

flabbergast *v.* to make speechless with amazement; astonish. Originally used in the eighteenth century.

flack *n.* press agent—*v.* to serve as a press agent.

flag down *v.* to signal a moving vehicle to stop. From the signal given for a train to stop at a small station.

flag is at half mast, one's the zipper on a pair of trousers is partially opened.

flag waver *n.* a chauvinist.

flak *n.* unanticipated negative reaction. Originally, a World War II term, the acronym for Flieger Ahwehr Kanone, German anti-aircraft fire.

flake *n.* an eccentric, unbalanced, irrational person.

flake off *v.* to depart. Often used as a command to cease annoying.

flake out *v.* to sleep.

flaky *adj.* 1. irresponsible 2. unreliable 3. out of touch with reality.

flamdoodle *n.* nonsense.

flame *n.* a beloved. Often used in the expression "old flame," a former romantic attachment.

flap *n.* 1. agitation 2. noise 3. distress.

flapdoodle *n.* nonsense.

flap one's chops *v.* to talk excessively.

flapper *n.* 1. a young woman of the 1920s, one who dressed in the latest fashions of the era and affected bold mannerisms 2. the hand.

flaps *n.* the ears.

flare *n.* [FOOTBALL] a short pass.

flare-up or **flare up** *n.* a burst of anger— *v.* to become angry.

flashback *n.* 1. a memory of the past 2. [DRUG CULTURE] an hallucination experienced some time after having taken an hallucinogenic drug 3. [BROADCASTING] a scene showing past action or the thoughts of a character reflecting the past.

flasher *n.* an exhibitionist, one who practices indecent exposure.

flash in the pan *n.* an expectation that appears promising but is disappointing; a failure.

flashy *adj.* ostentatious.

flat *n.* 1. a deflated tire 2. [ENTERTAINMENT] a wooden frame covered with canvas and painted to serve as scenery for a play—*adj.* 1. without money 2. of a woman, with extremely small breasts. Also, flat-chested—*adv.* completely.

flat apple *n.* [BOWLING] a dead ball.

flat broke *adj.* completely without money.

flat-chested *adj. See* flat.

flatfoot *n.* a policeman.

flathead *n.* a stupid person.

flatlander *n.* [SURFING] a clumsy body surfer.

flat-out *adj.* with concentrated effort at all stages; intensive. Usually used in politics or business, as in a "flat-out campaign"—*adv.* directly.

flatten *v.* to thrash; to knock down.

flat top *n.* 1. something having a flat or level surface (an aircraft carrier) 2. a hairstyle worn by men, popular in the 1950s.

flea *n.* a person of little importance.

flea bag *n.* a horse, usually a slow or old and weak one. *See* flea trap.

flea-bitten *adj.* old; shabby.

flea flicker *n.* [FOOTBALL] a dramatic play consisting of a long double pass.

flea market *n.* a sale of old odds and ends. A direct translation from the French *marche aux puces*, a market where one

is likely to pick up fleas along with the old pieces offered for sale.

flea trap, flea house *n.* a dilapidated, dirty hotel.

fleece *v.* to swindle.

flesh, in the *adv.* actually present.

flesh out *v.t.* to increase in size or scope, as in "to flesh out a story."

flesh peddler *n.* a pimp.

flesh pot *n.* 1. a brothel 2. anything purveying to lascivious tastes.

flick, flicker *n.* a movie.

flies *n.* [ENTERTAINMENT] the area above a stage, where scenery is stored suspended and from which necessary pieces are lowered during a play.

flimflam *n.* nonsense; trickery—*v.* to deceive; swindle.

flimsy *n.* thin paper.

fling *n.* 1. a spree 2. an attempt 3. a brief period during which the value of something is tested—*v.* "take a fling at something": to attempt something.

flip *adj.* impertinent—*v.* 1. to experience an extreme emotional reaction, either of pleasure or anger 2. to become mentally unbalanced.

flip-flop *n.* a complete reversal. Also used as a verb.

flip one's lid *v.* 1. to become angry 2. to become crazy.

flip one's lip *v.* to talk.

flip one's raspberry *v.* to lose one's temper.

flip one's wig *v.* to become angry.

flip out *v.* 1. [DRUG CULTURE] to lose contact with reality after the use of a narcotic 2. to lose one's self-control in an extreme emotional reaction.

flipper *n.* the hand.

flip side *n.* 1. the reverse side 2. the side of a phonograph record on which a song of secondary popularity is recorded.

fliv *n.* an automobile.

flivver *v.* to fail.

float *v.* to be happy.

float a flat *v.* [ENTERTAINMENT] to release a piece of scenery held suspended above the stage and rely on the current of air to slow its fall.

floating crap game *n.* [GAMBLING] an illegal gambling scheme to conduct games of dice, moving from location to location periodically to avoid detection by the police. Often the game is held in the back of a van or other vehicle, or in a hotel room.

floating on air, floating on the clouds *adj.* euphoric.

float one *v.* to cash a check.

flog *v.* [BRITISH SLANG] to sell, especially dishonestly or illegally.

flood *n.* an abundance of something, as in "a flood of letters"—*v.* to inundate with anything.

flooey, flooie *adj.* not in working condition.

floor *v.* 1. to surprise 2. to knock down.

floorboard *v.* to accelerate a vehicle to its limit of speed, i.e., to press the accelerator pedal down to the floor.

floozie, floozy *n.* a lewd woman.

flop *n.* a failure—*v.* 1. to fail 2. to lie down clumsily, heavily.

flophouse *n.* a cheap, filthy hotel often catering to prostitutes.

flopperoo *n.* a great failure.

flossy *adj.* garish; ostentatious.

flour *n.* cosmetic powder.

flower *n.* a male homosexual.

flower child *n.* any of the young people of the 1960s who alienated themselves from conventional society.

flub *n.* an error, usually verbal—*v.* to make an error.

flubdub *n.* a lack of ability.

fluff *n.* 1. a mistake, usually verbal 2. a girl or woman—*v.* to make a mistake.

fluff, get (or give someone) the *v.* to be rejected (or to reject someone) from friendship.

fluff off *v.* to leave.

fluff stuff *n.* [TRUCKERS' CB] snow.

fluke *n.* 1. a chance success 2. an unexpected occurrence.

flukum *n.* trinkets.

flumadiddle *n.* nonsense.

flummox *v.* to confuse, perplex.

flunk *v.* to fail, as in "he flunked the exam."

flunk out *v.* to be rejected from a school because of failing grades.

flush *adj.* wealthy; secure.

flush, in a *adv.* agitated.

flute *n.* a male homosexual.

fly *n.* 1. the zipper on a pair of men's trousers 2. a clever, knowledgeable person—*v.* 1. to be exceedingly happy 2. [DRUG CULTURE] to experience a pleasurable reaction to a narcotic—*adj.* alert and knowing; sharp; quick.

fly, let *v.* to express vehemently.

fly a kite, go *interj.* a command to stop annoying.

fly bait *n.* a corpse.

fly ball *n.* 1. [BASEBALL] a high ball which is either caught before it touches the ground or which lands outside the limits of the field, either among the spectators in the stands or over the fence 2. an eccentric person.

fly bob *n.* a policeman; a detective.

fly boy *n.* [AVIATION] the pilot or a member of an airplane crew.

fly-by-night *adj.* transitory and most often unscrupulous. Usually pertaining to a business set up to swindle customers, which takes a client's money and closes during the night.

fly cake *n.* a raisin cake. From the resemblance of a raisin to the body of a dead fly.

fly chaser *n.* [BASEBALL] an outfielder.

flychick *n.* an attractive, alert young woman.

fly cop *n.* a policeman; a detective.

fly dick *n.* a detective.

flyer *n.* 1. a risk 2. a printed announcement or advertisement usually distributed to pedestrians or delivered to residences.

fly light *v.* to be hungry.

fly off the handle *v.* to become excitedly angry. From the heavy blade of an axe which, if loose, could fly off the handle during vigorous use and cause much damage.

fly right *v.* to behave properly.

flyswatter *n.* [BASEBALL] a player who often hits fly balls.

fly the coop *v.* to leave an unpleasant place. Literally, a coop is a small house and pen where fowl are kept; it is a slang term for "jail." Following the bird terminology, "to fly the coop" means to escape from prison, and by extension, from any disagreeable place.

fly trap *n.* the mouth.

fob off *v.* to misrepresent an imitation as the genuine article.

fofarraw *n.* an uproar.

fog, in a *adv.* confused; distracted.

foggy *adj.* confused.

fog it in *v.* to throw with force.

fold *v.* to fail, of a business venture or a show.

folding cabbage, green, or **lettuce** *n.* paper money.

folding money *n.* a significant amount of money.

folknik *n.* a performer or devotee of folk songs.

follow suit *v.* to emulate. From the game of bridge, in which players must discard a card of the same suit the first player led with.

follow through *v.* to complete a project or solve a problem thoroughly and in all its aspects. Also used as a noun.

follow up *v.* to pursue a matter to completion.

fooey *interj.* nonsense. Also used as a noun.

foo foo *n.* perfume.

fool *n.* an especially enthusiastic devotee.

fool around *v.* 1. to waste time in idle behavior 2. to engage in casual sexual relations 3. to commit adultery.

foot *n.* [PRINTING] the bottom of a page, book or column 2. [SPORTS] a driver of a race car.

foot, give someone the *v.* to kick someone.

footing *n.* [HORSE RACING] the physical condition of a race track at any given time.

foot in it, put one's *v.* to make a blunder often verbal.

foot-in-mouth disease *n.* tactlessness. A humorous term based on the disease called foot-and-mouth.

foot in one's mouth, put one's *v.* to make a verbal blunder.

footsie *n.* the surreptitious touching or caressing of the foot of another with one's own foot in order to establish an initial physical intimacy—*v.* "play footsie": 1. to touch another's foot caressingly with one's own foot 2. [POLITICS] to negotiate unethical secret agreements of cooperation between a politician and an interest group or between two politicians 3. to pander to the one in authority to gain some advantage.

foot the bill *v.* to accept responsibility for payment.

foozle *n.* 1. an error 2. [GOLF] a clumsy stroke—*v.* to make an error.

for certain *adv.* surely. Also used as an interjection of affirmation.

for chrissake *interj.* an exclamation of dismay or surprise.

for crying out loud *interj.* an expression of surprise, happiness, dismay, etc., depending upon the context.

for free *adv.* without charge.

for heaven's sake *interj.* an exclamation of surprise or dismay.

for keeps *adv.* permanently; decisively.

fork over, fork out, or **fork up** *v.* to relinquish; to pay.

form *n.* strength, ability, and style to perform a feat.

for pete's sake *interj.* an expression of surprise, dismay, annoyance, etc., depending upon the context.

for pity's sake *interj.* an exclamation of surprise or dismay.

for real *adv.* to be taken seriously.

for sure *adv.* surely. Also used as an interjection of affirmation.

for the birds *adv.* preposterous.

for the love of mike *interj.* an exclamation of surprise, dismay, etc.

forty-five *n.* forty-five-caliber pistol.

forty ways from Sunday *n.* in great confusion.

forty winks *n.* sleep; a nap.

fossil *n.* an old or old-fashioned person.

foul ball *n.* 1. [SPORTS] a ball that is judged to be unplayable 2. any aborted attempt.

fouled up *adj.* confused.

foul mouth *n.* one who uses obscene or rude language—*v.* "have a foul mouth": to speak using obscene or rude language.

foul up *n.* an error, confusion—*v.i.* to fail, to err because of confusion—*v.t.* to ruin someone's plan or project.

four bagger *n.* [BASEBALL] a home run, i.e., a hit permitting the batter to run to all three bases, or bags, and then back to home base.

four eyes *n.* one who wears eyeglasses.

fourflusher *n.* [GAMBLING] a cheat. From the card game poker, in which five cards of the same suit make a flush. One who tries to pass off four cards of the same suit as a flush is a cheat.

four hundred, the *n.* the elite.

four-letter words *n.* obscene language.

four sheets to the wind *adv.* drunk.

fourth estate *n.* the press. An expression implying the great power of the press in forming opinions and influencing national policy. In Parliament, the three estates represented are: the first, the Church; the second, the nobles; the third, the common people.

fourwheeler *n.* [TRUCKERS' CB] a passenger car.

fox *v.* to behave cunningly.

foxhole *n.* [MILITARY] a ditch used by a soldier for protective shelter during warfare.

fox paw *n.* humorous variation of *faux pas,* the French term for a social blunder.

foxy *adj.* 1. sexy 2. sly.

fracture *v.* to cause an extreme emotional reaction in someone, usually expressed by laughter or tears.

fractured *adj.* drunk.

frag *v.* [MILITARY] to intentionally kill or wound.

fraidy cat *n.* a timorous person.

frail *n.* a young woman.

frame, frame up *n.* a purposeful deception causing an innocent person to appear guilty of a crime—*v.t.* to cause an innocent person to be accused of a crime.

frank *n.* abbreviation for frankfurter.

Frankenstein *n.* a project which seems promising but ultimately has ruinous effects on its creator. From the monster created by Dr. Frankenstein in the 1818 novel, *Frankenstein,* by Mary Wollstonecraft Shelley.

frat *n.* abbreviation for fraternity.

frater *n.* a member of a fraternity.

frau *n.* [GERMAN] wife.

frazzled *adj.* 1. drunk 2. nervous 3. exhausted.

freak *n.* 1. an eccentric 2. an enthusiastic devotee.

freak out *v.* [DRUG CULTURE] to lose one's self control. Originally used to indicate the state induced by the use of hallucinogenic drugs. Also used as a noun.

free agent *n.* a worker not under contract and therefore able to negotiate for new employment. Specifically, a professional athlete not available to be traded or sold by his team to another team against his will, or an actor not signed with one agent.

freebie *n.* anything given for free.

free-for-all *n.* a tumult; a fight.

free lance *adj.* hiring out one's services on a job-by-job basis to various employers. Also used as a verb. From the term applied to mercenary soldiers in medieval Europe—*n.* free lancer.

freeload *v.* to live at the expense of others; to lead a parasitic existence—*n.* freeloader.

free rider *n.* [LABOR] a non-union worker who gains the same benefits as the union workers who fought for them.

freeway sign *n.* an insulting gesture

made with an erect middle finger and other fingers folded: "the finger."

free wheeling *adj.* unconstrained.

freeze *n.* 1. a cessation 2. [ECONOMICS] maintenance of the status quo in price, wage, hiring, or production level, often by government intervention—*v.* 1. to remain in one position without moving 2. to stop.

freeze on someone, put the *v.* to reject someone.

freight, pull one's *v.* to leave.

French *n.* a euphemism for obscene language, used in the expression "pardon my French."

French kiss See soul kiss.

French leave *n.* leaving without permission. In French, the equivalent is called *filer a l'Anglaise,* English leave.

French walk See Spanish walk.

Frenchy *n.* a Frenchman.

fresh *adj.* impertinent.

fresh out of *adj.* having just sold or used up.

fried *adj.* drunk.

frig *v.* to coit.

frigging *adj.* detestable.

frill *n.* a young woman.

Frisco *n.* abbreviation for San Francisco.

frisk *v.* to search a person's garments to find any hidden object. Specifically, a search conducted by the police to find concealed weapons on the person of a suspected criminal. Also used as a noun.

frisking *n.* a search. *See* frisk.

fritter away *v.* to waste.

fritz *v.* to render inoperable—*adv.* "on the fritz": not in working order.

frogman *n.* one who works underwater wearing a diving suit and oxygen supply to be autonomous for a given period.

frogskin *n.* a one-dollar bill.

from A to Z *adv.* completely; thoroughly.

from hunger *adj.* inferior; ugly. From food that is unfit to eat but which will be accepted by someone sufficiently hungry.

from nothing *n.* nothing.

from nowhere *adj.* outmoded; inferior; unacceptable.

front *n.* [CRIME] 1. a legitimate appearance for a criminal enterprise 2. one who accepts to serve as figurehead for an enterprise in order to hide the actual power center in organized crime. Also used as a verb.

front and center *interj.* [MILITARY] a command to approach and face the speaker.

front-line state *n.* [POLITICS] an enemy state. From the military arrangement of lines of troops for battle, the front line facing the adversary directly.

front office *n.* the administration of an organization.

front runner *n.* 1. [POLITICS] the candidate most likely to win 2. [SPORTS] one who plays well only when the team is winning. Originally, a term from horse racing.

frosh *n.* a freshman; a first-year student in an institution of higher learning.

frozen *adj.* terrified.

fruit *n.* a homosexual.

fruitcake *n.* 1. an eccentric 2. an effeminate male.

fruit fly *n.* a woman who seeks the companionship of homosexual men.

fruit salad *n.* [MILITARY] service medals and ribbons worn on the chest of a uniform.

fruity *adj.* 1. crazy 2. homosexual.

frump *n.* an ill-kempt, ugly woman—*adj.* frumpy.

fry *v.* to die in the electric chair.

fuck *n.* 1. coitus 2. a stupid, mean person—*v.* 1. to coit 2. to treat in an unjust fashion.

fuck around *v.* 1. to engage in casual sexual relationships 2. to waste time.

fucked up *adj.* confused; bewildered; emotionally unstable.

fucking *n.* 1. coitus 2. an unjust treatment—*adj.* 1. detestable 2. excellent—*v.* "get (or give someone) a fucking": to treat (or be treated) unjustly.

fuck off *v.* to depart. Often used as a command to cease annoying.

fuck up *n.* 1. an incompetent 2. a failure—*v.* 1. to ruin 2. to frustrate.

fuck with *v.t.* 1. to coit with 2. to meddle with.

fuck you *interj.* an expression of annoyance and disdain.

fuddy duddy *n.* a prim, stodgy person.

fudge *v.* to cheat; to falsify.

full blast *adv.* to the highest degree possible.

full court press *n.* a concerted or desperate effort. From basketball, a play in which each player is covered by a player on the adversary team to prevent them from gaining the lead.

full house *n.* 1. [GAMBLING] in the card game of poker, all five cards in one's hand forming combinations 2. [ENTERTAINMENT] all seats in a theater occupied for a performance.

full of beans *adj.* 1. mischievous; naughty 2. bragging 3. lying.

full of bull *adj.* prone to exaggerate or lie.

full of hot air *adj.* pretentious; prone to exaggerate.

full of it *adj.* euphemism for "full of shit": lying, bragging.

full of oneself *adj.* pretentious; pompous; self-satisfied.

full of shit *adj.* lying; bragging.

full up *adj.* completely full.

fun *adj.* enjoyable.

Fun City *n.* New York City. Coined by Mayor John V. Lindsay in 1966.

fungo *n.* an error—*v.* to make an error.

fungoo *interj.* euphemism for fuck you. *See* fuck you.

funk *n.* a depressed mood.

funkiness *n.* 1. melancholy 2. insufficiency; poor quality.

funky *adj.* 1. odd, unusual, and imaginative 2. smelly.

funnies, the *n.* newspaper comic strips.

funny *adj.* odd; weird; crazy.

funny business *n.* deception.

funny house *n.* an insane asylum.

fuse, blow a *v.* to become angry.

fussbudget *n.* an excessively prim person, especially one who complains a great deal.

futz *v.* to trifle or meddle.

fuzz *n.* the police; a policeman.

fuzzled *adj.* drunk.

G

G *n.* one-thousand dollars, the abbreviation for one grand. Five G's means five-thousand dollars.

gab *n.* 1. idle chatter 2. exaggeration 3. one who talks excessively—*v.* to gossip; to chatter.

gabber *n.* one who talks excessively.

gabfest *n.* a social gathering for conversation or debate.

gabby *adj.* garrulous.

Gabriel *n.* a trumpeter. From the angel Gabriel, whose trumpet call will announce the day of final judgment.

gaff *n.* 1. counterfeit article 2. a sham—*v.* to cheat.

gaffe *n.* [FRENCH] a social blunder.

gaffer *n.* head electrician on a movie or TV set.

gag *n.* 1. a joke 2. something placed over the mouth to prevent speech or cries—*v.* 1. to joke 2. to stifle speech.

gaga *adj.* excited; crazy.

gage *n.* [DRUG CULTURE] marijuana.

gagers *n.* the eyes.

gage up, get one's *v.* to become angry.

gal *n.* a girl or woman.

galloping dominoes *n.* dice.

gam *v.* to boast.

game *adj.* willing.

game plan *n.* a strategy. Originally, a term used in football, now commonly used in reference to strategy in politics or business.

gamin *adj.* [FRENCH] boyish; literally, a street urchin. A feminine style of dress and general appearance imitating the looks and charm of a young street child.

gams *n.* legs, usually attractive legs. From the Italian *gamba*, leg.

gamy *adj.* having a strong, unpleasant odor.

gander *n.* a glance—*v.* "take a gander": to glance, peek.

gandy dancer *n.* a railroad worker. From the tool known as a gandy, manufactured by the Gandy Manufacturing Company of Chicago, a long iron bar with a pedal, used by workers to settle gravel around railroad ties. The bottom of the pole was plunged into the newly-poured gravel; one foot was placed on the pedal and the worker held the top with one hand and "danced" about in circles to tamp the gravel down.

gang bang *n.* a group rape of one victim.

gangster *n.* a criminal involved in organized crime.

gang up *v.* to band together, generally for purposes of aggression. Often in the construction "to gang up on someone": to band together against someone.

gapo *n.* offensive body odor; acronym for Gorilla Arm Pit Odor.

garbage *n.* 1. unappetizing food 2. worthless objects 3. nonsense 4. [BASKETBALL] an easily-scored basket.

garbage can *n.* a dilapidated ship.

gardening *n.* [MOUNTAIN CLIMBING] clearing away plant growth in order to have better footing on a climb.

gargle *v.* to drink.

garrison state *n.* [POLITICS] a country under military rule.

gas *n.* 1. idle chatter 2. exaggeration 3. anything amusing or excellent, as in "that's a gas"—*v.* to gossip.

gasbag *n.* 1. one who exaggerates 2. a braggart.

gash *n.* the mouth.

gasket, blow a *v.* to become enraged.

gasper *n.* [BRITISH SLANG] a cheap cigarette.

gassed *adj.* drunk.

gasser *n.* anything astonishing, amusing, or excellent.

gas, step on the *v.* to hurry; to move or act faster.

gas up *v.* 1. to fill the gasoline tank of a vehicle 2. to make more appealing.

gat *n.* a gun. Originally, a machine gun; the abbreviation for Gatling gun, the first machine gun.

gate *n.* the total receipts collected for admission to a spectator event.

gate crasher *n.* one who obtains admission to a social gathering or to a performance without an invitation or a ticket.

gate, get (or give someone) the *v.* to be rejected (or to reject someone) from friendship.

gator *n.* abbreviation for alligator.

gay *adj.* homosexual. Also used as a noun.

gazooney *n.* a naive person.

gear *adj.* [BRITISH SLANG] highly acceptable, attractive, etc.

geared *adj.* homosexual.

gee *interj.* an exclamation of surprise, disappointment, etc., depending upon the context.

geek *n.* 1. one who performs repulsive acts in a carnival, such as biting the head off of a live chicken; hence 2. a pervert.

geezer *n.* an eccentric old man.

geezil *n.* any object for which the proper name is not known.

geld, gelt *n.* [YIDDISH] money.

gent *n.* a man. Abbreviation for gentleman.

gents, the *n.* the men's lavatory.

george *v.* to dupe.

George do it, let *v.* to pass responsibility for a task to another. From Cardinal George d'Amboise, foreign minister under Louis XII of France, who had the reputation of getting things done.

geranium *n.* an attractive girl.

gesundheit *interj.* [GERMAN] literally, health; a wish for good health said when someone sneezes.

get *v.* 1. to understand, as in "I get it!" 2. to induce an emotional response 3. to notice 4. to annoy 5. to inflict revenge 6. to kill 7. to leave immediately 8. to receive sexual favors.

getaway *n.* an escape—*adj.* pertaining to escape, as in "I saw the getaway car."

get away with *v.t.* to go unpunished for.

get back *v.* to retaliate; to get revenge.

get by *v.* to survive.

get going *v.* 1. to begin 2. to leave.

get it *v.* 1. to understand something 2. to be punished.

get lost *interj.* a command to leave, to cease annoying.

get nowhere *v.* to make no progress despite efforts.

get off *v.* 1. [DRUG CULTURE] to feel pleasure after taking a narcotic; hence 2. to feel pleasure in anything.

get off my case *interj.* [BLACK SLANG] a command to stop annoying.

get off someone's back *v.* to cease annoying someone.

get on, get on in years *v.* to age.

get one's act together *v.* to determine one's goal and plan a course of action to achieve it. From the field of night-club entertaining, in which performers literally choose suitable material for and structure an act.

get one's brains fried *v.* [DRUG CULTURE] to be high on drugs.

get one's jollies *v.* to experience pleasure in something.

get one's shit together *v.* 1. to exploit one's talents to the maximum to achieve a goal 2. to solve one's problems.

get outa my face *interj.* [BLACK SLANG] a command to stop annoying, to leave.

get someone's goat *v.* to annoy, irritate, or frustrate someone.

get the jump *v.* to have an initial advantage.

get-together *n.* a social gathering.

get-up *n.* unusual apparel; a costume.

get-up-and-go *n.* vitality.

get wind of *v.t.* to learn inadvertantly of, usually in reference to a secret or a scheme.

get with it *v.* 1. to increase one's energy, enthusiasm, or output 2. to concentrate.

ghost *v.* to share lodging with another without the knowledge of the proprietor of the hotel, motel, etc., and without paying any additional charge.

ghostwriter, ghost *n.* one who writes something for pay which is then attributed to another. Politicians generally use ghostwriters to compose their speeches—*v.* ghostwrite, ghost.

GI *adj.* or *n.* [MILITARY] acronym for government issue; hence, humorously, a soldier in the United States Army.

gidget *n.* any small mechanical device for which the proper name is not known.

gift of gab *n.* the ability to persuade or to maintain interesting conversation.

gig *n.* a job; specifically, an engagement for a performer—*v.* "to give a gig to": to give employment to a performer.

GI Joe *n.* a typical soldier in the United States Army.

gilhooley *n.* 1. any object for which the proper name is not known 2. nonsense 3. lies.

gills *n.* the mouth.

gills, green around the *adj.* ill; nauseous.

gimmick *n.* a ploy, i.e., anything used to make something seem attractive or interesting.

gimmies, the *n.* selfishness.

gimp *n.* one who limps.

gimp stick *n.* a cane or crutch.

gimpy *adj.* crippled.

ginhead *n.* a drunk.

gin *n.* alcoholic liquor of any kind.

gink *n.* a fool.

gin mill *n.* a bar.

girlie, girly *n.* a girl or woman—*adj.* designating or of magazines, shows, etc., chiefly devoted to displaying nude young women.

girlie show *n.* a live show featuring scantily-clad women doing suggestive dances.

gism *n.* semen.

gismo, gizmo *n.* 1. any object for which the proper name is not known 2. a gadget 3. a contrivance 4. a gimmick.

give a pain *v.* to cause aggravation.

giveaway *n.* 1. anything that inadvertently reveals a secret 2. an object sold at such a low price as to be almost free, i.e., a great bargain 3. a free gift offered as an advertisement for or by a place of business.

give it to someone *v.* 1. to reprimand 2. to inflict bodily harm.

gizmo *n.* See gismo.

gladeye *adj.* an inviting or flirtatious glance.

glad hand *n.* a sincere, energetic, welcoming handshake—*v.* "give someone the glad hand": to give a hearty handshake.

gladiator *n.* a prize fighter.

glad rags *n.* one's best clothing.

glass arm *n.* [BASEBALL] a baseball pitcher's arm particularly susceptible to injury or easily weakened.

glass jaw *n.* [SPORTS] an athlete's, or specifically a prize fighter's, jaw that is easily broken.

glassy eyed *adj.* dazed; drunk.

glimmers *n.* the eyes.

glitch *n.* an error; a failure—*adj.* out of order.

glitterati *n.* the rich, elegant trend-setters who are said to glitter with style and wit.

globes *n.* the female breasts.

globe-trot(ting) *n., adj., v.* traveling from country to country.

glom *v.* to grab.

glop *n.* 1. unappetizing food 2. sentimentality.

glow on, have a *v.* to be intoxicated.

gluepot *n.* an old horse. From the fact that glue is often made using horses' hoofs.

gnomes of Zurich *n.* [POLITICS] the international bankers of Switzerland, a humorous if somewhat derogatory term.

go *n.* a chance. Usually in the expression "to have a go at something"—*v.* 1. to succeed 2. of a product, to be sold 3. to urinate or defecate—*adj.* [ASTRONAUT'S JARGON] in working order; functioning.

go-ahead *n.* permission to proceed.

go, all systems everything is in order and ready to begin.

go along with *v.t.* to agree with; to accept another's opinion.

go around together *v.* to be habitual social partners.

go all the way *v.* 1. finish; complete 2. support (someone or something) without reservation 3. have sexual intercourse.

goat *n.* 1. a lecherous man. Often in the expression "old goat." From the traditional representation of Pan, the Greek god of the fields, as half-man, half-goat 2. a scapegoat.

goat, get someone's *See* get someone's goat.

gob *n.* a sailor in the United States Navy.

gobble *v.* to eat greedily.

gobbledygook *n.* indecipherable writing or speech; nonsense.

gobs *n.* a large quantity.

go-by, get (or **give someone**) **the** *v.* to snub (or be snubbed by) someone.

god awful *adj.* dreadful.

go down on someone *v.* to perform fellatio or cunnilingus.

goes, what *v.i.* what's happening? Also used as an interjection.

gofer *n.* an aide who runs miscellaneous errands. From "go for."

go for *v.* to like.

go-getter *n.* an energetic and ambitious person.

gogo *adj.* lively, stylish in the manner popular in the discotheques of the 1960s—*n.* the discotheques of the 1960s.

going *adj.* successful.

going over *n.* 1. an examination 2. a beating.

goldbrick *n.* one who pretends to work industriously while actually relaxing— *v.* to shirk duty. From the swindle of the gold rush days in the American West, when bricks of lead were given a light gold coat and sold as pure gold to gullible investors; hence, a sham.

gold digger *n.* one who seeks financial benefit in emotional attachments. Usually applied to women who seek rich lovers.

golden shower *n.* a spray of urine.

goldfish bowl *n.* any place lacking privacy.

goldilocks *n.* any attractive woman or girl with blond hair.

gold star *adj.* excellent.

golf widow *n.* a woman whose husband is a golf enthusiast and often leaves her alone while he is playing. A humorous term based on the construction of "grass widow."

gone *adj.* 1. entirely involved in an activity 2. deceased.

gonef *n.* *See* gonif.

gone on *adj.* 1. enamored of (someone) 2. deceased.

gone, real *adj.* excellent; unusual. An expression popular in the 1960s and early 1970s.

goner, real goner *n.* one doomed to failure or death.

gong *n.* [BRITISH SLANG] a medal; especially a military medal.

gonif *n.* [YIDDISH] a thief; a swindler. Often used affectionately for a clever child.

gonof, gonoph *n.* *See* gonif.

goo *n.* 1. viscous matter 2. sentimentality.

goober *n.* a peanut.

goober grease *n.* peanut butter.

good deal *n.* 1. any favorable agreement or transaction 2. a large quantity.

good egg *n.* an agreeable and honest person.

good-for-nothing *n.* a lazy wastrel.

good head *n.* an intelligent, agreeable

person.

goodie, goody *interj.* an exclamation of gladness—*n.* a prig.

goodie-goodie *n.* a self-righteous prig.

good Joe *n.* a pleasant cooperative person.

good looker *n.* an attractive person.

good make *n.* one easy to seduce.

good, make *v.* to succeed.

goods, the *n.* 1. information; proof 2. the qualities necessary for success—*v.* "have the goods on someone": to have proof of someone's guilt.

goof *n.* 1. an error 2. a fool—*v.* 1. to make an error 2. to behave in a silly manner.

goof around *v.* to waste time.

goofball *n.* 1. a fool 2. [DRUG CULTURE] a barbiturate.

goof off *v.* to waste time in idleness, especially when expected to be working—*n.* one who wastes time in idleness.

goof up *v.* 1. to make a mistake 2. to become confused—*n.* one who becomes easily confused.

goofy *adj.* like or characteristic of a goof, i.e., stupid and silly.

goofy foot *n.* [SURFING] one who surfs with the right foot instead of the left foot in forward position.

googly *n.* protruding, of the eyes.

goo goo eyes *n.* romantic looks.

gook *n.* 1. a derogatory term for a Vietnamese 2. dirt.

go on *interj.* an exclamation of disbelief.

goon *n.* 1. [CRIME] a physically strong, mentally weak man paid to do another's unpleasant physical tasks, especially to beat or kill an enemy 2. a boor.

go one better *v.* [GAMBLING] to improve on another's performance, offer, etc. From the betting system in a game of poker in which any succeeding player can raise the sum of an initial bet.

goonk *n.* anything viscous and repulsive.

go, on the *adj.* active.

goony *adj.* 1. foolish 2. boorish.

goop *n.* 1. repulsive-looking food 2. nonsense 3. a naughty child, from the characters created by humorist Gelett Burgess, who are the epitome of bad manners.

goopy *adj.* sticky, gummy.

goose *n.* 1. a jab between the buttocks 2. a pinch on the buttocks—*v.* 1. to jab someone between the buttocks 2. to pinch someone on the buttocks.

goose bumps, gooseflesh *n.* a temporary roughening of the skin caused by an erection of the papillae in reaction to fear or cold.

goose egg *n.* the score of zero. From the shape of a large zero.

go out *v.* to lose consciousness.

gopher *See* gofer.

go places *v.* to succeed.

gorilla *n.* 1. a large, strong, often stupid person 2. a person regarded as a gorilla in appearance, strength, etc. 3. a gangster; a thug.

gosh awful *adj.* dreadful.

go-sho *n.* [AIRLINES] a customer who, without a reservation for a particular flight, waits at the airport hoping that someone will cancel his or her reservation. *See* no-sho.

gospel pusher *n.* a minister.

go steady *v.* to date one person exclusively.

go the distance *v.* [SPORTS] 1. of a baseball pitcher, to pitch a whole game 2. of a football player, to score a touchdown.

go to bat for *v.t.* to act in support of someone or something; to defend. From baseball, where a more suitable batter will replace the regular batter in a line-up when his particular style is necessary to the team.

go to pot *v.* to become dilapidated.

go to seed *v.* to fall into disrepair.

go to Sunday school *v.* [LUMBERJACK SLANG] to play a game of poker.

goulash *n.* confused information; nonsense.

go up (on one's lines) *v.* [ENTERTAINMENT] to forget one's lines of di alogue in a play, movie, etc.

gourd *n.* the head.

governor *n.* [BRITISH SLANG] a term of address to a man.

gow *n.* [DRUG CULTURE] opium.

go wrong *v.* to enter into a life of crime.

goy *n.* [YIDDISH] a gentile, i.e., a non-Jewish person.

grab *v.* to impress deeply. Often in the expression "how does that grab you?"—*v.* "have grab": to have the ability to induce a strong emotional response.

grabby *adj.* selfish; greedy.

grabs, up for *adj.* available.

grad *n.* abbreviation for graduate. Also used as an adjective, as in "grad school," meaning graduate school.

graffiti *n.* unauthorized scrawling on walls, etc., usually in public places. From *graffito*, an art popular in fifteenth-century Italy in which the top layer of white plaster is scratched from a wall in design form to reveal colored layers beneath.

graft *n.* bribery; a bribe.

grain of salt, with a *adv.* dubiously; with reservations as to the accuracy of a statement or the import of an action.

gramps *n.* a term of address for any older man; a variation of grandfather.

grand *n.* one-thousand dollars. No "s" is added to form a plural: two grand, two-thousand dollars.

grand bounce *n.* a complete rejection or dismissal.

grand slam *n.* 1. [BASEBALL] a home run hit when the bases are loaded; hence 2. anything overwhelmingly successful.

grandstand play *n.* [SPORTS] a ploy to impress spectators.

grandstand player, grandstander *n.* 1. [SPORTS] one who plays principally for the adulation of the spectators 2. a show-off.

grape *n.* wine.

grapefruit league *n.* [BASEBALL] major league baseball teams that have winter training in Florida.

grapes, the *n.* champagne.

grapevine *n.* the nebulous source of hearsay, gossip.

grass *n.* 1. [DRUG CULTURE] marijuana 2. [BRITISH SLANG] an informer's stool pidgeon.

grass cutter *n.* [BASEBALL] a low, forcefully-thrown ball.

grasshopper *n.* [MILITARY] a small, light airplane for scouting 2. an alcoholic beverage.

grassroots *adj.* [POLITICS] of the common people. Often used in the expression "grassroots support," as contrasted with the support of one's political party.

grass widow *n.* 1. a divorcee 2. originally, an unwed mother. From the grassy fields where many seductions took place.

graum *v.* to be troubled.

graveyard *n.* [BOWLING] a lane in which it is difficult to score—*adj.* 1. [LABOR] referring to the work shift between midnight and 8 a.m. 2. [POLITICS] top secret 3. of a job with no possibility for future advancement.

gravy *n.* a financial benefit; a considerable amount of money.

gravy, in the *adj.* rich.

gravy train *n.* a source of easy wealth.

gray matter *n.* intelligence. From the construction of the human brain: the highly convoluted gray area is the cerebrum, which controls acquired knowledge.

grease *n.* 1. hair tonic 2. money 3. a bribe—*v.* to bribe.

greaseball *n.* one who looks dirty or behaves in a slovenly manner. Often a derogatory term for Latin immigrant men who wore a lot of grease in their hair.

greased *adj.* drunk.

greased lightning *n.* anything rapid.

grease joint *n.* a cheap, low-quality restaurant.

grease monkey *n.* a mechanic.

greaser *n.* a teenaged boy of the 1950s

who used greasy hair tonic liberally and whose attitude was characterized by sullenness or toughness.

grease someone's palm *v.* 1. to tip 2. to bribe.

greasy *adj.* untrustworthy.

greasy grind *n.* an overly diligent student.

greasy spoon *n.* a cheap, low-quality restaurant.

great *n.* a person of importance—*adj.* wonderful. Also used as an interjection.

great guns, go *v.* to display style, energy, and ambition.

Great White Father *n.* [POLITICS] the President of the United States. A name given by the Indians in the early nineteenth century, now used sarcastically in regard to the paternalism the image evokes.

greedy up *v.* to eat rapidly and greedily.

greefa *n.* [DRUG CULTURE] a marijuana cigarette.

green *adj.* inexperienced, as a young tree before the bark begins to form.

green-eyed monster *n.* jealousy.

green folding *n.* dollar bills.

greenhorn *n.* 1. a recent immigrant 2. a neophyte.

green ice *n.* emeralds.

greenie *n.* 1. an inexperienced, naive person 2. [DRUG CULTURE] a green-colored pep pill.

green light, give the *v.* to permit an action to begin.

green money, green stuff *n.* dollars.

green room *n.* [ENTERTAINMENT] a backstage room used by performers as a lounge between appearances in a play or show.

green thumb *n.* a talent for making plants flourish.

grid, gridiron *n.* [SPORTS] the playing field in a game of football—*adj.* pertaining to football.

griefo, grifa *n.* [DRUG CULTURE] a marijuana cigarette.

grift *n.* money earned dishonestly—*v.* to earn money dishonestly.

grifter *n.* one who earns money in dishonest business ventures.

grill *v.* [POLICE] to question intensively, as if slowly cooking over flames.

grind *n.* 1. a boring task 2. an overly diligent student—*v.* 1. to study with great intensity 2. to gyrate the pelvis.

grinder *n.* a huge sandwich made with Italian bread.

grind something out *v.* to produce supposedly creative works with little effort.

gringo *n.* a derogatory Hispanic term for an American. Originally, an eighteenth-century Spanish term for one with a strange accent.

grip *n.* [ENTERTAINMENT] a backstage worker who moves scenery in a theater.

gripe *n.* a complaint—*v.* 1. to complain 2. to annoy, as in the construction "something gripes someone."

gripe session *n.* a meeting for the purpose of expressing one's complaints.

gripe someone's cookies *v.* to annoy or trouble someone greatly.

gripes, the *n.* a tendency to complain.

grit *n.* 1. nerve 2. courage.

groaner *n.* a singer.

groceries *n.* a meal. *See* bring home the groceries.

groghound *n.* one fond of alcoholic beverages.

grog mill *n.* a bar.

groove, in the *adj.* [MUSIC] modern, admirable, excellent. An expression popular among jazz musicians in the 1930s; from the phonograph needle, which must be in the groove of the record to play music.

groovy *adj.* exciting; admirable.

gross *adj.* vulgar, disgusting, repulsive.

gross out *v.t.* to offend someone's sensibilities with disgusting behavior or talk.

grotty, groaty *adj.* abbreviation for grotesque.

grouch bag *n.* [ENTERTAINMENT] a small bag carried by performers on tour in which money and valuables are secured.

group grope *n.* 1. an orgy 2. [BUSINESS] mutual appreciation within a group of creative business people, sometimes including stealing each other's ideas.

groupie *n.* an ardent follower of a group of rock-and-roll singers, or by extension, of any public figure or performer.

grouse *v.* to complain.

growl *v.* to display displeasure in one's tone of voice.

grub *n.* food.

grubstake *n.* 1. money advanced to help establish a new household or business 2. one who lends money for such purposes—*v.* to lend money for a new enterprise, with risk of foregoing repayment if the venture fails. From the days of the gold rush in the American West, when shopkeepers would advance food to prospectors against future repayment when they discovered gold.

gruesome twosome *n.* a humorous term for a couple seen frequently together.

grunge *n.* a bore.

grungy *adj.* dirty, sloppy, foul, unpleasant.

grunt *n.* a bill incurred in a restaurant or bar.

grunt and groaner *n.* a professional wrestler, especially one who seeks to excite the audience by loud sounds of struggle.

G-string *n.* a loincloth, an abbreviated covering of the genitals worn by striptease dancers. From the heaviest string on a violin.

guck *n.* any thick, viscous, sticky, or slimy substance.

guess hitter *n.* [BASEBALL] a hitter who tries to anticipate the style of a pitch.

guff *n.* exaggeration; nonsense; rudeness.

guinea *n.* 1. a derogatory term for an Italian 2. [HORSE RACING] a stable boy. From the salary paid stable hands in the past in England.

guinzo *n.* a derogatory term for a foreigner, particularly an Italian.

gull *n.* 1. a dupe 2. a prostitute—*v.* to deceive.

gum, beat one's gums *v.* to talk idly.

gum beater *n.* one who chatters.

gum beating *n.* chatter.

gumbo *n.* [HORSE RACING] thick mud on a race track.

gum boot *n.* a detective—*v.* to walk quietly; to sneak.

gum foot *n.* a policeman.

gummer *n.* a toothless person who cannot chew, but mashes food with the gums.

gummixed up *adj.* confused.

gumshoe *n.* a detective—*v.* to walk quietly; to sneak.

gum up *v.t.* to hinder, impede. Often in the expression "gum up the works": to impede progress.

gun *n.* [SURFING] a heavy and large surfboard—*v.* 1. to shoot 2. to rev a motor.

gunboats *n.* 1. large feet 2. large shoes.

gung ho *adj.* enthusiastic; zealous. From the name of the Chinese industrial co-operatives of the mid-1930s, the words meaning "work together."

gun, give something the *v.* to increase the speed of a motorized vehicle.

gunk *n.* grime.

gun moll *n.* 1. a female criminal working with male gangsters 2. the girlfriend of a criminal.

gunsel *n.* 1. [CRIME] a young criminal 2. anyone lacking experience. From the German *ganzel*, a gosling.

gussied up *adj.* well-groomed and dressed in one's best clothing.

gut *n.* the abdomen—*v.* to destroy the interior of something—*adj.* deeply felt; emotionally powerful. Frequently used in the expression "gut reaction."

gut bucket *n.* a seedy saloon.

gut course *n.* a college course requiring little work or preparation.

gut issue *n.* a political or sociological problem that creates a powerful emotional reaction beyond reason.

gutless *adj.* lacking courage, daring, perseverance.

guts *n.* 1. courage 2. nerve.

gutsy *adj.* 1. courageous 2. daring.

gutter, in the *adj.* 1. base 2. hopeless.

gutty *adj.* daring; intrepid.

guzzle *v.* 1. to drink sloppily 2. to drink liquor.

guzzler *n.* one who guzzles. *See* guzzle.

gyp *n.* 1. a swindle 2. a swindler—*v.* to cheat.

gyp artist *n.* an accomplished swindler.

gyp joint *n.* a business establishment where customers are systematically cheated.

gyp sheet *n.* a paper containing information necessary to pass an examination and which a dishonest student attempts to conceal and consult during the examination.

gyrene *n.* a United States Marine.

H

H *n.* [DRUG CULTURE] heroin.

habit *n.* [DRUG CULTURE] drug addiction.

habit, off the *adj.* no longer addicted to drugs.

hack *n.* 1. a taxicab 2. a bad cough 3. a routine, drudge worker, especially one who produces mediocre creative works automatically for pay 4. [CRIME] a prison guard—*v.* 1. to drive a taxicab 2. to cough—*adj.* ordinary; mediocre; quickly produced.

hack around *v.* to waste time.

hack it *v.* to succeed; to struggle with a problem to ultimate success.

hack it out *v.* to negotiate a solution to a problem, as if hacking one's way through a jungle.

had *adj.* duped.

hag *n.* an ugly old woman.

haha *n.* a joke.

haimish *adj.* [YIDDISH] reminiscent of home; nostalgic.

hair, get in someone's *v.* to annoy someone.

hair, let down one's *v.* to relax; to dispense with formalities.

hair off the dog, take *v.* to become older and wiser.

hair of the dog that bit you, a *n.* a drink of the same alcoholic beverage that caused one's present hangover.

hairpin *n.* a woman.

hairy *adj.* 1. involving risk or danger 2. difficult to accomplish.

hairy buffalo *n.* a strong alcoholic beverage made with any combination of liquors mixed together.

half *n.* [SPORTS] a halfback in the game of football.

half a load *n.* [DRUG CULTURE] fifteen three-dollar bags of a narcotic.

half a shake *n.* a short period of time. *See* two shakes of a lamb's tail.

half-assed *adj.* mediocre; idiotic; foolish.

half-baked *adj.* 1. callow, of a person 2. incomplete, of a thought or action.

half buck *n.* fifty cents.

half cocked *adj.* insufficiently prepared, as a gun must be fully cocked to be fired.

half pint *n.* 1. a short person 2. a young person.

half-shot *adj.* drunk.

half-stewed *adj.* drunk.

half-truth *n.* a statement which discloses only part of the known information, in itself not false, but since information has been withheld, it is misleading.

halvsies, go *v.* to share something equally between two people.

ham *n.* 1. a short-wave radio hobbyist 2. [ENTERTAINMENT] a minimally talented actor or performer who overemotes on stage or screen. Abbreviation of hamfatter, from the ham fat actors used to remove theatrical makeup when face creams were too expensive 3. a person who constantly tries to attract attention to himself.

hamburger *n.* a face covered with contusions.

hamburger heaven *n.* a restaurant specializing in quick meals.

hamburger out of, make *v.t.* to thrash soundly.

ham it up *v.* to overemote.

ham joint *n.* a cheap restaurant.

hammy *adj.* like or characteristic of a ham (actor); overacting.

hand *n.* applause.

handbasket, go to hell in a *v.* to lead a dissolute life.

H and C *n.* [DRUG CULTURE] a mixture of heroin and cocaine.

handful *n.* a difficult or exhausting task.

hand it to someone *v.* to congratulate someone.

handkerchief head *n.* [BLACK SLANG] a mildly derogatory term for a black person who is self-abasing before whites.

handle *n.* 1. a name 2. insight or understanding—*v.* "to handle someone": to manage someone's career.

hand-me-down *n.* or *adj.* a used article passed on for use to someone else.

handout *n.* 1. something given without cost, usually as charity 2. [JOURNALISM] information supplied to a reporter by a politician's press agent.

hand over fist *adv.* rapidly and greedily.

handshaker *n.* an overly affable person.

hang a few on *v.* to have several drinks of liquor.

hang a right (or a left) *v.* 1. [SKIING] to turn right (or left) 2. [DRIVING] to turn right (or left).

hang around *v.* to idle about.

hangdog *adj.* pertaining to a sad or cringing aspect.

hanger on *n.* a parasite.

hang five *v.* [SURFING] to stand toward the front of the surfboard with one's five toes gripping the front rim.

hang in for someone *v.* 1. to replace someone at a task, i.e., to substitute for another 2. [ENTERTAINMENT] to understudy.

hang in there *v.* to face difficulty courageously or tenaciously; to persevere.

hang loose *v.* to relax.

hang one on *v.* to become drunk.

hangout *n.* any informal gathering place.

hang out *v.* to spend time idly.

hang out, let it all *v.* to make one's thoughts, feelings, and opinions obvious.

hang out with someone *v.* to socialize, usually habitually, with someone.

hangover *n.* the physical discomfort experienced after having drunk too much liquor.

hang papers *v.* to hand out subpoenas.

hang, the *n.* the ability to function gained through familiarity with a procedure—*v.* "get the hang of something": to become familiar with a procedure and adept at performing it.

hang tough *v.* to be obstinate in pursuit of a goal; to persevere.

hang-up *n.* a psychological obstacle.

hang up *v.* to replace a telephone receiver in its cradle, thus ending a telephone call.

hankie *n.* abbreviation for handkerchief.

hanky panky *n.* 1. mischief 2. sexual misconduct 3. unethical behavior.

happening *n.* a phenomenon of the 1960s. An event—usually with political or artistic overtones—with certain aspects planned, but leaving room for spontaneous improvisation by the perpetrators and the spectators, who were encouraged to interact.

happenstance *n.* an occurrence.

-happy *suffix* a devotee of; addicted to; as in "moneyhappy."

happy *adj.* drunk.

happy money *n.* money to be spent frivolously.

hard-boiled *adj.* insensitive.

hard-core *adj.* unredeemable, irremediable, firmly committed, extreme.

hard drug *n.* [DRUG CULTURE] an addictive drug.

hard hat *n.* 1. a construction worker. From the hard plastic hats worn by construction workers at building sites 2. a political reactionary. From the beatings of student protestors by construction workers in the 1960s—*adj.* pertaining to a reactionary point of view.

hard head *n.* one who is stubborn.

hard hearted *adj.* cruel; unemotional.

hard line *n.* an unyielding position—*adj.* uncompromising.

hard money *n.* coins, as opposed to paper currency.

hard-nosed *adj.* unyielding; forceful.

hard rock *n.* a style of loud, rhythmic, fast rock-and-roll music.

hard sell *n.* aggressive, high-pressure sales tactics.

hard time *n.* difficulty, usually purposefully inflicted.

hard up *adj.* in extreme need. Usually in reference to financial or sexual needs.

hardware *n.* weapons, especially guns.

harebrained *adj.* foolish.

harp polisher *n.* an ardently religious person. From the traditional image of angels playing harps in heaven.

has-been *n.* one who has had success and fame in the past but is no longer renowned.

hash *n.* 1. food 2. [DRUG CULTURE] hashish—*v.t.* 1. to examine or discuss an idea thoroughly 2. to make a mistake 3. to spoil something.

hash and trash *n.* [TRUCKERS' CB] interference noises that hamper radio transmission.

hashhouse *n.* a cheap restaurant.

hash marks *n.* fecal stains left on underwear.

hash out *v.* to examine or discuss an idea thoroughly.

hash over *v.* to discuss an idea repeatedly for added clarity.

hash slinger *n.* a cook, waiter, or waitress in a cheap restaurant.

hassle *n.* 1. a disagreement 2. an annoyance 3. a frustration—*v.* 1. to importune 2. to annoy.

hatch *n.* the mouth.

hatchet, bury the *v.* to reconciliate.

hatchet job *n.* calumny; the destruction of someone's reputation.

hatchetman *n.* 1. [POLITICS] a ruthless political aide whose function is to "do the dirty work" for an official 2. [CRIME] a paid assassin.

hatchet, take up the *v.* to prepare for a fight or quarrel.

hate someone's guts *v.* to vehemently hate someone.

hat in the ring *n.* [POLITICS] declaring candidacy. From a boxing term used in the American West, showing a man's willingness to fight any combatant by literally throwing his hat into the ring where the fight would be held.

hat, pass the *v.* to solicit or collect financial contributions.

hatrack *n.* a skinny person.

hat, wear more than one *See* wear more than one hat.

haul ass *v.* to move quickly.

hausfrau, housefrau *n.* [GERMAN] a housewife, especially in reference to a strong, homely woman.

have a bead on *v.t.* 1. to have an unobstructed view of a target 2. to have under control 3. to be aware of.

have a bun on *v.* to be drunk.

have a buzz on *v.* to be drunk.

have a crush on someone *v.* to have a strong romantic or sexual attraction to someone. Usually said of adolescents.

have a screw loose *v.* to be eccentric, crazy.

have a thing about *v.t.* to have a strong emotional reaction, either positive or negative, to.

have a thing going *v.* to be in the midst of a successful love affair, enterprise, etc.

have had it *v.* to be annoyed.

have it *v.* to possess an intangible quality of attraction; to have charisma.

have it for someone *v.* to be romantically attracted to someone.

have it in for someone *v.* to seek revenge, to resent someone.

have it, let someone *v.* to attack someone verbally or physically.

have-nots *n.* [POLITICS] those people or political structures that possess neither wealth nor power nor resources.

have one's druthers *v.* to have one's choice, one's preference.

haves *n.* [POLITICS] those people or political structures that possess wealth, power, and resources.

have something going *v.* to be engaged

in a project.

have something going for oneself *v.* to have the qualities necessary for success.

hawk *n.* [POLITICS] one who believes in the necessity of war to establish military power firmly.

hay *n.* 1. an insignificant amount of money 2. bed, specifically as a place for sexual intercourse. Often used in the construction "I'll get her in the hay."

hay, hit the *v.* to go to sleep.

hay, make *v.* to take advantage of a propitious situation.

haymaker *n.* a powerful blow with the fist, intended to cause a knockout.

hayseed *n.* a naive country dweller.

haywire *adj.* 1. crazy 2. confused 3. inoperable.

haze *v.* to initiate a new member into a fraternity with sometimes violent pranks.

hazing *n.* the act of initiating someone into a fraternity. *See* haze.

head *n.* 1. [PRINTING] the top of a page or book 2. [NAUTICAL] the toilet on a boat 3. [DRUG CULTURE] one who uses drugs.

head, off (or out of) one's *adj.* crazy.

headache *n.* any vexation.

headbuster, headcrusher *n.* [CRIME] a criminal who uses extreme physical force to collect outstanding debts or to inflict punishment.

head doctor *n.* a psychiatrist, psychologist, or psychoanalyst.

head, have a *v.* to feel the aftereffects of being drunk, i.e., to have a hangover.

headhunter *n.* 1. [CRIME] a paid assassin 2. [SPORTS] a particularly violent player.

head, in over one's *adv.* in difficulty, as if in water too deep for safety.

head is at, where one's *n.* 1. one's state of mind at any given moment 2. one's opinions.

headliner *n.* a person of prominence, especially a star performer.

head off *v.t.* 1. to avoid 2. to overtake.

head over heels *adv.* euphorically.

head shop *n.* a store selling paraphernalia associated with the drug culture, including pipes for hashish or opium, cigarette papers for marijuana cigarettes, psychedelic posters, special lighting equipment, etc.

head shot *n.* a photograph of the face.

head shrinker *n.* a psychiatrist, psychologist, or psychoanalyst.

heap *n.* 1. a large quantity 2. a dilapidated vehicle.

hear footsteps *v.* to sense the presence of an opponent.

heart *n.* courage, bravery, determination.

heart, have a *v.* to be kind or understanding.

hear the birdies sing *v.* to be unconscious.

heartland *n.* [POLITICS] the central portion of the United States, implying traditional moral and political values as well as location; Middle America.

hearts and flowers *n.* sentimentality.

heart throb *n.* a beloved. Often a male public figure who inspires adoration in females.

heat *n.* 1. pressure 2. [CRIME] pressure exerted on criminals by police investigation into their activities 3. [SPORTS] a preliminary competition held to eliminate some of the less proficient contestants before a major competition.

heat, in *adj.* of an animal, desirous of sexual relations. Also used for particularly promiscuous humans.

heater *n.* a pistol.

heat on, put the *v.* to keep a thorough watch on another's activities in order (a) to detect anything illegal, or (b) to find fault with their performance.

heave *v.* to regurgitate.

heaves, the *n.* nausea to the point of repeated regurgitation.

heave-ho *interj.* a call to indicate that something is being thrown.

heave-ho, give someone the (old) *v.* to eject someone forcibly.

heavy *n.* 1. [ENTERTAINMENT] the villain in a show 2. [SURFING] a big wave—*adj.* 1. profound 2. admirable 3. [HORSE RAC-

ING]of a race track, covered with heavy, sticky mud.

heavy date n. an important social engagement, often one which includes some sort of sexual activity.

heavy foot n. one who drives a vehicle too fast, i.e., who presses the accelerator pedal too hard.

heavy handed adj. 1. clumsy 2. lacking subtlety.

heavy hearted adj. depressed; sad.

heavy money n. a large sum of money.

heavy necking, petting n. sexual foreplay.

heavy sugar n. a large sum of money.

heckle v. to mock volubly.

hedge n. a defense—v. to avoid direct confrontation.

hedge a bet v. [GAMBLING] to counterbalance a bet with other bets to avoid loss.

heebie-jeebies n. nervousness, anxiety, disquietude. Coined by cartoonist Billy de Beck.

heel n. an unscrupulous person.

heesh n. [DRUG CULTURE] hashish.

heifer n. a woman.

heist n. a robbery—v. to rob.

helicopter n. [SKIING] a full twist in the air.

hell, give someone v. to reprimand someone severely.

hell, go to interj. an expression of disdain, anger, irony, etc.

hell and gone, to adj. lost forever.

hell and high water n. any major obstacle.

hell bender n. 1. a debauch 2. one who is debauched.

hell bent adj. recklessly obdurate.

hell cat n. a strong-willed, evil woman.

heller n. a person who is noisy, wild, reckless, etc.

hellhole n. any unpleasant place.

hell of a time n. 1. a difficult, unpleasant time 2. an excellent time.

hell on wheels adj. 1. dynamic 2. an unsettling force 3. unpredictable 4. mean 5. violent.

hell's bells interj. an exclamation of impatience.

hell to pay n. responsibility for one's misdeeds, as in "for that, you will have hell to pay!"

help, on the adv. [PRISON]employed at a prison job, of an inmate.

he-man n. an especially virile man.

hemp n. [DRUG CULTURE] marijuana.

hen n. a woman.

henchman n. a subordinate, especially one who performs unpleasant tasks.

hen party n. a social gathering of women.

hen-peck v. of a woman, to dominate a man by persistent nagging.

hen-pecked adj. of a man, dominated by a woman by persistent nagging.

hep adj. knowledgeable; aware. From the military call to march in the tempo, hep-2-3-4. One who is hep fits right into the proper rhythm of life.

hepcat n. one who is knowledgeable and aware.

herb, the n. [DRUG CULTURE] marijuana.

here's how interj. a drinking toast. From the American Indian greeting "how."

Herkimer Jerkimer n. a fool.

hero n. a huge sandwich made with Italian bread, one that requires a "heroic" effort to eat.

hey Rube interj. [CIRCUS SLANG] a cry of distress; a rallying call of circus people in fights with local residents.

hi interj. a greeting of welcome.

hick n. a naive country dweller.

hickey n. a bruise mark on the skin, usually near the neck, as the result of overly zealous kissing.

hick town n. a small rural town.

hideaway n. a secret refuge.

hideout n. a secret refuge used by criminals to escape capture.

hides n. drums. From the covering made of animal hide.

hifi n. abbreviation for high fidelity: a phonograph giving excellent sound quality.

high adj. 1. drunk 2. under the influence

of drugs 3. happy.

high as a kite *adj.* very drunk, drugged, or happy.

highball *v.* to proceed at great speed.

highbrow *n.* an intellectual—*adj.* pertaining to intellect or culture. From the belief that a brow which is high is the sign of intellectual superiority.

high-class *adj.* elite, refined, stylish.

higher than a kite *adj.* extremely drunk, drugged, or happy.

higher-ups *n.* superiors.

highfalutin *adj.* 1. snobbish 2. elite.

high-hat *n.* a snob—*v.* to behave snobbishly.

high horse, on one's *adj.* vainglorious; pretentious. In fourteenth-century England, persons of the highest rank mounted the largest and tallest horses in the royal pageants, according to the writings of John Wyclif.

high jinks, hijinx *n.* spontaneous fun.

high mucky-muck *n.* [AMERICAN INDIAN] an important person. From the Algonquin, "has much food."

high on something *adj.* enthusiastic about something. From the feeling of euphoria in a drug-induced state.

high on the hog *adv.* extravagantly. Said of living a lavish lifestyle.

highpockets *n.* a tall person.

high rise, hi-rise *n.* a tall building—*adj.* pertaining to a tall building.

high roller *n.* 1. [GAMBLING] an avid dice player 2. an expensive prostitute 3. one pursuing an extravagant lifestyle.

high sign *n.* a secret signal, usually indicating permission to proceed.

high-tail, high-tail it *v.* to leave rapidly.

high time *adj.* a gay, exciting, enjoyable time.

high tone *adj.* [BLACK SLANG] 1. light-skinned 2. elegant, snobbish, of a person 3. exclusive, of an organization, a place.

high-ups *n.* people of importance.

high, wide, and handsome *adv.* with case, aplomb, assurance.

high yellow *n.* a light-skinned black person.

hijack *v.* to take command of a vehicle illegally by force—*n.* hijack, hijacking.

hike *n.* an increment—*v.* to increase.

hill *n.* [BASEBALL] the pitcher's mound.

hillbilly *n.* an uneducated, unsophisticated mountain dweller.

hill, go over the *v.* [MILITARY] to desert from the armed forces. *See* over the hill.

hill of beans *n.* something of little significance. Often in the expression "something amounting to a hill of beans," i.e., nothing of significance.

hitchhike *v.* to travel by getting free rides from passing vehicles.

hitchy *adj.* nervous, irritable.

hit it off *v.* to please mutually.

hit, make a *v.* 1. to be a great success 2. to murder.

hitman *n.* [CRIME] a paid assassin.

hit someone for something *v.* to borrow something from someone.

hitter *n.* [CRIME] a gun.

hits *n.* [DRUG CULTURE] pills.

hit the books *See* books, hit the.

hit the bottle *v.* to drink hard liquor, usually in great quantity; often used to imply habitual drunkenness.

hit the bricks *v.* to walk, often in search of employment.

hit the bull's eye *v.* to succeed.

hit the ceiling *v.* to become angry suddenly and violently.

hit the deck *v.* 1. [NAUTICAL] to present oneself for work 2. to begin a project.

hit the dust *v.* 1. to fall to the ground, usually to avoid danger.

hit the jackpot *See* jackpot.

hit the mattress *v.* [CRIME] to go into hiding.

hit the road *v.* to leave, depart. Often used as a command to leave.

hit the sack *v.* to go to bed.

hit the spot *v.* of a refreshment, to satisfy.

hoagy, hoagie *n.* a huge sandwich made with Italian bread.

hobnob *v.* 1. to frequent socially 2. to seek advantage by associating with people of wealth and importance.

hock *v.* to pawn; to borrow money against the value of an object left with the lender.

hock, in *adj.* owing money.

hockable *adj.* suitable to pawn.

hockey puck *n.* a hamburger.

hockshop *n.* a pawn shop.

hocus-pocus *n.* 1. an incantation used by magicians performing tricks 2. trickery, deception.

hodad, hodaddy *n.* [SURFING] an incompetent surfer; a non-surfer.

hodge-podge *n.* an odd mixture or combination; a jumble.

hoedown *n.* a lively country dance. The time to put the hoe down and enjoy oneself.

hog *n.* 1. a selfish person 2. a Harley-Davidson motorcycle—*v.* to behave selfishly.

hogwash *n.* nonsense.

hog-wild, go *v.* to become greatly excited.

hoist by one's own petard *v.* to be destroyed by one's own devices. From the medieval practice of planting a bomb (petard), which sometimes backfired, in the wall of a castle under attack.

hoke, hokum *n.* 1. nonsense 2. deception.

hoke up *v.* to add gross comedic or maudlin elements to a creative work in order to have a greater immediate popular appeal.

hokey, hoky *adj.* nonsensical, silly, maudlin.

hokus *n.* [DRUG CULTURE] a narcotic.

holding the bag *adv.* duped into accepting another's responsibilities.

hold out *n.* 1. one who refuses to follow a group dictum 2. [SPORTS] one who refuses to accept contractual terms offered by management—*v.* to refuse to accept a group dictum, often to await some special consideration.

hold, put someone on *v.* 1. to place a telephone call in abeyance electronically 2. to keep someone waiting.

hold the line *v.* to maintain control over something.

hold up *n.* an armed robbery—*v.* to rob with threatened violence and using weapons.

hole *n.* any decrepit, dirty place.

hole, in a *adv.* in a dilemma; in a difficult situation.

hole, in the *adv.* 1. owing money; needing money 2. [CRIME] in prison; in solitary confinement 3. [SPORTS] scheduled to play after two other players have had their turns 4. held in abeyance.

hole in one's head *n.* vacuity; absent-mindedness.

hole in the wall *n.* 1. a small dingy residence or place of business 2. [TRUCKERS' CB] a tunnel.

hole up *v.* to go into hiding.

Hollywood *adj.* 1. affected; insincere 2. gaudy; ostentatious.

holy cow *interj.* an exclamation of surprise, disbelief.

holy Moses *interj.* an exclamation of dismay or disbelief.

holy terror *n.* a hellion. Usually in reference to an uncontrollable child given to tantrums or mischief.

holy Toledo *interj.* an exclamation of surprise.

hombre *n.* [SPANISH] a man.

home *n.* the ultimate goal, especially in sports.

home cooking *n.* anything satisfying or pleasurable.

home free *adj.* certain to succeed.

home in *v.* [AVIATION] to be guided by radar to a target.

home piece *n.* [PRISON] a fellow inmate who was one's friend before imprisonment.

homer *n.* [BASEBALL] a home run. Also used as a verb.

homo *n.* or *adj.* abbreviation for homosexual.

hon *n.* *See* honey.

honcho *n.* [JAPANESE] a leader. Used most often in business and politics.

honest Injun *interj.* an exclamation attesting to the veracity of a statement.

honey *n.* 1. anything excellent 2. anything prized 3. a term of endearment (also, "hon").

honker *n.* [AUTO RACING] a particularly speedy car.

honky *n.* a derogatory term for a white person.

honky-tonk *n.* 1. a cheap, noisy saloon 2. originally, a style of jazz music often played in saloons—*adj.* 1. garish, gaudy 2. lively.

hooch *n.* 1. homemade liquor 2. a Korean or Vietnamese grass hut, often one used by young prostitutes and soldiers.

hood *n.* a criminal; abbreviation for hoodlum.

hooey *n.* nonsense.

hoof *n.* the foot—*v.* 1. to walk 2. to dance.

hoofer *n.* a dancer.

hoo-ha *n.* [YIDDISH] noise, tumult, commotion.

hook *n.* 1. any gimmick used to entice or lure 2. [STUDENT SLANG] the grade of "C" in a course—*v.t.* 1. to entice or lure 2. to entrap—*v.* "hook someone on something": to induce an addiction to something in someone.

hook, get (or give someone) the *v.* to be dismissed (or to dismiss someone) from employment. From the custom in vaudeville to remove a player from the stage by means of a large hook.

hooked *adj.* 1. married 2. addicted.

hook, off the *adj.* removed from responsibility.

hook, on the *adj.* entrapped; at someone's mercy.

hooker *n.* a prostitute.

hook, line, and sinker *adv.* completely, usually implying gullibility. From the fish that accept bait readily and, as a result, get caught.

hooks *n.* the hands.

hooky *n.* an unexcused absence from school—*v.* "play hooky": to stay out of school without a legitimate excuse.

hooligan *n.* 1. a tough, disruptive, ill-mannered person 2. [AUTO RACING] a race of secondary importance held for competitors not qualifying for a major race.

hoop-a-doop, hoop-de-do *n.* 1. a joyous, raucous celebration or party 2. joyful noise.

hoopla *n.* 1. [POLITICS] excitement and enthusiasm surrounding a campaign or rally 2. publicity.

hoosegow *n.* [COWBOY SLANG] a jail. From the Spanish, *juzgado*.

hootch *See* hooch.

hootenanny *n.* 1. a social gathering, specifically for singing folksongs 2. a euphemism for "damn," in the expression "not to give a hootenanny."

hop *n.* 1. a short distance 2. a dance. A term popular in the 1940s through 1950s.

hop head *n.* [DRUG CULTURE] an opium addict.

hopped up *adj.* 1. excited, nervous 2. under the influence of drugs.

hops, full of *adj.* foolish, senseless.

hop up *v.* 1. to energize 2. to take narcotics or administer them.

horn, blow (or toot) one's own *v.* to brag, boast.

hornblowing *n.* vigorous publicity or advertising.

horn in *v.* to insinuate oneself.

hornswoggle *v.* to swindle.

horny *adj.* sexually excited.

horse *n.* 1. [DRUG CULTURE] heroin 2. one-thousand dollars 3. a stubborn person 4. [SPORTS] a strong offensive player.

horse around *v.* to play roughly.

horse collar *n.* [BASEBALL] a score of zero. From the similarity of shape between a zero and a large round collar—*v.* of a baseball pitcher, to pitch a game allowing no runs to the adversary team.

horsefeathers *n.* nonsense. Coined by cartoonist Billy de Beck.

horsehide *n.* a baseball.

horse laugh *n.* a raucous laugh.

horse opera *n.* [ENTERTAINMENT] a cowboy movie.

horse play *n.* good-natured, rough romping.

horse sense *n.* instinctual wisdom.

horse's mouth, straight from the *adj.* of information, direct from the source. To determine the age of a horse, one examines its teeth. Its first permanent teeth appear at age 2½, the next pair appears at 3½, and the third pair appears at 4½. Therefore, to find the true age of a horse, one goes directly to its mouth.

hose *v.* to beat, as with a hose.

hosed *adj.* tricked.

hot *adj.* 1. lucky 2. popular 3. excellent 4. sexually excited 5. stolen 6. angry.

hot air *n.* exaggeration; bragging; lies.

hotbed *n.* any environment conducive to nurturing any given vice, i.e., a hotbed of crime, of hate, of sedition, etc. From the glass-enclosed bed of fertilized soil used by horticulturists to grow certain plants.

hot corner *n.* [BASEBALL] third base.

hot damn, hot diggity damn, hot diggity dog *interj.* an expression of great delight or surprise.

hot dog *n.* an expert. Also, hot dogger— *v.* [SPORTS] to perform in a showy manner for the benefit of the spectators; to show off.

hot foot *n.* a prank involving lighting a match surreptitiously stuck between someone's toes or in someone's shoe in order to burn the foot and surprise the victim. Often used in the construction "to give someone a hot foot."

hot foot it out *v.* to leave rapidly.

hot for *adj.* desirous of.

hot grease *n.* trouble.

hothead *n.* an irascible person.

hot ice *n.* [CRIME] stolen diamonds.

hot line *n.* [POLITICS] the direct teletype linkage between countries, specifically the United States and the USSR, to permit immediate communication in a crisis in order to avoid an all-out war. *See* all-out war, cold war.

hot mama *n.* a sexy woman.

hot mike *n.* [ENTERTAINMENT] a micro- phone that is working.

hot one *n.* something surprising or amusing.

hot pants *n.* desire for frequent sexual activity, as in "to have hot pants for someone."

hot potato *n.* a political problem that no one wishes to handle because of the difficulty involved or the stigma associated with an unpopular stand on the issue. Therefore, as a potato too hot to hold, it is passed from one to another.

hot property *n.* an assuredly successful client to manage or a valuable product or creative work to handle. Used in politics, business, and entertainment.

hot rod *n.* an automobile, usually an old one stripped of extraneous parts.

hot rodder *n.* a person, typically a teenager, who drives hot rods. *See* hot rod.

hot seat *n.* 1. the electric chair 2. a difficult or potentially embarrassing situation.

hots, have the *v.* to be desirous of sexual activity.

hot shit *n.* anything excellent. Often used derisively for one who has an inflated self-image: "to think one is hot shit." Also used as an interjection.

hot shoe *n.* [AUTO RACING] an excellent racing driver.

hot shot *n.* 1. an energetic and ambitious person 2. a self-satisfied braggart.

hotsie-totsie *adj.* in good condition, safe, fine. Coined by cartoonist Billy de Beck.

hot spot *n.* 1. a night club or any extremely popular place for social engagements 2. a difficult or potentially embarrassing situation.

hot stove league *n.* [SPORTS] a humorous concept of what baseball fans do during the winter when no games are held nationally: they sit around a hot stove and discuss baseball.

hot stuff *n.* 1. anything of excellence or great popularity 2. a mildly derogatory term of address to an attractive person.

hot tamale *n.* a sexy woman.

hot under the collar *adj.* 1. angry 2. nervous 3. embarrassed 4. frightened.

hot walker *n.* [HORSE RACING] a stable hand who walks a horse around after a race in order to cool it off.

hot water *n.* trouble. From a sixteenth-century practice of repelling an enemy by throwing scalding water.

hound *v.* 1. to annoy 2. to persecute.

hounds *n.* the feet.

house *n.* 1. [ENTERTAINMENT] the audience in a theater 2. the auditorium in which the audience sits 3. a house of prostitution.

house, on the *adj.* paid for by the management; free.

house cleaning *n.* restructuring responsibilities within an organization.

household word *n.* [POLITICS] a familiar politician. Coined in reference to Spiro T. Agnew, Richard Nixon's running mate (*see* running mate) in 1968, who at that time was not well-known nationally.

house nigger *n.* [BLACK SLANG] a derogatory term for a black person who is self-abasing before whites.

housewife time *n.* [BROADCASTING] late morning and early afternoon hours when the radio and television audience is composed largely of housewives.

how come *interj.* why? From the Dutch *hoekum,* "why."

how-de-do *n.* 1. a greeting 2. a surprising turn of events. Often in the expression "that's a fine how-de-do."

howl *n.* anything provoking riotous laughter—*v.* to laugh heartily.

howling *adj.* great, as in "a howling success."

hubba hubba *interj.* 1. a command to move quickly 2. an exclamation of admiration.

hubby *n.* abbreviation for husband.

huddle *n.* a private, informal conference.

hue and cry *n.* a great clamor.

huff, in a *adv.* in anger, outrage.

hugger-mugger *n.* confusion.

hullabaloo *n.* commotion; noise; confusion.

humble pie *n.* humiliation—*v.* "eat humble pie." Originally, a humorous play on "umble pie," a pie made of the internal organs of deer and served to servants and other lowly helpers while the masters ate the better cuts of meat after the hunt.

humbug *n.* 1. nonsense 2. deception 3. an imposter. Also used as an interjection.

humdinger *n.* anything of excellence.

humdrum *adj.* dull; boring.

hump *n.* 1. a sexually desirable person 2. a partner in coitus—*v.* to coit.

hump, over the *adj.* having finished the most difficult part of a task.

humpty dumpty *n.* [POLITICS] a candidate doomed to lose.

humpy *adj.* sexually excited.

hunch *n.* an intuition.

hundred proof *adj.* 1. the most excellent 2. the worst. From the grading system measuring the alcohol content in alcoholic beverages.

hungover *adj.* feeling the aftereffects of drunkenness.

hung up *adj.* afflicted with a psychological problem.

hunk *n.* 1. a large piece 2. a muscular, attractive man 3. a sexually desirable person.

Hunky-dory *adj.* in good condition, safe, fine.

hurt *v.* to be in need. Often in the construction "to hurt for something": to be in need of something.

hush-hush *adj.* secretive.

husk *v.* to remove one's clothing.

hustle *n.* 1. a dance popular in the 1970s 2. an energetic and persuasive sales pitch—*v.* 1. to perform a task with energy and enthusiasm 2. to sell narcotics 3. to prostitute oneself.

hustle on, get a *v.* to speed up.

hype *n.* 1. a strong advertising campaign 2. [DRUG CULTURE] abbreviation for hypodermic syringe 3. one who sells drugs to addicts, i.e., a pusher—*v.* 1. to intensify 2. to speed up 3. to sell drugs.

hyped up *adj.* 1. false, exaggerated, of a claim 2. nervous, irritable.

hyping *v.* to stimulate, excite, enliven, etc., artificially as or by the injection of a drug.

hypo *n.* a hypodermic needle.

I

ice *n.* one or more diamonds—*v.* to become silent and unresponsive.
ice, on *adv.* 1. of a person, in prison 2. of a plan, kept in abeyance ready for use at the propitious moment 3. of a competition, certain to be won.
ice, on thin *adv.* precariously.
iceberg *n.* a person who shows little emotion.
icebox *n.* any place that is extremely cold.
ice breaker *n.* 1. any element which serves to initiate a new relationship 2. one adept at making personal overtures.
icky *adj.* unpleasant, usually in the sense of viscous.
idiot box *n.* a television set.
idiot cards *n.* [BROADCASTING] large sheets of heavy paper upon which a script is written to prompt the actors in an on-camera production.
iffy *adj.* problematical; uncertain.
illuminated *adj.* drunk.
image *n.* [POLITICS] an idealized impression of a personality which is presented as truly representing the person in question. Also in wide use in business and entertainment.
immense *adj.* very good; excellent.
immie *n.* a marble. Abbreviation for "imitation agate."
in *n.* an advantage—*adj.* currently acceptable; popular.
in, get *v.* of a man, to coit.
in a pickle *adj.* in difficulty.
indeedy *interj.* a coy form of "indeed."
Indian giver *n.* one who takes back a gift.
influence peddler *n.* [POLITICS] one who serves as a paid intermediary for a private interest seeking the support of a public official with whom the intermediary is supposed to have influence.
info *n.* abbreviation for information.
in for it, be *v.* to anticipate imminent revenge or chastisement.
in front *adv.* in advance, usually of a payment.
ink *v.* to sign one's name to.
inky dinky *adj.* [BLACK SLANG] elegant; exclusive; pompous. Also used as a noun.
in like Flynn *adj.* secure, comfortable, fortunate. From the Chicago political boss Flynn, who never lost an election. Later from the film star Errol Flynn, whose success with young women is legendary.
inman *n.* [CRIME] a criminal who forces entry into premises to be burglarized.
inner-directed *adj.* of a reflective nature; introverted.
in one *adv.* [ENTERTAINMENT] playing in the downstage area close to the audience.
in orbit *adj.* 1. excellent 2. excited 3. ecstatic.
in place *n.* [POLITICS] a political spy placed in the ranks of the opposing party.
input *n.* the total of all information, skill, and effort brought to a project.
inside job *n.* [CRIME] a theft perpetrated with the collusion of or by an employee, a friend, etc., i.e., an insider.
insider *n.* 1. one accepted as a member of a group 2. one privy to information.
inside straight, draw an *v.* 1. to hope for the impossible 2. to take a chance on

77

something that might not succeed. From the game of poker, in which such a winning hand is unlikely to be drawn.

in spades *adv.* 1. with great conviction 2. forcefully 3. with no possible doubt. From the card game of bridge, in which the spades are the most powerful suit.

in the altogether *adj.* naked.

in the know *adj.* aware; knowledgeable.

in there *adv.* exerting great effort to succeed. From boxing, indicating that a prize fighter is truly making his presence felt in the ring.

into *adv.* absorbed in; involved in; interested in.

intro *n.* abbreviation for introduction.

invitation *n.* [TRUCKERS' CB] a summons issued by the police.

invite *n.* an invitation.

IOU *n.* a promissory note, the acronym for "I owe you."

Irish Mafia *n.* [POLITICS] the tightly knit group of Bostonians of Irish descent that formed the core of President John F. Kennedy's aides and supporters.

iron *n.* [CRIME] a gun.

iron curtain *n.* [POLITICS] the ideological separation between the European communist nations and the Western capitalist countries. Coined by Winston Churchill on March 5, 1946, in a speech at Westminster College in Fulton, Missouri.

Irving *n.* a boring person.

it *n.* sex appeal. A term particularly popular in the 1920s, when the actress Clara Bow was called the "It Girl."

it *See* give it to someone, have it for someone, have it in for someone *and* make it (with someone).

itch *n.* a desire.

itchy *adj.* 1. nervous 2. anxious.

ivories *n.* 1. piano keys 2. teeth 3. dice 4. billiard balls.

ivory thumper *n.* a pianist.

Ivy League *n.* and *adj.* a group of prestigious universities located in the northeastern United States. Originally, four colleges forming an intercollegiate athletic league in the nineteenth century: Harvard, Yale, Columbia, and Princeton. In Roman numerals the four is IV, pronounced ivy, hence the name. Later other colleges were included but the name remained.

ixnay *interj.* nix; no. *See* pig Latin.

J

J *n.* [DRUG CULTURE] abbreviation for joint, a marijuana cigarette.

jab a vein *v.* [DRUG CULTURE] to inject a narcotic into a vein.

jack *n.* money.

Jack *n.* a general term of address for a man whose name is not known.

jack around *v.* to spend time idly.

jackass *n.* 1. a fool 2. a boor.

jackeroo *n.* a cowboy. From the Spanish *vaquero*.

jack off *v.* to masturbate.

jack out *v.* to display a gun one is carrying on one's person.

jackpot *n.* 1. a great deal of money 2. the best prize awarded in a contest. From the game of poker, in which bet money accumulates in the pot until a player can open the game with a pair of jacks or better—*v.* "hit the jackpot": 1. to have a great victory 2. to gain a lot of money suddenly.

jackroller *n.* [CRIME] a criminal who specializes in robbing debilitated victims, i.e., the aged, drunkards, etc.

jack someone's wig *v.* to pull someone's hair.

jack up *v.* to increase, specifically to raise a price.

jag *n.* 1. a spurt of frenetic and uninterrupted activity, e.g., "crying jag," "shopping jag," "writing jag" 2. a male prostitute.

jagged *adj.* drunk.

jag house *n.* a brothel catering to male homosexuals.

jailbait *n.* a girl under the age of maturity viewed as a sex object with whom coitus would be considered statutory rape, and thus result in legal prosecution of the male, who would face a prison term.

jailbird *n.* 1. a prisoner 2. an ex-convict.

jake *adj.* satisfactory; acceptable; fine.

jalopy, jalop *n.* a dilapidated old vehicle.

jam *n.* 1. a difficult situation; a predicament 2. anything simple or easy to accomplish—*v.* 1. to play music, especially jazz, spontaneously and informally 2. to stick.

jammed up *adj.* or *adv.* in trouble or confusion.

jammer *n.* a musician who plays at a jam session.

jamoke *n.* coffee.

jam session *n.* an informal gathering of jazz musicians at which jazz music is played spontaneously.

jam up *n.* a congestion—*v.* to congest.

jane *n.* 1. a woman 2. one's female beloved 3. a woman's toilet.

jap *v.t.* 1. to dupe 2. to ambush.

jasper *n.* 1. a man 2. a dupe.

java *n.* coffee. From the island of Java, the place of origin of certain coffee beans.

jaw *n.* conversation—*v.* to converse, argue, discourse.

jawbone *v.* 1. to buy on credit 2. to persuade by threats 3. to gossip.

jaw breaker, jaw cracker *n.* 1. a piece of candy that is particularly hard to chew 2. anything hard to say, to pronounce.

jay *n.* 1. a dupe 2. a fool 3. a neophyte.

jaywalk *v.* to traverse a street at other than the designated pedestrian crosswalk or against the traffic light.

jaywalker *n.* one who jaywalks. *See* jaywalk.

jazz *n.* 1. a style of music, originally improvisational, characterized by syncopated rhythm and melancholy strains of trumpet, trombone, or saxophone 2. energy; enthusiasm 3. lies; exaggeration.

jazz bo *n.* one who is well-dressed, knowledgeable, and alert.

jazz up *v.* to enliven.

jazzy *adj.* exciting; excellent; lively.

jeans *n.* denim trousers.

jeasly *adj.* of little value; inferior; insignificant.

jeebies *n.* trembling from fear, nervousness—*v.* "have the jeebies": to tremble from fear.

jeep *n.* [MILITARY] a small powerful motor vehicle with four-wheel drive. From G.P. (general purpose), the Army designation for its use.

jeeter *n.* one repulsive in appearance or behavior. From the character in Erskine Caldwell's *Tobacco Road*.

Jeeves *n.* a familiar, disrespectful term of address to any butler.

jeez *interj.* an exclamation of surprise or dismay.

jelly *n.* anything easy or simple to accomplish.

jellyroll *n.* [BLACK SLANG] 1. coitus 2. a good lover.

jenny *n.* an airplane.

jerk *n.* 1. a fool 2. a boor.

jerk, soda or **beer** *n.* one who works dispensing drinks at a soda fountain or a bar. Originally, beer jerk meant "drunkard," but has come to mean one who serves the drink.

jerk off *n.* 1. a boor 2. a fool 3. an idler—*v.* 1. to masturbate 2. to spend time idly.

jerk town *n.* a small rural town.

jerkwater *n.* a small rural town. From the railroad trains that stopped at such towns for water where the water had to be jerked up with a pump—*adj.* backwards, naive, or having any other of the characteristics associated with small rural towns.

jerky *adj.* stupid, foolish, etc.

jerry *n.* 1. a manual laborer 2. [BRITISH SLANG] a derogatory term for a German, especially a German soldier.

Jersey green *n.* [DRUG CULTURE] a type of marijuana.

jet up *v.* 1. to intensify 2. to improve performance.

jew, jew down *v.* to bargain.

jibberjabber *n.* chatter. Also used as a verb.

jiffy bag *n.* a small bag used for carrying toilet articles.

jiffy, jiff *n.* 1. an instant 2. a short period of time.

jig *n.* 1. a derogatory term for a black person 2. a party where the main activity is dancing.

jigamaree *n.* any object for which the proper name is not known.

jig chaser *n.* a derogatory term for a white person viewed as a persecutor of blacks.

jigger *n.* a one and one-half ounce glass used for liquor.

jiggerman *n.* [CRIME] a lookout.

jiggery pokery *n.* deception.

jiggins *n.* a fool.

jigglies *n.* [BROADCASTING] television scenes showing actresses moving their bodies in sexually suggestive ways.

jig is up, the an expression indicating that an action is finished and the consequences will ensue. In seventeenth-century England, "jig" meant a practical joke.

jig-swiggered *adj.* a euphemism for "damned."

jillion *n.* a great number.

jim *v.t.* to ruin.

Jim Crow *n.* and *adj.* discriminatory practices against blacks in the United States. As early as the eighteenth century, Jim Crow appeared as the name of a dance and eventually became associated with black-face entertainers. In 1840, the Boston Railroad had a segregated car for blacks, known as the Jim

Crow car.

jimdandy *adj.* excellent. Also used as a noun.

jimjams *n.* a state of extreme nervousness or fright; trembling from fear.

jimmies *n.* candy sprinkles usually used to top ice cream cones or on cookies.

jimmy *n.* [CRIME] a burglar's tool used to open locks—*v.* to open a lock with a special tool, usually to burglarize the premises.

jingle *n.* 1. a little song, usually as an advertisement 2. a telephone call.

jingoism *n.* [POLITICS] bellicose chauvinism. From "by jingo" in the refrain of a popular music hall song in London, boasting of national strength during the time preceding the Crimean War.

jinx *n.* bad luck—*v.* to cause bad luck.

jism *n.* 1. energy 2. excitement 3. semen.

jitney *n.* 1. a small vehicle used as a bus 2. a nickel—*adj.* 1. cheap 2. inferior.

jitney bag *n.* a purse.

jitter *v.* to tremble from fear, cold, etc.—*n.* the jitters.

jitterbug *n.* a dance popular in the 1940s, characterized by quick movements of the hands and feet, i.e., jittering; also, one who does the dance.

jittery *adj.* nervous.

jive *n.* banter. Originally, the talk or jokes of jazz musicians while they play—*v.* to tease, deceive.

job *v.* to deceive, cheat, trick.

jock *n.* 1. a jockey 2. an athlete 3. a boorish fellow with great strength and little intelligence 4. abbreviation for jock strap, an athletic supporter.

jockey *n.* one who operates a specified vehicle, machine, etc.

jod on the job *adj.* attentive to one's task or duty.

joe *n.* 1. coffee 2. a man. *See* good Joe.

Joe Blow *n.* 1. any man whose name is not known 2. the personification of the average man 3. one who exaggerates or brags.

Joe College *n.* a typical eager and enthusiastic college student who participates fully in the social aspects of campus life.

joey *n.* [CIRCUS SLANG] a clown. From the great early nineteenth-century English clown Joseph Grimaldi.

john *n.* 1. a toilet 2. a prostitute's customer.

John Bull *n.* the personification of the British people. From a satire by Dr. John Arbuthnot written in 1712 on the War of the Spanish Succession, in which animals personify the nations involved in the struggle.

John Doe *n.* 1. the average man 2. the name generally applied to a man whose name is not known or to a male foundling.

John Hancock *n.* a signature. From the signature of John Hancock, which appears large and clear on the Declaration of Independence so that King George would not need his spectacles to read it.

John Law *n.* a policeman.

johnny-come-lately *n.* 1. a newcomer 2. a neophyte.

johnny-on-the spot *n.* an opportunist; one who seeks to be at the right place at the right time.

Johnny Rebel, Johnny Reb *n.* a soldier of the Confederacy during the Civil War.

John Q. Public *n.* the average citizen.

Johnson *n.* the penis.

joint *n.* 1. a social gathering place 2. [DRUG CULTURE] a marijuana cigarette 3. a gun 4. the penis—*adj.* excellent.

joint hop *v.* to move from one place of entertainment to another.

joker *n.* 1. one who tries to appear clever 2. a fool.

jollies *n.* pleasure, enjoyment, excitement. Often in the construction "to get one's jollies."

jollop *n.* a large quantity.

jolly *adj.* [BRITISH SLANG] pleasing.

jolt *n.* 1. a drink of liquor 2. [DRUG CULTURE] an injection of heroin.

Joneses, keep up with the *v.* to emulate one's peers; specifically, to acquire material goods to maintain social status. From the 1913-1931 comic strip, "Keeping Up With the Joneses," by A. R. Momand.

josh *v.* to tease; to joke.

josher *n.* one who teases or jokes.

joshing *n.* the act of teasing or joking.

jostle *v.* to pick pockets, steal valuables from pocketbooks, etc., usually in a crowd.

jostler *n.* one who jostles. *See* jostle.

joy juice *n.* liquor.

joy knob *n.* the steering wheel of a vehicle.

joy pop *v.* [DRUG CULTURE] to inject a narcotic under the skin, but not into a main blood vessel.

joy powder *n.* [DRUG CULTURE] morphine.

joy ride *v.* 1. [DRUG CULTURE] to use narcotics occasionally 2. to steal a car for the purpose of taking a ride—*n.* joyrider.

joy stick *n.* 1. the steering wheel of a vehicle 2. a pipe for smoking marijuana 3. the penis.

juane *n.* [DRUG CULTURE] marijuana.

Judy *n.* any female.

jug *n.* 1. a jail 2. a bottle of liquor.

juggins *n.* a fool.

jughead *n.* a stupid person.

jugs *n.* the female breasts.

juice *n.* 1. liquor 2. any fuel or source of power, such as gasoline or electricity 3. [CRIME] interest on a usurious loan 4. narcotics, drugs 5. [POLITICS] importance, influence—*v.t.* to administer narcotics, especially to a race horse or an athlete before a competition.

juice bar *n.* a social gathering place where non-alcoholic beverages are served but which often becomes a center of illicit drug use.

juice dealer *n.* [CRIME] a usurer.

juiced, juiced up *adj.* 1. drunk 2. drugged; under the influence of a narcotic.

juice head *n.* a drunkard.

juju *n.* [DRUG CULTURE] a marijuana cigarette.

juke *v.* 1. to fake 2. to deceive.

juke box *n.* a coin-operated phonograph in the shape of a large music box. Preceded by the juke organ, a coin-operated music box playing loud gay music, like that of a hurdy-gurdy, and often found in brothels.

juke house *n.* a brothel. From the Gullah *juke*, disorderly.

jumbo *adj.* huge. From the name of the elephant purchased by P. T. Barnum in 1883 and exhibited as the main attraction in his circus.

jump *n.* an advantage—*v.t.* to ambush—*v.i.* to be exciting, lively, of a place.

jump a claim *v.* to encroach on another's mining rights.

jump all over someone *v.t.* to criticize someone.

jump bail *v.* to neglect to appear in court after having been released on bail.

jump down someone's throat *v.* to become furious and verbally abuse someone.

jumped up *adj.* ill-prepared.

jump, get the *See* get the jump.

jumping-off place *n.* a desolate, out-of-the-way spot. Originally, from the belief that the world is flat and that at the end of the earth there is void.

jump off the deep end *v.* 1. to overreact 2. to lose one's self-control, one's temper.

jump on *v.t.* to criticize severely.

jump, on the *adj.* active.

jump on the bandwagon *See* bandwagon, jump on the.

jumps, the *n.* nervousness.

jump the broomstick *v.* to wed. From the custom of having the couple jump the broomstick at a slave wedding instead of exchanging formal vows.

jump the cable *v.* to send an electric charge through wire cable in order to reactivate a dead battery or to start a vehicle without the ignition key.

jump the gun *v.* to begin prematurely. From the starter's pistol signaling the beginning of a race; an anxious racer would try to begin before the gun is actually fired.

jump the hurdle *v.* to marry.

jump up the line, take a *v.* to advance.

June around *v.* 1. to experience the effects of spring fever 2. to be restless.

jungle *n.* a place of danger and survival of only the strong, especially in reference to the fierce competition of the business world and to the crime in modern cities.

juniper juice *n.* gin, which is made from juniper berries.

junk *n.* [DRUG CULTURE] heroin.

junk food *n.* food consumed principally as between-meal snacks and having little nutritional or gastronomical value.

junk heap *n.* a dilapidated vehicle.

junkie *n.* [DRUG CULTURE] an addict.

junk mail *n.* letters of little interest sent unsolicited through the mail, usually business advertisements, requests for donations, etc.

junk up *v.t.* [CRIME] to administer narcotics to. Often to an athlete or a horse about to compete.

K

K *n.* [BASEBALL] an out resulting from three strikes.

kadigin *n.* any object for which the proper name is not known.

kafooster *n.* idle chatter, gibberish, nonsense.

kale *n.* money.

kamikaze *n.* [SURFING] falling or jumping purposely from a surfboard. From the Japanese suicide air missions during World War II.

kangaroo court *n.* an unauthorized tribunal set up to mete out justice either where no regular court is available or in defiance of government courts.

kaput *adj.* [GERMAN] 1. inoperable 2. destroyed.

kayo *See* KO.

keek *n.* a voyeur.

keep a stiff upper lip *v.* to maintain one's courage and self-confidence under adverse circumstances.

keep company *v.* to date on a steady basis.

keep-lock *n.* [PRISON] the punishment of confining a prisoner to a cell with no recreation.

keep the ball rolling *v.* to maintain steady activity or discussion.

keep up with the Joneses *See* Joneses, keep up with the.

keerect *interj.* correct.

kef *n.* [DRUG CULTURE] marijuana.

keister, keyster, kister, kiester *n.* the buttocks.

kept *adj.* fully supported financially by one's lover.

kerflooie, go *v.* 1. to fail 2. to explode 3. to become inoperable.

kerflummixed *adj.* confused.

kettle of fish *n.* a troublesome situation. Usually, "a fine kettle of fish."

key *n.* [DRUG CULTURE] a kilogram of a drug, of marijuana.

keynoter *n.* [POLITICS] one who delivers the tone-setting speech at a gathering, convention, etc.

keynote speech *n.* [POLITICS] the speech that expresses party policy at a political gathering.

keys *n.* the piano.

keystone sack *n.* [BASEBALL] second base.

kibbitz *v.* [YIDDISH] 1. to joke 2. to meddle 3. to offer unwanted advice—*n.* kibbitzer.

kibosh on someone, put the *v.* to hinder, to impede, to squelch.

kick *n.* 1. a complaint 2. pleasure, satisfaction, gratification 3. power, strength, potency 4. a temporary but consuming interest—*v.* to complain.

kick around *v.t.* 1. to discuss 2. to mistreat.

kick back *n.* [CRIME] an illegal sharing of profits. Also used as a verb.

kick, be on a *v.* to pursue a sudden intense interest.

kicker *n.* 1. an outboard motor 2. a surprise ending, ironic twist, etc.

kick in *v.* to contribute.

kick it *v.* to free oneself of a habit.

kick off *n.* [FOOTBALL] the beginning of a football play. Also used as a verb—*v.* to die.

kick out *v.t.* to eject forcibly.

kick party *n.* [DRUG CULTURE] a social gathering for taking drugs, specifically LSD.

kick stick *n.* [DRUG CULTURE] a marijuana cigarette.

kick the bucket *v.* to die.

kick up *n.* commotion; trouble—*v.* to cause trouble.

kick up a storm *v.* to cause trouble.

kick up one's heels *v.* to enjoy oneself, i.e., to gambol like a young animal.

kicky *adj.* stylish, lively, amusing.

kid *n.* 1. a child 2. an inexperienced person—*v.* 1. to joke 2. to tease.

kidder *n.* one who jokes or teases.

kiddo *n.* a mildly disrespectful term of address.

kid stuff *n* a task or activity simple enough for a child to accomplish.

kife *v.* to cheat.

kike *n.* a derogatory term for a Jewish person. From "kikel," a small circle used as a signature by illiterate immigrants who refused to make an "X" because of its resemblance to a cross, the symbol of Christianity.

kill *v.t.* 1. to shut off 2. to finish, end anything 3. to spoil, ruin 4. [BROADCASTING] to edit out a portion of a prerecorded show 5. [PRINTING] to destroy type matter which is no longer needed 6. to amuse greatly.

killer *n.* 1. anything difficult to accomplish 2. anything startling or exceptional.

killing *n.* a huge financial success.

killjoy *n.* one who impedes another's pleasure.

kill the clock *v.* [SPORTS] to retain possession of the ball or puck during the last minutes of play in order to prevent the opposing team from scoring points.

kilo connection *n.* [DRUG CULTURE] a narcotics wholesaler, one who deals in drugs by the kilogram quantity.

king pin *n.* [SPORTS] a leader, a person of the greatest importance in any given field. From the central pin in the arrangement of bowling pins.

kings *n.* a package of king-size cigarettes.

kink *n.* a perversion.

kinky *adj.* odd, unusual, outlandish, perverse.

kip *n.* 1. a rooming house 2. a bed 3. sleep—*v.* to sleep.

kipe *v.* to steal.

kiss *v.* [SPORTS] to touch lightly, specifically in billiards, of one ball to touch another lightly. Also used as a noun.

kisser *n.* 1. the mouth 2. the face.

kissing cousin *n.* anyone close enough to kiss as a greeting.

kiss of death *n.* 1. anything initially pleasant that presages eventual doom 2. [POLITICS] support from a source that severely reduces a candidate's chances for election, sometimes a deliberate dirty trick masterminded by an opposing party.

kiss off *n.* 1. a rejection 2. a dismissal— *v.t.* 1. to reject 2. to dismiss.

kiss something goodbye *v.* to resign oneself to a loss.

kiss the dust *v.* to die.

kit and caboodle *n.* a group of things in its entirety.

kite *v.* [BUSINESS] to use nonexistent or falsified collateral to increase business loans and escalate one's investments.

kite flying *n.* the use of falsified documents or bank checks for which there are no funds to obtain money.

kitsch *n.* [GERMAN] creative works having little artistic merit but wide popular appeal. From *kitschen*, to smear.

kittens, have *v.* of a person, to become upset, angry.

kitty *n.* [GAMBLING] the prize money in a game composed of penalties or bets from all the players involved; hence, any collection of money.

klepto *n.* a kleptomaniac, one who steals out of compulsion.

klupper *n.* one who works particularly slowly.

klutz *n.* [YIDDISH] one who is clumsy.

kneebender *n.* an exceptionally religious person.

kneecapping *n.* [CRIME] shooting a victim in the legs, a technique particularly used by political terrorists.

knee-high to a grasshopper *adj.* young; small.

kneesies *n.* surreptitiously touching or caressing the knees of another with one's own knees in order to establish an initial physical intimacy.

knick-knack *n.* a small object with only decorative value.

knock *v.* to criticize harshly; to calumniate.

knock a nod *v.* to go to sleep.

knock about *v.t.* to manhandle, mistreat.

knock around *v.* to spend time idly.

knock down *v.* to reduce a price.

knock-down-drag-out *n.* 1. a violent brawl 2. violence. Also used an an adjective.

knocked out *adj.* exhausted.

knocked-up *adj.* pregnant.

knockers *n.* the female breasts.

knock heads together *v.* to mete out punishment.

knock it off *interj.* a command to desist from certain behavior.

knock it over the fence *v.* 1. [BASEBALL] to hit a fly ball over the fence, allowing a home run; hence 2. to have a great success.

knock off *v.t.* 1. to produce automatically or rapidly 2. to stop 3. to subtract 4. to rob 5. to kill.

knock off work *v.* to stop work. From the slave galley in a ship, where one man would beat rhythmically on a block of wood to insure an even pace in rowing. A special beat indicated permission to cease work and change shifts.

knock oneself out *v.* to work with great diligence to the point of exhaustion.

knockout *n.* 1. a stunningly attractive woman 2. anything wonderful. *See* KO.

knockout drops *n.* a drug in liquid form administered in a drink to stupefy or render the victim unconscious.

knock over *v.* [CRIME] to rob.

knock someone down to size *v.* to deflate an inflated ego.

knock someone for a loop *v.* to stun, confuse.

knock someone's block off *v.* literally, to knock someone's head off; hence, to strike or thrash someone.

knock them dead *v.* [ENTERTAINMENT] to impress an audience with one's performance.

knock them in the aisles *v.* [ENTERTAINMENT] to delight an audience with one's performance.

knock up *v.* to make pregnant.

knothead *n.* a stupid person.

know-how *n.* knowledge and ability to perform a task.

know-it-all *n.* one who arrogantly professes to have vast knowledge.

know-nothing *n.* an ignoramus.

know one's business *v.* to be expert in a particular field.

know the ropes *v.* to be familiar with all aspects of a certain situation. From the many various ropes used on masted sailing vessels, which a sailor had to know the function of.

know the score *v.* to be knowledgeable, aware. From literally knowing the score in a sports game.

know what's what *v.* to be aware of all the ramifications of any given situation.

knuckle buster *n.* a fist fight.

knuckle down *v.* to concentrate one's efforts in serious work.

knuckle dusters *See* brass knuckles.

knucklehead *n.* a stupid person.

knuckle under *v.* 1. to be defeated 2. to yield.

KO *n.* [BOXING] the acronym for knock out, a punch which causes a loss of consciousness or an inability to rise and continue the fight. Also used as a verb—*adj.* "KO'ed": knocked out.

kodiak *n.* [TRUCKERS' CB] a policeman; a variation of the bear terminology referring to the police in CB slang, based on Smokey the Bear.

kook *n.* an eccentric.

kooky *adj.* eccentric.

kosher *adj.* [HEBREW] authentic; honest. Originally, of food prepared according to Jewish ritual law; now applied to any dealing which is clearly acceptable and honest.

kowtow *v.* [CHINESE] to abase oneself in flattery. Originally, to show respect by touching the forehead to the ground.

kraut, krauthead *n.* a derogatory term for a German.

kvell *v.* [YIDDISH] to feel pride; to gloat.

kvetch *n.* [YIDDISH] a complainer—*v.* to complain.

L

labonza *n.* the buttocks.

lace into *v.t.* to attack verbally.

lacy *adj.* effeminate.

la-de-da *adj.* affected; snobbish. Also used as a noun and an interjection.

ladies' man *n.* a man pleasing to women by his suave manner.

lady *n.* [DRUG CULTURE] cocaine.

lady bear *n.* [TRUCKERS' CB] a policewoman.

lady killer *n.* a man known for his sexual conquests of women.

lag *n.* a criminal—*v.* to arrest.

lagniappe *n.* [FRENCH] a tip; a small bonus.

laid back *adj.* relaxed.

laid, get *v.* to coit.

laid out *adj.* drunk.

laid up *adj.* ill.

lam *n.* a quick escape—*v.* 1. to escape 2. to thrash.

lamb *n.* 1. a naive person 2. a dupe.

lambaste *v.* 1. to criticize severely 2. to thrash.

lambasting *n.* 1. severe criticism 2. a thrashing.

lame *n.* a social misfit—*adj.* not conversant with current social mores.

lame brain *n.* a foolish person.

lame brained *adj.* foolish.

lame duck *n.* [POLITICS] a politician who is finishing a term in office, not having been re-elected. Also used as an adjective.

lame duck bill *n.* [POLITICS] a bill of legislation that has little chance for adoption or implementation.

lam, on the *adv.* escaping quickly—*v.* "take it on the lam": to escape quickly.

lam out of somewhere *v.* to leave somewhere quickly.

lamp *n.* the eyes—*v.* to look at.

land *v.t.* 1. to obtain 2. to win.

land a blow *v.* to hit.

landline *n.* [TRUCKERS' CB] a telephone.

land office business, do *v.* to run a financially successful, active enterprise. From the nineteenth-century American government land offices, which were always busy during American expansion westward.

landslide *n.* [POLITICS] an overwhelming election victory for a candidate.

landsman, lantzman *n.* [YIDDISH] a person from one's home town.

lard ass, lard bucket *n.* a fat person.

lard head *n.* a stupid person.

large charge *n.* 1. anything exciting 2. an important person. Often used derisively to indicate one with an inflated self-image.

last ditch *adj.* [MILITARY] desperate. Often in the expression "last ditch effort." From the era when combat forces fought mainly from ditches. When the advancing enemy had wiped out all the others, the soldiers in the last ditch waged a deperate struggle.

last laugh, have the *v.* to enjoy an ultimate triumph, especially after a humiliation. From the moral of an Aesop fable, "he who laughs last laughs best."

last licks *n.* 1. the privilege of a loser in a contest to take a last turn even when the opponent has a definite victory 2. the last chance.

last straw *n.* the final indignity that precipitates a strong reaction. From the fable about an overloaded camel and the last straw added to the burden, which broke the camel's back.

latch onto someone *v.* to cling to someone for moral support, affection, etc.

latch onto something *v.* 1. to discover a valuable piece of information 2. to grasp something tenaciously.

lather, in a *adv.* in a state of anger; furiously.

laugh *n.* something worthy of scorn, derision, ridicule.

laugher *n.* [SPORTS] a competition with an easy victory.

laugh out of the other side of one's mouth *v.* to change abruptly from happiness to sorrow, anger, frustration, annoyance, etc.

laugh up one's sleeve *v.* to be secretly amused; often, to gloat at another's misfortune. From the garments of the fifteenth century, with huge sleeves suitable to use as pockets or to conceal one's facial expression.

launching pad *n.* [DRUG CULTURE] any place where addicts usually go to administer injections of narcotics to themselves.

launder *v.t.* to channel illegally gained money into legitimate businesses, thus to remove the stigma of its origin.

laundry *n.* [CRIME] any legitimate enterprise into which illegally gained money is channeled.

laundry list *n.* [POLITICS] the list of political favors owed after an election.

lawn mower *n.* a sheep.

lay *n.* 1. a partner in coitus 2. in certain games of cards, a group of several related cards which may be placed face up on the table in order to score points—*v.* to coit.

lay a fart *v.* to emit intestinal gas.

lay an egg *v.* to blunder; to fail in a very visible way.

lay down on the job *v.* to shirk responsibility.

lay down the law *v.* to insist on a certain standard of behavior.

lay into *v.t.* 1. to attack 2. to castigate severely.

lay it on the line *v.* to express one's opinion truthfully, boldly.

lay it on thick *v.* 1. to exaggerate 2. to flatter blatantly.

lay low *v.* to stay in hiding.

lay-off *n.* 1. [LABOR] a discharge from employment 2. [CRIME] a rich criminal who accepts large bets placed by small-time bookmakers to cover their possible losses on competitions or races which attract heavy betting.

lay off *v.* 1. [LABOR] to discharge from employment 2. [CRIME] of a bookmaker, to make a large bet to cover possible losses from a competition attracting heavy betting 3. to cease, desist.

lay one on *v.i.* to become drunk—*v.t.* to strike someone.

lay one's cards on the table *See* put one's cards on the table.

lay someone off *v.* 1. to dismiss someone from employment 2. to put someone's telephone call "on hold."

lay someone out *v.* 1. to knock someone down 2. to render someone unconscious.

lay something on someone *v.* to accuse someone of something.

lay something on the line *v.* to risk something.

lay them in the aisles *v.* [ENTERTAINMENT] to win an audience's enthusiastic approbation.

l'chayim *interj.* [HEBREW] a wish of good luck, good health, etc., used as a drinking toast. Literally, "to life."

lead *n.* bullets.

lead balloon *n.* anything that fails to have the positive effect predicted. Often in the construction "go over like a lead balloon."

lead by the nose *v.* 1. to dominate someone; to gain mastery over someone 2. to show someone the best course of action.

leaders *n.* [PRINTING] diacritical markings on a page that attract attention and lead the viewer's glance to a desired object, such as a series of dots in a table of contents, which lead from chapter headings to page numbers.

leadfooted *adj.* slow; clumsy.

lead-in *n.* 1. an introduction 2. an electrical wire leading to an antenna.

lead in one's pants, have *v.* to move or work slowly.

lead in one's pencil, have *v.* 1. to be prepared for any challenge 2. to show energy and enthusiasm.

lead off *n.* [SPORTS] the first player at bat in a game of baseball. Also used as a verb and an adjective.

lead out, get the *v.* to quicken one's pace; to hurry.

lead out, shake the *See* shake the lead out.

lead pipe cinch *n.* an assured success; a certainty.

lead poisoning *n.* [CRIME] death from a gunshot wound.

leaf *n.* [DRUG CULTURE] cocaine, processed from the cocoa leaf.

leak *n.* unauthorized disclosure of secret information. Also used as a verb.

leak, take a *v.* to urinate.

lean on *v.t.* 1. to exert psychological pressure 2. to coerce 3. to force.

leaped up *adj.* angry.

leap up *v.t.* to flatter.

leather *n.* 1. a football 2. sado-masochistic sexual activity.

leatherneck *n.* a United States Marine. Probably from the leather lining in the collar of the uniform.

leathers *n.* the leather garments typically worn by motorcycle riders.

leather trade *n.* a clientele composed of homosexuals favoring sado-masochistic sexual activity.

leave *n.* 1. a brief vacation from military duty, prison, school, etc. 2. [BOWLING] the pins left standing after the first ball of a frame has been played.

lech, letch *n.* 1. a lecherous person 2. a lecherous desire, craving.

leech *n.* a parasitic person.

left *n.* [POLITICS] 1. the pro-communist forces 2. political radicals, usually liberal in philosophy. From the practice in European parliaments of seating radicals to the left of the room and the ultraconservatives to the right.

left field, be out in *v.* to be misled or mistaken.

left foot *n.* a protestant.

left-handed *adj.* 1. homosexual 2. ill-prepared 3. of a compliment, actually a carefully-veiled insult.

left holding the bag *See* holding the bag.

leftie, lefty *n.* 1. a left-handed person 2. one whose political sympathies lie with the radical left.

leftist, left wing *n.* 1. a communist sympathizer 2. a socialist. Also used as an adjective.

leg *v.* 1. to leave 2. to escape on foot.

leg, pull someone's *See* pull someone's leg.

leg, shake a *See* shake a leg.

leg, shake a wicked *See* shake a wicked leg.

legal beagle *n.* 1. a lawyer 2. one who hunts down evidence.

legal eagle *n.* a respected and adept lawyer.

legger *See* bootlegger.

legit *n.* [ENTERTAINMENT] a stage play, originally as opposed to a vaudeville show, now as opposed to television, radio, cinema, etc.—*adj.* legitimate.

leg man *n.* a male who finds a woman's beautiful legs to be the most visually pleasing part of her anatomy.

leg show *n.* an entertainment featuring scantily-clad women with beautiful legs.

legs, with *See* with legs.

lemon *n.* [GAMBLING] anything defective, unpleasant, or causing a loss. On a slot machine, the lemon has no match, and therefore its appearance obviates any winning combination and assures a loss—*v.* in a game of billiards, to play in a manner not up to professional standards.

lend a hand *v.* to aid in a task.

lepper *n.* [HORSE RACING] a horse trained to jump obstacles and run in steeplechase races.

let go with *v.t.* to release that which is suppressed.

let it all hang out *v.* to hide nothing.

let it roll *v.* to maintain, or especially to increase, the speed of a motor vehicle

letterman *n.* a player on a school sports team who has been awarded the school monogram for excellence in playing.

lettuce *n.* paper money.

level, on the *adj.* honest, legitimate, authentic.

level-headed *adj.* sensible.

level with *v.* to speak honestly, forthrightly to.

levis *n.* denim trousers or overalls. From those originated and manufactured by Levi Strauss and popular among cowboys because of the strength of the material and the practicality of the design: small metal studs reinforce the seam junctures.

liberate *v.* to steal or loot, especially from a defeated enemy.

liberty *n.* 1. a sailor's permission to go ashore for forty-eight hours 2. a respite; a brief vacation from one's job, studies, etc.

liberty, at *adj.* without a job; unemployed.

library shots *n.* [BROADCASTING] film footage taken of general subject matter, such as the ocean, a monument, animals, etc., which is kept on file to be inserted in any show when needed.

lick *v.t.* to thrash—*n.* licking.

lickety-split *adv.* as quickly as possible.

lick one's chops *v.* to anticipate something with satisfaction.

licorice stick *n.* a clarinet.

lid *n.* 1. [DRUG CULTURE] one ounce of marijuana 2. a hat.

lid, flip one's *v.* 1. to become excited or angry 2. to lose one's self-control.

lid on something, put the *v.* to conceal something.

Life, the *n.* prostitution

life of the party *n.* an affable humorous extrovert.

lifer *n.* a prisoner serving a life sentence.

lifestyle *n.* the manner in which one chooses to live, including matrimonial state, career, etc. Coined by psychologist Alfred Adler in 1929.

lift *v.* to steal.

lifties *n.* shoes made specially to increase the height of the wearer.

light, out like a *adj.* 1. sound asleep 2. unconscious.

light, see the *v.* to understand.

light-fingered *adj.* prone to steal; proficient at stealing.

lightfooted *adj.* homosexual.

light into *v.t.* to criticize harshly; to castigate.

lightning *n.* inferior homemade liquor.

light of, make *v.* to ridicule; to diminish the importance of.

light out *v.* to leave quickly.

lights out *n.* 1. the hour of curfew 2. death.

lightweight *n.* a person of little importance.

like, make *v.* 1. to pretend 2. to imitate.

like crazy *adv.* speedily, energetically, enthusiastically.

like hell *interj.* an emphatic negation— *adv.* speedily, energetically, enthusiastically.

like mad *adv.* speedily, energetically, enthusiastically.

lily *n.* a male homosexual.

lily livered *adj.* cowardly.

lily white *adj.* totally without guilt.

lily whites *n.* 1. a lady's hands 2. hands.

limb, out on a *adv.* in a precarious situation.

limbo, in *adj.* or *adv.* 1. straying; lost 2. [ENTERTAINMENT] of scene or costume design, not specific enough to designate a locale, period, etc.

limey *n.* an English person, specifically a British sailor. From the British navy practice of providing limes for sailors to eat during sea trips to avoid scurvy.

limit, go the *v.* to spare no effort to

achieve a goal.

limp *adj.* drunk.

limp wrist *n.* an effeminate man; a homosexual—*adj.* limp-wristed.

line *n.* 1. an occupation; a specialty 2. insincerity—*v.* "hand someone a line": to seek to dupe someone with deceptive speech.

line, hold the *v.* 1. to maintain a given limit 2. of a telephone caller, to be obliged to wait a short while until the other speaker has finished other business.

line, down the *adv.* each one of a group or series.

line, draw the *v.* to set limits.

line, give a *v.* to make an excuse.

line, in *adj.* 1. proper; conforming to accepted standards 2. prepared; in order.

line, lay it on the *See* lay it on the line.

line on, get a *v.t.* to find information about.

line, out of *adj.* unwarranted; improper.

lines, read between the *v.* to infer; to find a hidden significance in another's words or deeds.

line, the *n.* a line of chorus girls.

line, toe the *v.* 1. to obey with alacrity 2. to conform to established standards. From a racer poised at the starting line, waiting for the signal to begin competition.

line ball *n.* [SPORTS] a ball which hits the line demarcating the boundaries of a playing area, in such games as tennis, handball, squash.

line drive, liner *n.* [BASEBALL] a baseball batted low and following a straight trajectory.

line out *v.* [BASEBALL] of a baseball player, to hit a line drive which is caught by the opposing team, thus causing the player to be out.

line-up *n.* 1. [BASEBALL] the batting order of a baseball team 2. [POLICE] a group of possible suspects of a crime placed in a row for identification by a witness or victim.

lip *n.* 1. rudeness 2. insolent talk.

lip, bite one's *v.* to restrain oneself from indiscreet speech.

lip, keep a stiff upper *See* keep a stiff upper lip.

lippy *adj.* rude; impertinent.

lip service *n.* an expression of intentions, opinions, etc., never substantiated by actions.

lip sync *v.* [BROADCASTING] 1. to coordinate lip movement with pre-recorded audio track in a film 2. to mouth pre-recorded words in a live appearance. Also used as a noun.

liquidate *v.t.* to kill.

lit *n.* abbreviation for literature—*adj* drunk.

litterbug *n.* one who drops trash about

little black book *See* black book.

little shaver *n.* a young boy.

little woman, the *n.* a humorous term for one's wife.

lit to the gills *adj.* drunk.

lit up like a Christmas tree *adj.* drunk.

live *adj.* [BROADCASTING] of a performance, not pre-recorded.

livebag *n.* a net kept in water in which a fisher can keep caught fish alive until they are let free or killed.

live ball *n.* [SPORTS] a ball that is in play at any given moment of a game.

live down *v.t.* to suffer humiliation because of a foolish action or misdeed.

live in *See* sleep-in.

live it up *v.* 1. to enjoy oneself 2. to celebrate.

live one *n.* 1. an energetic, vivacious person 2. an eccentric 3. an unusually gullible person; a dupe.

live up to *v.t.* to be worthy of.

live wire *n.* an energetic, enthusiastic, vivacious person.

living doll *n.* an extremely agreeable, pleasant, helpful person.

living end, the *n.* the most extraordinary, exciting, etc.

lizzie *n.* an old, dilapidated automobile.

loaded *adj.* 1. drunk 2. rich 3. of a statement or question, suitable to entrap and destroy. From a loaded firearm ready for use.

load off one's chest, get a *v.* to confess, thus relieving oneself of the burden of conscience.

load off one's feet, take a *v.* to sit down.

load off one's mind, take a *v.* 1. to unburden oneself of a problem 2. to stand up.

load of postholes *n.* [TRUCKERS' CB] an empty truck.

load of rocks *n.* [TRUCKERS' CB] a truck carrying a load of bricks.

load of something, get a *v.* to look at something, often something unusual or startling.

load of sticks *n.* [TRUCKERS' CB] a truck carrying lumber.

loads *n.* a great quantity.

loaf *n.* [BRITISH SLANG] 1. the head 2. the brain.

loan shark *n.* [CRIME] a usurer. From the predatory nature of the shark.

lob *n.* 1. a dupe; a fool 2. an act of throwing an object 3. [TENNIS] hitting the ball high, aiming at the rear of an opponent's side of the court; also, a ball hit high 4. [BASEBALL] a high fly ball— *v.* 1. to move slowly, clumsily; 2. to throw or hit (a ball), aiming high.

lobber *n.* [BASEBALL] a baseball player adept at hitting high, slow fly balls.

lobster shift *n.* [LABOR] the work shift between 8 p.m. and 4 a.m. or midnight and 8 a.m. From "lobster," a dupe; that is, one who would work those hours is a fool.

local yokel *n.* [TRUCKERS' CB] a local police officer, as opposed to state or county police.

lock, stock, and barrel *adv.* completely. The three items are the major components of a gun.

loco *adj.* crazy.

loco weed *n.* [DRUG CULTURE] marijuana.

loggerheads, at *adv.* opposed to each other; fighting. From a military instrument, a heavy iron ball attached by a chain to a long wooden handle, used in the fourteenth century.

logo *n.* an emblem, a symbol, especially one which identifies a product or a business.

logrolling *n.* [POLITICS] exchange of political favors by legislators who vote on issues to benefit each other.

lollapalooza *n.* anything exceptional or excellent.

loner, lone wolf *n.* one who prefers solitude to society.

long and short of something, the *n.* a full explanation of something, usually in summary.

long arm *n.* a police officer.

long dozen *n.* thirteen.

long drink of water *n.* a tall person.

long green *n.* dollar bills; money.

longhair *n.* one interested in and knowledgeable about the arts, especially classical music—*adj.* longhaired.

longhandle underwear *n.* winter underwear with long sleeves and legs.

long hitter *n.* a drunk.

long home *n.* the grave.

longhorn *n.* a Texan.

long in the tooth *adj.* old. From the horse's gums, which recede with age.

long Johns, longies, long ones *n.* winter underwear with long sleeves and legs.

long run, in the *adv.* ultimately.

longshoe *n.* a self-confident, urbane person.

long shot *n.* anything unlikely to succeed, but which would bring great advantage if it did. Often used in gambling: "the horse is a long shot."

long suit *n.* one's specialty. In the game of bridge, a player's strength often lies in having many cards of the same suit to lead off with in succession.

long time no see a casual greeting meaning that one has not seen one's friend in a long time.

looey, looie *n.* [MILITARY] a lieutenant.

loogan *n.* beer.

look-alike *n.* a person who resembles another almost identically.

look alive *v.* to appear energetic, intelligent. Also used as an interjection.

look at someone cross-eyed *v.* to suspect someone of wicked intentions. Usually in the construction "one can't look at someone cross-eyed without (provoking something)."

look daggers at *v.t.* to regard with great hostility.

look down on *v.t.* to regard with scorn.

looker *n.* a very attractive person.

look-see *n.* a cursory examination—*v.* "take a look-see," "have a look-see."

look up *v.i.* to appear more promising— *v.t.* to call or visit someone.

look up and down *v.t.* to examine, scrutinize. Often with a sexual connotation.

look up to *v.t.* to admire.

loon *n.* a crazy person—*adj.* loony.

loony bin *n.* an insane asylum.

looped *adj.* drunk.

loose *adj.* 1. relaxed 2. licentious; immoral 3. generous, or too generous.

loose ends, at *adj.* confused; disordered.

loot *n.* money.

lose face *v.* 1. to be embarrassed 2. to lose respect, esteem.

lose one's cool *v.* to lose one's composure.

lost, get *See* get lost.

lot hopper *n.* a motion picture employee hired to play small roles with no dialogue in various films, and who must go from lot to lot, where the scenes are being filmed.

lot lice *n.* [CIRCUS SLANG] townspeople who watch as a circus tent is pitched and the grounds are set up for the show.

loud *adj.* gaudy; ostentatious.

loudmouth *n.* one who talks loudly, excessively, boastfully.

lounge lizard *n.* an indolent, pleasure-seeking man who frequents lounges.

louse *n.* a repulsive person.

louse up *v.t.* to spoil, ruin.

lousy *adj.* despicable, dreadful, inferior.

lousy with *adj.* full of.

lovebird *n.* a beloved.

love-in *n.* a casual and relaxed gathering where people meet and celebrate loving feelings. A late-1960s, early 1970s term.

lover boy *n.* a man who seeks to win favor with women.

lovey-dovey *adj.* 1. sentimental 2. excessively affectionate.

low *adj.* 1. melancholy 2. despicable.

lowbrow *n.* a person with no intellectual interests. Coined by Will Irwin in 1902-3. Also used as an adjective.

lowdown *n.* 1. information 2. truthful appraisal—*adj.* mean, unfair, despicable.

lower the boom *v.* to mete out well-deserved punishment or criticism. From the nautical term for stowing cargo in the hold of a ship.

low-life *n.* a despicable person.

low profile *n.* an unrevealing public image.

lox *n.* liquid oxygen.

LP *n.* a long-playing phonograph record.

LSD *n.* [DRUG CULTURE] lysergic acid diethylamide tartrate, an hallucinogenic drug.

lube *adj.* lubrication.

lubricated *adj.* drunk.

luck, out of *adj.* unfortunate; without a chance of success.

luck boy *n.* [CIRCUS SLANG] one who runs a gambling concession at a circus.

luck out *v.* 1. to experience a great stroke of good fortune 2. to experience misfortune.

lude *n.* [DRUG CULTURE] abbreviation for Quaalude, a brand name for a depressant drug.

lug *n.* 1. the face 2. a boorish person.

lugger *n.* [CRIME] one with great strength used to lift heavy objects in a burglary.

lug on someone, put the *v.* to make a request for a loan from someone.

lulu *n.* 1. [POLITICS] expense money given a politician "in lieu" of a carefully documented expense account 2. a big mistake.

lummox *n.* a clumsy, awkward person.

lump *v.t.* to endure an annoyance.

lump it *v.* to accept misfortune stoically.

Often used as an interjection.

lumps *n.* a beating—*v.* "give someone their lumps," "get or take one's lumps": to give, get, or suffer a beating.

lunatic fringe *n.* [POLITICS] extremists, a term used by detractors.

lunger *n.* [OLD SLANG] a person who has tuberculosis.

lunk *n.* a stupid, clumsy person.

lunkhead *n.* a stupid person.

lush *n.* a drunk.

lush roller *n.* a criminal who preys upon helpless drunks as robbery victims.

M

M *n.* 1. [DRUG CULTURE] morphine 2. money.

Ma Bell *n.* a humorous personification of the Bell Telephone system.

Mac *n.* a fellow; used as a general term for a man or boy.

macaroni mills *n.* saw mills.

macher *n.* [YIDDISH] 1. an ambitious, clever manipulator 2. a person of importance.

machine politics *n.* organized self-serving groups sponsoring candidates and issues that will advance their interests.

machismo *n.* [SPANISH] aggressive masculinity.

macho *adj.* [SPANISH] strong; aggressive; masculine.

macho drama *n.* a play, movie, etc., with a theme or treatment glorifying masculinity.

Mack *n.* a familiar term of address for any man whose name is not known.

mad about, be *v.t.* 1. to be enamored of someone 2. to be highly attracted to something.

madame *n.* the female head of a brothel.

made *adj.* [CRIME] accepted into organized crime after having committed murder on assignment.

made, have it *v.* 1. to be successful 2. to be certain of security or success.

mad, like *adv.* with great speed, energy, or enthusiasm.

mad money *n.* money to be spent frivolously.

magazine *n.* [PRISON] a prison sentence of six months. From the expression "throw the book at someone," meaning to give someone a long sentence, thus six months is not a book but only a magazine.

magic marker *n.* [ENTERTAINMENT] a humorous, derogatory term for a dancer who uses only minimal energy in rehearsal.

magoo *n.* 1. an important person 2. a custard pie thrown in someone's face.

Mag's snatch, look like *v.* to be unkempt.

maiden *n.* [RACING] a racing horse or dog who has never won a race.

main drag, main stem *n.* the main street in a town.

main guy *n.* [CIRCUS SLANG] the rope holding up the center pole in a circus tent.

mainline *n.* those rich suburban Philadelphians living along the route of the Pennsylvania railroad to New York City; hence, the elite—*v.* [DRUG CULTURE] to inject a drug into a major vein.

mainliner *n.* 1. a member of the elite 2. [DRUG CULTURE] an addict who injects narcotics intravenously.

main queen *n.* an attractive, passive male homosexual.

main stem *See* main drag.

mainstream *n.* the center of current activity. Used in politics and sociology to indicate the major areas of middle-class thought, action, etc.—*v.t.* to place in or guide to the accepted standards of the middle class.

make *n.* [POLICE] a description—*v.t.* 1. to recognize or identify someone or something 2. to coit with someone.

make, on the *v.* 1. to be in search of a lover 2. to be sexually active and aggressive.

96

make a hit *v.* 1. to please 2. [CRIME] to murder 3. to rob.

make a monkey out of someone *v.* 1. to make someone appear foolish 2. to deceive someone.

make a pitch *v.* to attempt to persuade.

make a point *v.* [GAMBLING] to succeed, i.e., to accomplish a desired goal. From the number a player must throw on the dice to win a game of craps.

make a scene *v.* to cause trouble by loud speech or angry gestures.

make both ends meet *v.* to succeed in balancing a budget. Originally, the word "mete" meant equal. From the bookkeeper's debits and credits.

make good *v.* to succeed.

make good one's debts *v.* to repay one's creditors.

make hay while the sun shines *v.* to take advantage of an opportunity.

make it *v.* to achieve success.

make it with someone *v.* to coit with someone.

make like *v.* 1. to pretend 2. to imitate.

make no bones about something *v.* to speak or act directly and honestly.

make or break *v.t.* to cause the ultimate success or imminent failure of.

make out *v.i.* to engage in kissing, caressing, fondling—*v.t.* to discern.

make-out artist *n.* a successful lover.

make points *v.* 1. to ingratiate oneself with one's superiors 2. to advance in one's field. Also, "to score points."

make something out of nothing *v.* to misinterpret an action and take offense.

make the grade *v.* 1. to be acceptable 2. to succeed.

make the rounds *v.* to go from place to place in search of employment.

make the scene *v.* to be present in the center of activity.

make time with someone *v.* to woo someone.

make tracks *v.* to leave.

make-up *n.* a special examination given a student who was absent for a scheduled test in school or who failed the first test.

make waves *v.* to exacerbate a situation.

makings, makins *n.* the required ingredients.

malarky *n.* 1. exaggeration 2. lies.

male chauvinist pig *n.* 1. a male who seeks to repress women and keep them in a subservient position.

mama's boy *n.* a male excessively attached to his mother; hence, a weakling, a sissy.

Mama Smokey *n.* [TRUCKERS' CB] a policewoman.

man *interj.* an exclamation of astonishment, disbelief, satisfaction, etc.

Man, the *n.* 1. anyone in a position of authority 2. a term used by blacks for a white man, especially one in authority, or white people in general.

man-about-town *n.* a sophisticated, elegant man who spends much time socializing at the most luxurious night spots.

managed news *n.* [POLITICS] carefully edited news provided to the media by the government; often this news is less than complete or so slanted as to change its actual import.

manana *n.* [SPANISH] tomorrow; hence, any time in the future, especially used humorously to indicate an indefinite postponement, a lazy attitude.

mangy with *adj.* full of.

man in the street *n.* the average citizen.

man-sized *adj.* large.

map *n.* the face.

maple *n.* a bowling pin.

marbles *n.* [AUTO RACING] pebbles, gravel, dust, etc., making an area of a racing course slippery.

marbles, lose one's *v.* to become insane.

marfak *n.* butter.

Marge *n.* a female homosexual.

maricon *n.* [SPANISH] a male homosexual.

mark *n.* the victim of a swindle; a dupe

marker *n.* a promissory note.

martooni *n.* a martini.

married *adj.* [STUDENT SLANG] having dated each other exclusively for more than a year.

Mary *n.* a male homosexual.

Mary Jane, Jane, Mary Warner *n.* [DRUG CULTURE] marijuana.

mash *v.* to make sexual overtures.

masher *n.* a man who tries to force his attentions on women.

mash note *n.* a letter expressing love and desire.

mask *n.* the face.

massacre *n.* a definitive defeat. Also used as a verb.

massage parlor *n.* a business establishment where the masseuses are usually prostitutes and offer such services to the clients.

mass media *n.* any means of communication that reaches vast audiences, such as television, newspapers, etc.

mastermind *n.* the leader of a group; one who devises a plan of action. Also used as a verb.

master of ceremonies *n.* a host at a social gathering who introduces guests and supplies witty commentary.

matchmaker *n.* [BOXING] one who arranges boxing matches.

matey, matie *n.* 1. a shipmate 2. a friend or companion.

matman *n.* [SPORTS] a wrestler.

Maud *n.* a woman; any woman.

mauler *n.* 1. a wrestler 2. a boxer.

maverick *n.* [POLITICS] one who eschews political party loyalties and whose views are independent of those of fellow party members.

mavin *n.* [YIDDISH] 1. an expert 2. a connoisseur.

max *n.* abbreviation for maximum.

maxi *n.* a woman's garment with a hemline that extends to the ankle; popular in the late 1960s.

mayday *n.* a distress call. From the French *aider*, to help An internationally accepted code word used by ships, etc., in emergencies

mazel *n.* [HEBREW] luck

mazel tov *interj.* [HEBREW] literally, good luck; an expression of congratulations.

mazuma *n.* [YIDDISH] money.

MC *n.* acronym for master of ceremonies, the official host or spokesperson at a gathering. Also, emcee.

McCoy *n.* the real person or real thing as opposed to a substitute.

MCP *n.* acronym for male chauvinist pig.

MDA *n.* [DRUG CULTURE] methyldiamphetamine, a stimulant.

meal on wheels *n.* [TRUCKERS' CB] a truck carrying a load of cattle.

meal ticket *n.* any source of income, especially one gained with little or no effort.

mean *adj.* 1. excellent 2. skillful 3. effective.

meanie *n.* a malicious person.

meat *n.* 1. the essential element of something 2. one's field of specialized interest 3. a male considered appealing, as a sex partner 4. the penis 5. a dupe; a weakling.

meat and potatoes *adj.* 1. basic 2. essential 3. satisfying.

meatball *n.* a stupid, clumsy person.

meathead *n.* a stupid person.

meat hooks *n.* the hands or fists.

meatrack *n.* any place used by homosexual males to meet, appraise, and make contact with other homosexual males for sex acts.

meat show *n.* any entertainment exciting prurient interests.

meat wagon *n.* [TRUCKERS' CB] an ambulance.

mechanic *n.* [CRIME] an expert at cheating in card or dice games.

med *adj.* pertaining to medicine or medical studies.

media *n.* various means of mass communication: television, cinema, newspapers, etc.

medico *n.* a doctor; a medical student.

meet *n.* a sports contest.

megabucks *n.* 1. a million dollars 2. a great deal of money.

megadeaths *n.* [MILITARY] 1. millions killed 2. a great number of deaths, as in a war.

megillah *n.* [HEBREW] a long, complicated, or boring story or explanation. Often in the expression "the whole megillah": anything in its tedious entirety.

mellow *adj.* pleasantly drunk.

mellow out *v.* 1. [DRUG CULTURE] to feel a pleasurable, comfortable sensation after having taken a narcotic 2. to become relaxed.

mensch *n.* [YIDDISH] an admirable and well-mannered person.

mental *n.* abbreviation for mental case; hence, a crazy person.

merry-go-round *n.* a rapid series of events.

mesc *n.* [DRUG CULTURE] abbreviation for mescaline, an hallucinogenic drug.

meshuga *adj.* [YIDDISH] crazy.

mess *n.* a person who is confused, distracted, irrational.

mess around *v.* to spend one's time idly.

mess around with *v.t.* 1. to spend one's time idly with 2. to annoy 3. to have sex with.

mess up *v.t.* 1. to confuse someone 2. to frustrate someone's efforts 3. to thrash someone.

meth *n.* [DRUG CULTURE] abbreviation for Methedrine, a brand name for an amphetamine.

Mexican red *n.* [DRUG CULTURE] a type of marijuana.

mezz *n.* 1. [DRUG CULTURE] a marijuana cigarette 2. the abbreviation for mezzanine.

MF *n.* acronym for mother fucker, i.e., a despicable person.

mib *n.* a marble in a children's game of marbles.

Michigan roll *n.* a roll of worthless papers cut to the size of dollar bills with one real bill placed on the outside to deceive the victim of a swindle who believes the whole wad to be of dollars.

mick *n.* a derogatory term for an Irish person.

mickey *n.* [CANADIAN SLANG] a thirteen-ounce bottle of whiskey.

Mickey Finn *n.* a drug administered surreptitiously in a drink to make someone ill or unconscious.

Mickey Mouse *n.* 1. an easy task 2. [POLITICS] a candidate who has an easy victory. Also used as an adjective.

micro *n.* a style of dress or skirt with the hemline reaching just below the panties; popular in the late 1960s.

microdecisionmakers *n.* [POLITICS] voters.

Middle America *n.* the politically and socially conservative middle class in the United States; specifically, the middle class in the Midwest.

middle brow *n.* a non-intellectual with a typically middle-class outlook on life. Also used as an adjective.

middle-of-the road *adj.* 1. resisting extremes, especially of politics 2. mediocre.

middy *n.* 1. a midshipman 2. a child's or woman's blouse imitating the style of a sailor's shirt.

midi *n.* a style of dress or skirt with the hemline reaching mid-calf; popular in the late 1960s and early 1970s.

miff *v.* 1. to offend 2. to annoy.

MIG *n.* [MILITARY] a small, powerful jet-powered fighting plane. Named for its inventors, Russians Artem Mikoyan and Mikhail Gurevich.

mig, miggle *n.* a cheap clay marble in a children's game of marbles.

mighty *adv.* very.

mighty mezz, the *n.* [DRUG CULTURE] marijuana.

mike *n.* a microphone.

mild downturn *n.* [BUSINESS] a slight reversal.

milk *v.* to induce a desired reaction by persistent action.

milk wagon *n.* a police wagon.

mill *n.* a beating—*v.* to punch; to strike; to beat.

mill, put someone through the *v.* to subject someone to a physically and mentally exhausting experience.

milquetoast *n.* a self-effacing, shy, weak person. From the character Caspar Milquetoast in H.T. Webster's 1920s comic strip, *The Timid Soul.*

Milwaukee goiter *n.* a protruding abdomen; a beer belly. Milwaukee is the center of beer production in the United States.

mincemeat of, make *v.t.* 1. to thrash someone 2. to defeat someone decisively.

mince pies *n.* the eyes.

mind bender *n.* 1. [DRUG CULTURE] an hallucinogenic drug 2. anything astonishing or overwhelming.

mind blower *n.* 1. [DRUG CULTURE] an hallucinogenic drug 2. anything astonishing or overwhelming.

mind boggling *adj.* astonishing, amazing, difficult to comprehend.

mind fuck *v.* to intentionally confuse someone.

mind fucker *n.* one who intentionally tries to confuse someone.

mind one's p's and q's *v.* to be precise, polite.

mind spacer *n.* [DRUG CULTURE] an hallucinogenic drug.

mingle *n.* a dance.

mini *n.* a dress or skirt with the hemline above the knee, often mid-thigh; popular in the 1960s.

mintie *n.* a male homosexual.

minute, up to the *adj.* the latest; the most recent.

mish mash *n.* an odd mixture; a haphazard combination of elements.

miss *v.* to fail to menstruate at the proper time.

Miss Emma *n.* [DRUG CULTURE] morphine.

missionary worker *n.* [LABOR] a worker allied to management who attempts to break a strike by fostering a feeling of hopelessness in the striking workers by spreading insidious rumors of doom and futility.

Missouri meerschaum *n.* a humorous term for a corn cob pipe.

miss the boat *v.* 1. to fail to understand 2. to be too late to take advantage of an opportunity.

missus, the *n.* one's wife.

mister, the *n.* one's husband.

Mister Big *n.* 1. the most important person in any organization 2. the hypothetical leader of an enterprise.

Mister Charlie *n.* [BLACK SLANG] a white man.

Mister Right *n.* a woman's ideal beloved.

Mister Tom *n.* [BLACK SLANG] a mildly derogatory term for a middle-class black man. *See* Uncle Tom.

mitt *n.* the hand.

mitts *n.* 1. the hands 2. handcuffs.

mitt, tip one's *v.* to betray oneself.

mix *n.* [BROADCASTING] one image or sound fading as another appears or emerges—*v.* 1. to fight 2. to interact socially 3. [BROADCASTING] to have one image or sound fade as another appears or emerges.

mixed bag *n.* a variety of elements.

mixer *n.* 1. soda or water used to dilute a strong alcoholic beverage 2. a party or social gathering for the purpose of introducing people one to the other.

mix it up *v.* to fight vigorously.

mixologist *n.* a bartender.

mix up *n.* 1. a confusion 2. a fight—*v.* to confuse.

MJ *n.* [DRUG CULTURE] marijuana.

MO *n.* [POLICE] acronym for *modus operandi*, the way one usually does something: the clues in a crime which indicate to the police which criminals might be guilty of a crime because of similarities with past crimes perpetrated by them.

mo *n.* a moment.

moan, put on the *v.* to complain.

mob *n.* organized crime.

mobster *n.* a criminal working with organized crime.

mockie *n.* 1. a derogatory term for a

Jewish person 2. one who literally mocks someone or something.

mojo *n.* [DRUG CULTURE] any narcotic.

moke *n.* 1. a stupid person 2. a derogatory term for a black person.

mola *n.* a homosexual.

moll *n.* 1. a female criminal 2. the mistress of a criminal.

mollycoddle *n.* a weakling—*v.* to pamper.

Molotov cocktail *n.* a homemade bomb, made with gasoline or another combustible substance, which is placed in a glass container and is wrapped in a rag and which is to be ignited and thrown at a target. Named for the Soviet leader V.M. Molotov.

mom-and-pop *adj.* pertaining to a small business, typically run by a husband and wife.

momism *n.* the theory that dominant mothers influence and often destroy their offsprings' lives.

momzer *n.* [YIDDISH] bastard.

Monday morning quarterback *n.* 1. one who reflects on the weekend football games just played and expounds wordily on how the plays could have been improved 2. an expert in retrospect.

moneybags *n.* a rich person.

moneygrubber *n.* one exclusively devoted to the accumulation of wealth.

money, in the *adj.* 1. rich 2. secure.

money player *n.* [SPORTS] a player who performs well under pressure.

money talks a maxim meaning that wealth makes one powerful, influential.

moniker *n.* a person's name or nickname.

monkey *n.* 1. a man 2. an energetic, active child 3. an addiction 4. [GAMBLING] a bet of five-hundred dollars.

monkey around *v.* to spend one's time idly.

monkey business *n.* 1. deception, trickery 2. foolish or frivolous behavior.

monkey jacket *n.* a short, tight jacket. From its resemblance to the costume of an organ grinder's monkey.

monkey drill *n.* [MILITARY] calesthenic exercises.

monkey off one's back, get the *v.* to break a drug addiction.

monkey on one's back, have a *v.* to be addicted to narcotics.

monkeyshines *n.* playful or foolish behavior.

monkey suit *n.* a suit of formal clothing.

mono *n.* mononucleosis.

monster *n.* 1. [BUSINESS] an item which attains sudden and overwhelming popularity 2. [DRUG CULTURE] a drug having lasting deleterious effects on the nervous system 3. [SPORTS] a football lineman who plays wherever his strength is needed at the moment.

Montezuma's revenge *n.* diarrhea, especially dysentery caught by American tourists in Mexico, where Montezuma was king of the Aztecs, defeated by the Spaniards under Cortes.

month of Sundays *n.* 1. a time so long past as not to be remembered 2. a rare occasion.

moo *n.* 1. milk 2. steak.

mooch *v.* 1. to beg 2. to fish for salmon by dragging a baited line behind a slow-moving boat.

moocher *n.* a person who begs.

moo juice *n.* milk.

moola, moolah *n.* money.

moon *v.* to expose one's bared buttocks as a joke or a sign of disrespect.

moonie *n.* a follower of Reverend Sun Myung Moon, i.e., a member of the Unification Church.

moonlight *v.* to work at a second job during one's hours free from the first.

moonshine *n.* homemade or illegally-distributed liquor.

mope *n.* a listless person—*v.* 1. to lack energy 2. to spend time idly.

mope around *v.* to behave listlessly.

moped *n.* a small "mo"torized bicycle that can also be driven by "ped"aling.

mop up *v.* to win a decisive victory.

morning drive *n.* [BROADCASTING] the

morning rush hour when people drive to work and listen to the radio, forming the largest audience of the day.

morning glory *n.* [HORSE RACING] a horse that runs well in workouts but never wins a race.

morph *n.* morphine.

mosey, mosey along *v.* to meander. From the Spanish *vamos*, "let's go."

most, the *n.* 1. anything excellent 2. the best of a group of things.

mostest *adj.* variant of "the most," as in "the hostess with the mostest."

mossback *n.* 1. an unsophisticated country dweller 2. [POLITICS] a reactionary.

mother *n.* 1. an older male homosexual 2. anything frustrating or troublesome; a euphemism for "mother fucker."

mother fucker *n.* 1. a despicable person 2. an arduous or frustrating task.

mother fucking *adj.* 1. despicable 2. inferior.

Mother Hubbard *n.* a long, loose-fitting dress.

mother-in-law *n.* [BOWLING] the left rear pin in the pin formation.

motion lotion *n.* [TRUCKERS' CB] vehicle fuel.

motor mouth *n.* [TRUCKERS' CB] a talkative person.

mound *n.* [BASEBALL] the slightly-raised ground in the center of a baseball diamond, where the pitcher stands.

mountain dew *n.* homemade liquor.

mountain oysters *n.* the testicles of an animal as food.

mouse *n.* 1. a black eye 2. an affectionate term of address for a little girl or young woman.

mousetrap *v.t.* to deceive someone.

mouth *n.* impertinence.

mouth, down in the *adj.* unhappy.

mouth, have a big *v.* to speak loudly, excessively, indiscreetly.

mouthful *n.* 1. a statement that seems significant, truthful, wise 2. a tirade.

mouthpiece *n.* 1. a spokesperson 2. a lawyer.

move *v.t.* to sell merchandise, thus to move it out of the store.

move on, get a *v.* to hurry.

movie *n.* a motion picture.

moxie *n.* bravery, courage, resilience.

Mr. Clean *n.* [POLITICS] a humorous slightly deprecating term for an inexperienced and idealistic politician.

Mr. Nice Guy *n.* one whose main goal is to be liked and who would sacrifice integrity for this.

Mr. X *n.* one whose identity cannot be revealed.

mucker *n.* a coarse or vulgar person, especially one without honor; a cad.

muckraker *n.* [POLITICS] one who unearths deleterious material about an opponent's activities that have been contrary to the country's good.

muck up *v.t.* to soil.

mucky-muck *n.* [AMERICAN INDIAN] an important person. From the Algonquin: "has much food." Also, high mucky-muck.

mud *n.* 1. coffee 2. slander 3. [DRUG CULTURE] opium.

mudder *n.* [HORSE RACING] a horse that runs best on a muddy track.

mud puppy *n.* a salamander.

mud slinging *n.* an attempt to discredit someone with insults and by leveling scandalous charges against them. Also used as an adjective.

muff *n.* 1. a clout 2. [SPORTS] a fumble of a ball 3. the *mons veneris*—*v.* 1. to make an error 2. [SPORTS] to fumble a ball.

muff one's lines *v.* [ENTERTAINMENT] of an actor, to forget or misspeak the lines of dialogue.

mug *n.* 1. the face 2. the mouth 3. a photograph of a criminal kept in police files 4. a stupid, rough, or clumsy person 5. a grimace—*v.i.* to grimace—*v.t.* [CRIME] to accost someone and rob them with the use of force or threatened violence.

mugger *n.* [CRIME] one who accosts someone and robs them with the use of force or threatened violence.

muggle *n.* [DRUG CULTURE] a marijuana cigarette.

mug shot *n.* a photograph of a criminal's face kept in police files.

mugwump *n.* [POLITICS] one who deserts a political party to join the opposition. From the Algonquin *mugquomp*, chief: one who tries to be chief in another camp when it is impossible to be one in one's own.

mule *n.* 1. a stubborn person 2. [DRUG CULTURE] a narcotics smuggler 3. [AUTO RACING] a car used for practice.

mulligan *n.* 1. a stew made of bits of meat and vegetables, especially as prepared by hoboes 2. [GOLF] in informal golf games, a courtesy shot given when the last shot was poorly executed.

mulligrubs, the *n.* a state of depression.

mum *n.* 1. a chrysanthemum 2. silence 3. a term of address for one's mother.

mumbo-jumbo *n.* 1. superstition 2. gibberish.

mummy bag *n.* a sleeping bag which fits tightly around the body and the head, leaving only the face visible.

mump *v.* 1. to beg 2. to cheat.

mumsie *n.* a term of address for one's mother.

munchies *n.* [DRUG CULTURE] snack items, particularly sweets, strongly desired by users of marijuana.

murder *n.* 1. anything difficult to accomplish 2. an exacting superior 3. a difficult situation—*v.t.* to defeat decisively.

murder, get away with *v.* to escape the consequences of one's acts.

murderer's row *n.* [BASEBALL] the heavy hitters in a line-up of a baseball team.

murphy *n.* 1. an Irish potato 2. [CRIME] a confidence racket in which the victim pays for a sealed document of purported value, only to discover that it is a blank piece of paper. Also used as a verb.

Murphy's Law *n.* a wry parody of a scientific principle stating that if anything can go wrong, it will.

muscle *n.* 1. strength 2. influence.

muscle, on the *adj.* eager to engage in combat.

musclehead *n.* a stupid person.

muscle in *v.* 1. to insinuate oneself in a group 2. to force one's way in by sheer strength.

muscle out *v.* to force someone out of a group.

muscle up *v.* to use one's maximum strength to perform a feat.

mush *n.* 1. sentimentality 2. the mouth.

mushhead *n.* a stupid person.

mushmouth *n.* one who speaks without enunciating clearly.

mushroom *v.* to grow quickly to great proportions, as does the fungus.

mushroom cloud *n.* the cloud of atomic waste, fire, and smoke rising in the shape of a mushroom after an atomic explosion.

musical chairs, playing *n.* 1. scheming and counterscheming to gain an advantage 2. vacillating between several choices 3. changing sexual partners frequently 4. bureaucratic confusion. From the children's game in which participants march around a group of chairs to music, and when the music stops each must sit on a chair. The child left without a chair is eliminated, one chair is removed, and the game continues until only one child is left.

muss *n.* 1. a squabble 2. a row 3. commotion—*v.* to make a mess.

mussy *adj.* disordered.

Mustache Pete *n.* [CRIME] an Italian-American crime boss of the early twentieth century; at that time, an individual of this type characteristically had a long mustache.

mutt *n.* a mongrel dog.

muttonchops *n.* a man's whiskers extending from the front of the ear to the middle of the cheek around the jawline, resembling a chop of mutton in shape: thinner at the top and rounded at the bottom.

muttonhead *n.* a stupid person—*adj.* muttonheaded.

muzzle *v.* 1. to silence 2. to suppress criticism.

my ass, my foot *interj.* an exclamation of disbelief, disdain, etc.

N

nab *v.t.* 1. to catch 2. to arrest.

nag *n.* 1. a scold 2. an old horse—*v.* to scold.

nail *n.* 1. a cigarette 2. [DRUG CULTURE] a hypodermic needle—*v.t.* 1. to arrest 2. to catch 3. [SPORTS] to stop an opponent.

name *n.* a celebrity. Also used as an adjective.

name dropper *n.* one who mentions the names of important people, intimating close association in order to gain prestige or some advantage.

name of the game *n.* 1. the essence of a situation; the pivotal issue 2. the major goal; the actual purpose.

nana *n.* an affectionate term for one's grandmother.

nance *n.* a homosexual.

Nancy *n.* a homosexual.

nappy-headed *adj.* foolish; stupid.

naps *n.* [BLACK SLANG] kinky hair.

narc *n.* 1. a member of federal or local law enforcement agencies dealing with the illegal use and distribution of narcotics 2. an informer—*v.* to inform.

nark *interj.* [BRITISH SLANG] 1. stop it 2. keep quiet.

narky *adj.* 1. argumentative 2. overly sensitive.

narreshkeit *n.* [YIDDISH] foolishness.

natch *adv.* naturally; of course.

natty *adj.* well dressed; stylish—*adv.* nattily.

natural *n.* 1. anyone naturally suited to a given task, opportunity, etc. 2. anything sure to succeed 3. [BLACK SLANG] an afro hairstyle. *See* afro.

natural English *n.* [BILLIARDS] body position and movement to impel the ball hit to follow a straight trajectory after bouncing off another ball or the side of the billiard table.

nature boy *n.* 1. a virile man, one fond of the outdoors 2. an unkempt male.

navigate *v.* to walk.

Neanderthal *n.* a boorish, crude, and clumsy person. From the remains of primitive people found in the Neanderthal Valley in Germany.

near miss *n.* [MILITARY] 1. a destructive weapons attack that misses the exact target but does damage to the enemy nonetheless; hence 2. anything that succeeds despite a momentary setback.

near side *n.* the left side of a horse.

neat *adj.* 1. of an alcoholic beverage, served without water, soda, or ice 2. excellent.

neat-o *interj.* an exclamation of admiration.

nebbish *n.* [YIDDISH] an ineffectual, foolish person.

necessary, the *n.* 1. money 2. a toilet.

neck *v.* to kiss and caress—*n.* necking.

neck, get it in the *v.* to be severely punished or abused.

neck, risk one's *v.* to put one's security or one's life in danger.

neck, stick out one's *See* stick one's neck out.

necktie *n.* a hangman's noose.

necktie party *n.* 1. a lynching 2. a lynch mob.

needle *n.* a hypodermic needle—*v.t.* 1. to annoy 2. to provoke.

needle, on the *adj.* addicted to drugs.

nellie *n.* an effeminate person—*adj.* effeminate.

nerd *n.* a fool.

nerf *v.* [AUTO RACING] to hit another auto lightly during a race.

nerf bar *n.* [AUTO RACING] a bumper guard often mounted all around the bottom of a racing car to prevent its wheels from being bumped during a race.

nerts *interj.* an expression of mild frustration, annoyance.

nerve *n.* insolence—*adj.* nervy.

nerved *adj.* [HORSE RACING] pertaining to cutting the nerve in a horse's foot to alleviate pain and permit it to race even after a minor injury.

nervous Nellie *n.* a timid person who is easily upset and is hesitant to act.

nervous pudding *n.* fruit gelatin dessert.

nest egg *n.* money saved for future security.

never to chew one's tobacco twice *See* chew one's tobacco.

never-never *n.* [BRITISH SLANG] the installment plan—*adj.* imaginary, fantasized, unrealistic, etc.

never-was *n.* a person who has never succeeded. *See* has-been.

new ball game *n.* a changed situation demanding a re-evaluation of one's position.

newshawk *n.* a newspaper reporter.

newspaper *n.* a prison sentence of thirty days. From the expression "throw the book at someone," to give someone a harsh sentence, thus thirty days is not the book, but only a newspaper.

newt *n.* a stupid person.

next off next, in a series.

next to someone, get *v.* to become friendly with someone.

N.G., n.g. *adj.* no good.

nibs, his or **her** *n.* self-importance.

nice guy *n.* a pleasant, agreeable, likeable person. *See* Mr. Nice Guy.

nice little piece of furniture *n.* a sexually attractive woman.

nice nellie *n.* an overly fastidious person.

nicey-nice *n.* an overly solicitous person. Also used as an adjective.

nick *n.* [BRITISH SLANG] prison—*v.* 1. to arrest 2. to nab.

nickel bag *n.* [DRUG CULTURE] five dollars worth of narcotics.

nickel defense *n.* [FOOTBALL] a defensive play using five defensive backs.

nickel nurser *n.* a miserly person.

nicker *n.* [BRITISH SLANG] one pound sterling.

nick of time, in the *adv.* at the critical moment.

nicotine drawers *n.* underpants with fecal stains. From the brown nicotine stains left on the fingers of habitual smokers.

nifty *adj.* 1. clever 2. wonderful 3. stylish.

nigger *n.* a derogatory term for a black person when used by a white person.

nigger heaven *n.* the upper balcony of a theater.

niggertoe *n.* a Brazil nut.

nightcap *n.* 1. a drink taken before retiring to bed 2. [BASEBALL] the second game of a double header. *See* double header 3. [HORSE RACING] the last race of the day.

nightingale *n.* 1. a singer 2. an informer.

night people *n.* those who function best or who work at night.

night routers *n.* [POST OFFICE JARGON] postal workers who sort and box carrier mail at night to be delivered the next morning.

night spot *n.* a night club.

nighty-night *interj.* baby talk for "good night."

-nik *suffix* [YIDDISH] an adherent; a devotee.

nincompoop *n.* a fool.

nineteenth hole *n.* [GOLF] a humorous term for the bar at a golf club where most players go after having played the eighteen-hole golf course.

nine-to-five *n.* a boring, routine job, one beginning at 9 a.m. and ending at 5 p.m. every weekday. Also used as a verb.

nine-to-fiver *n.* an unimaginative office worker.

nip *n.* a derogatory term for a Japanese

person—*v.* to steal; to snatch.

nipper *n.* 1. a young boy 2. handcuffs or leg irons.

Nips and Chinks *n.* [STUDENT SLANG] Oriental studies.

nitery *n.* a place of entertainment.

nit-picker *n.* one who is concerned with minute details, who finds fault—*v.* nit-pick.

nitty-gritty *n.* the basic details.

nitwit *n.* a stupid person.

nix *v.* to negate. Also used as a noun and an interjection.

no account *adj.* 1. worthless 2. irresponsible. Also used as a noun.

nob *n.* 1. the head 2. a rich or cultured person.

no bargain *n.* an undesirable person or thing.

nobble *v.* to disable a horse, as by drugging it to win a race.

nobby *adj.* stylish.

nobody, a *n.* an insignificant person.

nod *n.* [DRUG CULTURE] a drug-induced stupor. Also used as a verb.

nod, get the *v.* 1. to be granted permission 2. to be chosen.

no dice *interj.* an emphatic negation.

no-frills *adj.* [AIRLINE JARGON] of a cheap airplane travel plan providing for no amenities during the flight.

noggin *n.* the head.

no go *adj.* [ASTRONAUTS' JARGON] inoperative; not functioning.

no-good, no-goodnik *n.* an irresponsible, untrustworthy person.

no great shakes *adj.* not exceptional; unsatisfying.

no holds barred *adv.* by any means whatsoever. From wrestling, permitting any technique of fighting necessary to win.

noise *n.* 1. arguments 2. nonsense.

no kidding *interj.* 1. an exclamation averring one's sincerity 2. an expression of incredulity.

no-man's land *n.* 1. a neutral territory separating warring powers; hence 2. any perilous, unprotected area.

non com *n.* [MILITARY] a noncommis-

sioned military officer.

no never mind *n.* 1. no attention 2. little importance. In the expressions "pay someone no never mind" and "make no never mind."

no-no *n.* anything forbidden.

noodle *n.* the head.

noodling *n.* [SPORTS] catching fish with one's hands, usually by grabbing them at the gills.

nookie, nooky *n.* coitus.

no-op *adj.* [AIRLINE JARGON] does not operate; inoperative.

nope *interj.* no.

nose, by a *adv.* [HORSE RACING] barely; by a slight margin. From the smallest measure by which a horse is deemed winner of a race over another horse.

nose candy *n.* [DRUG CULTURE] cocaine.

nose-dive *n.* a sudden devastating misfortune.

nose hit *n.* [BOWLING] directly hitting the front pin in the pin formation.

nose job *n.* a rhinoplasty, i.e., surgery to change the shape of a nose.

nose, on the *adv.* precisely; accurately. The director of a radio show signals from the control room with the gesture of placing a finger on the nose to indicate that the timing of the show is perfect.

nose out *v.* 1. to succeed 2. to win, usually at another's expense.

nosh *v.* [YIDDISH] to snack. Also used as a noun.

no-sho *n.* [AIRLINE JARGON] one who reserves a seat on a scheduled flight and then neither cancels it nor uses it.

no soap *interj.* absolutely not.

no sweat *interj.* an affirmation that something can be done without difficulty.

nosy *adj.* 1. curious 2. prying—*n.* nosybody.

not all there *adj.* 1. crazy 2. eccentric 3. stupid.

notchery *n.* a brothel.

not dry behind the ears *adj.* young and inexperienced.

nothing *n.* 1. an ineffectual, boring, foolish person 2. an inconsequential thing—*adj.* 1. boring 2. insubstantial.

nothing doing *interj.* an emphatic negation.

nothing, know from *v.* to profess ignorance.

not up *adj.* [SPORTS] of a ball in tennis, handball, squash: out of play, usually because it has bounced twice.

now *adj.* 1. currently acceptable or desirable 2. modern.

no way *interj.* an emphatic negation.

nowhere *adj.* 1. outlandish 2. old-fashioned 3. unacceptable.

nozzle *n.* the nose.

nudie *n.* a pornographic entertainment.

nudnik *n.* [YIDDISH] 1. a persistent bore 2. a nag.

nudzh *n.* [YIDDISH] a pest—*v.* to annoy.

nuke *n.* a nuclear weapon.

numb *adj.* stupid.

numb-brained *adj.* stupid.

number *n.* a person, especially someone extraordinarily attractive, eccentric, etc.

number, get (or have) someone's *v.* 1. to understand someone's motives 2. to obtain personal information about someone.

number is up, one's the time of one's punishment or one's death has come.

number one *n.* 1. oneself 2. [BABY TALK] urine—*adj.* the most important; the best.

numbers, by the *adv.* properly; according to the rules.

number's game *n.* [POLITICS] the use of statistics to bolster an argument, often the use of such statistics in a deceptive way.

number two *n.* [BABY TALK] feces.

numbhead *n.* a stupid person.

nurse *v.* 1. to sip (a drink), making it last a long time 2. to cajole, to entreat, to induce (a person to perform according to one's wishes).

nursery race *n.* [HORSE RACING] a race for two-year-old racing horses.

nut *n.* 1. the head 2. a crazy or eccentric person 3. a devotee 4. bribery accepted by a member of the police force.

nut, off one's *adj.* crazy.

nutcracker *n.* 1. [FOOTBALL] a strenuous practice session 2. anything difficult to accomplish.

nut factory *n.* an insane asylum.

nut house *n.* an insane asylum.

nuts *n.* the testicles—*adj.* crazy—*interj.* an exclamation of frustration, annoyance, disappointment, etc.

nuts about, be *v.t.* to be extremely fond of.

nuts and sluts *n.* [STUDENT SLANG] a sociology course.

nutty, nutty as a fruitcake *adj.* crazy.

O

oats, feel one's v. to feel strong, energetic, happy.

ochre n. money.

OD v. [DRUG CULTURE] acronym for overdose: to suffer the ill effects of taking too large a dose of narcotics. Also used as a noun.

oddball n. an eccentric.

off v.t. to kill—adj. crazy.

off, get v. to attain a state of euphoria.

off base adj. 1. behaving improperly 2. misled. From the baseball player who is not where he should be.

offbeat adj. 1. [MUSIC] in jazz, having the accent on the second beat of a measure of a piece written in 4/4 time 2. odd, eccentric, unusual.

off-color adj. obscene.

off one's rocker adj. crazy.

off one's track adj. crazy.

off-putting adj. 1. annoying 2. repellent.

off the cuff See cuff, off the.

off the record adv. unofficially. Also used as an adjective.

off the reservation n. [POLITICS] the withholding of support for the candidate of one's own party.

off the top of one's head adv. spontaneously; in an unstudied or irresponsible manner.

off the wall adj. crazy, weird.

off-year election n. [POLITICS] an election for public office held in a year when there is no presidential election.

oil n. flattery—v.t. to bribe someone.

oil burner n. an old dilapidated car.

oil someone's palm v. to bribe someone.

okay n. an assentment, approval—v.t. 1. to approve of 2. to permit—adj. 1. ac-

ceptable 2. admirable—interj. an expression of assentment.

okey-dokey interj. an expression of assentment; a variation of okay.

old fogey, fogy n. [MILITARY] an elderly man. From "fogey," a military pension, hence one who receives it.

old goat n. 1. an elderly lascivious man 2. an unpleasant old person.

old guard n. [POLITICS] a staunch Republican, usually very conservative. Also used as an adjective.

old hat n. anything old-fashioned, outmoded, or too familiar. Also used as an adjective.

oldie n. 1. anything that is old 2. [BROADCASTING] a hit tune from the past; an old song.

old Joe n. venereal disease.

old lady n. 1. one's mother 2. one's wife or lover.

old man n. one's father 2. one's husband or lover.

old pro n. one who is experienced and talented in any area of achievement.

old saw n. a folk saying or proverb.

old Sol n. the sun. From the French soleil, the sun.

on prep. [DRUG CULTURE] addicted to. Often in the construction "on pills."

once in a blue moon adv. rarely.

once-over n. a scrutinizing glance.

once over lightly adv. 1. rapidly 2. cursorily.

one and only n. one's lover.

one-armed bandit n. [GAMBLING] a gambling device into which a coin is inserted, then a lever pressed, which activates a mechanism to spin three rows of pictures; the pictures must match one another when the spinning stops in order for a gambler to win.

one bagger *n.* [BASEBALL] a hit of the ball permitting the player to run to first base.

one down *interj.* a tally indicating that the first of a series of opponents has been defeated, or one of a series of tasks accomplished.

one for the road *n.* a final drink of the evening.

one-horse *adj.* 1. small 2. rural 3. unsophisticated.

one-horse town *n.* a small rural town. A nineteenth-century American term, indicating a town so small that one horse was all that was needed for the amount of work or transportation needed there.

one-liner *n.* [ENTERTAINMENT] a brief witty quip or joke.

one-lunger *n.* [CRIME] a wristwatch or other mechanical device shoddily made but usually bearing the counterfeit label of a reputable firm.

one-night stand *n.* 1. [ENTERTAINMENT] a performance scheduled to be presented only once in a given place 2. a casual act of coitus with a stranger one will probably never see again.

one of the boys *n.* an accepted member of a group.

one-on-one *n.* a direct confrontation between two opponents.

one-shot *adj.* occurring only once.

one too many, have *v.* to become drunk.

one-track mind *n.* an interest in only one thing.

one-two *n.* [BOXING] a punch with the left fist followed by a cross jab with the right.

oneupsmanship *n.* the desire to appear always to be the most intelligent, skillful, strong, etc., especially in direct comparison and competition with another strong, skillful, intelligent person.

ongepotchket *adj.* [YIDDISH] 1. overly decorated; garish 2. sloppy.

on hold *See* hold, put someone on.

onion *n.* the head.

onions, know one's *v.* to be knowledgeable, alert, aware.

on the arm *adv.* on credit.

on the cuff *See* cuff, on the.

on the make *adj.* sexually aggressive.

on the pad *adj.* receiving regular bribery payments.

on the point *adj.* [POLITICS] ahead of other candidates in popularity before an election. Originally, a military term for the soldier leading an advance of troops.

on the rims *adj.* 1. poor 2. operating with little money.

on the rocks *adj.* 1. of a drink, served with ice 2. in danger 3. destroyed.

on the ropes *adj.* [SPORTS] beaten. From the boxer backed up to the ropes by the blows of his opponent.

on the take *adj.* 1. greedy 2. receiving bribes.

on the town *adj.* celebrating; seeking entertainment, especially in public places such as discos, theaters, restaurants, etc.

on to, be *v.t.* 1. to be aware of 2. to have information about.

oodles *n.* a large amount, as in "oodles of money."

oomph *n.* 1. an attractive personality 2. sex appeal 3. energy, enthusiasm. Also used as an adjective.

oops *interj.* an exclamation of surprise.

ooze *v.* to move slowly.

op art *n.* a style of painting utilizing geometric shapes and patterns to create various optical effects.

open *adj.* 1. candid, honest 2. [SPORTS] of a competition, with both professional and amateur competitors 3. [SPORTS] of a player, unguarded.

open bodyguard *n.* [POLICE] a police bodyguard openly accompanying the person being guarded to discourage attack.

open contract *n.* [CRIME] an assignment to murder someone which may be carried out by any mob member at any time.

openers, for *adj.* or *interj.* 1. to begin with 2. first. From the game of poker, in which a player must hold at least a pair of jacks in order to open the betting.

open shop *n.* [LABOR] a place of work employing both union and non-union members.

open up *v.* 1. to reveal one's thoughts candidly 2. to speak confidentially 2. to use one's full strength after having operated at a minimal level.

operator *n.* a charming, clever manipulator.

OR *n.* [HOSPITAL JARGON] acronym for operating room.

oral *n.* a test given orally, as opposed to a written examination.

orbit, in *adj.* ecstatic.

Oregon *n.* [POST OFFICE JARGON] a tub in which mail is sorted at the post office.

or else *interj.* a threat of retribution if certain acts are not performed.

oreo *n.* a derogatory term used mainly by blacks to describe a black person who takes on the values of a white society and is disloyal to fellow blacks: one who is "black on the outside with a white soul." From the Oreo cookie, chocolate crackers sandwiching white cream filling.

Oscar *n.* a golden statuette presented as an award annually by the Academy of Motion Picture Arts and Sciences for outstanding contributions to cinema.

ossified *adj.* drunk.

ostrich *n.* a person who refuses to acknowledge harsh reality.

other body *n.* [POLITICS] the House of Representatives to a senator, the Senate to a congressperson.

ouch *interj.* a cry of pain.

ouch wagon *n.* [TRUCKERS' CB] an ambulance.

ounce man *n.* [DRUG CULTURE] a narcotics retailer.

out *adj.* unfashionable, outmoded, unacceptable.

outage *n.* the state of being out of order, i.e., broken.

outer-directed *adj.* extroverted; of an active, sociable nature.

outfox *v.t.* to outwit.

out from under *adj.* no longer in difficulty.

out front *adj.* honest—*adv.* in advance. Also, up front.

out in left field *adj.* entirely mistaken.

out of it *adj.* 1. distracted; dazed 2. outmoded.

out of line *adj.* 1. impertinent 2. presumptuous.

out of one's mind, one's head *adj.* crazy

out of pocket *adj.* 1. paid for with one's own money 2. no longer in contact (with someone).

out of shape *adj.* 1. in poor physical condition 2. [AUTO RACING] having lost control of one's automobile.

out of sight *adj.* 1. beyond the ordinary 2 spectacular. Also used as an interjection. Especially popular in the 1960s.

out of sync *adj.* [BROADCASTING/FILM] with sound and image not properly coordinated so that the speaker's lips form words already heard or not yet spoken in a pre-recorded or filmed production.

out of the woods *adv.* having finished the most difficult or major part of a task.

out of this world *adj.* unbelievably excellent.

out-of-towner *n.* someone from a different town.

output *n.* the results of work on a project; the cumulative amount of work done.

outro *n.* [BROADCASTING] the opposite of introduction: the comments of a disc jockey as a recording ends, which often form a verbal bridge between two recordings.

outs, on the *adj.* 1. quarreling 2. in opposition.

outside chance *n.* a marginal chance of success.

outside piece *n.* [POST OFFICE JARGON] a parcel too large to fit in a mailbag.

outtake *n.* [BROADCASTING/FILM] that which is deleted in the process of editing a pre-recorded show or film.

out to lunch *adj.* crazy.

over a barrel *adj.* at someone else's mercy.

overboard *adj.* highly emotional.

overexposure *n.* the state of being too long in the public eye.

overkill *n.* [MILITARY] having more power than is actually necessary to destroy an enemy completely.

over-the-counter *adj.* 1. of stocks, sold directly to customers without passing through a stock exchange 2. of drugs, sold without a doctor's prescription.

over the falls, go *v.* [SURFING] to ride the curl of a breaking wave.

over the hill *adj.* old; past the prime of life.

ox *n.* a clumsy person.

oyster *n.* a person who talks very little.

ozone *n.* fresh air.

P

package *n.* a sexually attractive woman.

package deal *n.* a business transaction in which all features must be accepted as offered.

pack a piece *v.* [CRIME] to carry a gun.

pack a wallop *v.* to be strong, forceful.

packet *n.* [BRITISH SLANG] a large amount of money.

pack in *v.t.* 1. to accommodate 2. to find time for.

pack rat *n.* a person who pilfers.

pack them in *v.* to have large audiences.

pad *n.* 1. a bed 2. a residence—*v.* 1. to add fictitious expenditures to one's expense account 2. to add excess verbiage to a written piece.

pad, on the *adv.* [CRIME] receiving regular bribery payments.

padding *n.* anything extraneous added to increase the size, length, or volume of something.

paddle one's own canoe *v.* to depend upon one's own efforts.

paddy *n.* an Irishman.

paddy boy *n.* [BLACK SLANG] a derogatory term for a white male.

paddy wagon *n.* a police vehicle used to transport criminals, suspects.

paddy whack *n.* a thrashing.

padiddle *n.* [TRUCKERS' CB] a car with only one working headlight.

padre *n.* [MILITARY] a chaplain. From the Italian *padre*, meaning "father."

page *n.* one who ushers audience members to their seats before a performance.

pageboy *n.* a woman's hairdo characterized by medium length straight hair turned under at the ends.

page-one *adj.* [JOURNALISM] exciting, in-teresting. From the fact that the most interesting news stories appear on page one of a newspaper.

pain, give someone a *v.* to annoy someone.

pain in the ass, in the neck *n.* an annoyance.

paint remover *n.* inferior liquor.

paint the town red *v.* 1. to indulge in celebration, merriment 2. to go on a spree.

pal *n.* a friend; a comrade.

pal around with *v.t.* to fraternize with.

palace guard *n.* [POLITICS] the close advisors to the President, who serve as a buffer between him and those seeking an audience.

pale *n.* a white person.

palm, grease someone's *v.* to bribe someone.

palm, have an itchy *v.* to desire money.

palm something off on someone *v.* to deceive someone into accepting something unnecessary or substandard.

palooka *n.* 1. an inept prizefighter 2. a strong but slow-witted person.

palsy-walsy *adj.* overly friendly.

pan *n.* 1. the face 2. [ENTERTAINMENT] an unfavorable review of a performance 3. [BROADCASTING] a sweeping camera shot—*v.* 1. of a critic, to give an unfavorable review of a production 2. to move a camera horizontally while shooting a picture.

Panama red *n.* [DRUG CULTURE] a type of marijuana.

panhandle *v.* to beg for money on the streets—*n.* panhandler.

panic *n.* a person or thing considered

extremely humorous—*v.* to convulse (a listener, an audience) with laughter, delight, etc.

panic button, push the *v.* to become nervous or upset over something.

panic deck *n.* [AVIATION] a special seat designed to eject a pilot with parachute from the plane when the proper lever is activated.

panman *n.* a musician who plays the steel drums.

pan out *v.* to succeed.

pansy *n.* a male homosexual.

pantywaist *n.* a sissy; a weakling. From a decidedly unmasculine undergarment worn by women and children at the turn of the century to help hold up their panties.

pap *n.* money and favors from political patronage.

papa *n.* a male lover.

paper *n.* 1. [ENTERTAINMENT] free tickets to a performance 2. [POLICE] a summons for a parking violation—*v.* to distribute free tickets to a theatrical event in order to have a large audience 2. of the police, to give parking tickets.

paper hanger *n.* a person who passes forged checks or counterfeit paper money.

paper tiger *n.* [POLITICS] one who would be fierce but poses no real threat.

paralyzed *adj.* drunk.

par, up to *adj.* 1. in normal condition 2. in good health.

pard *n.* abbreviation for partner. Used as a term of address.

parimutuel *n.* [GAMBLING] a gambling system in which the odds are determined by the amounts bet on each competitor and the amount of money won is dependent upon the number of winning bettors.

park *v.i.* 1. to rest 2. to engage in sexual activity in a parked car—*v.t.* to leave something or someone somewhere.

park bench orator *n.* a citizen given to speaking out on public affairs.

parlay *v.* [GAMBLING] to bet one's poten-

tial winnings in a first race or contest on a second one.

parley-voo *v.* to speak or understand a language. A corruption of the French *parlez-vous*, meaning "do you speak?"

parlor house *n.* a brothel.

parlor pink *n.* [POLITICS] one who espouses leftist philosophies while remaining comfortably rich.

partner *n.* a friend; a companion.

party *n.* a person.

party boy *n.* a young male hedonist.

party girl *n.* 1. a young female hedonist 2. a prostitute.

party line *n.* 1. [POLITICS] the position on issues officially assumed by a political party 2. a single telephone circuit serving more than one residence.

party poop *n.* a dull person, one who would spoil the fun for others.

pass *v.* 1. [SPORTS] to throw a ball to a teammate 2. [GAMBLING] to retire from competitive bidding or betting in a game of cards.

pass at, make a *v.* to make a sexual overture to someone.

pass away *v.* to die.

passion pit *n.* a drive-in movie, as used by young people parked in cars for sexual activity.

pass off *v.t.* to cause something or someone to be accepted as truly part of a certain category.

pass on *v.i.* to die—*v.t.* "pass on something": 1. to approve something 2. to refuse to consider, to skip something. Also, "pass something on": 1. to bestow something 2. to repeat news.

pass out *v.* to faint.

pass up *v.t.* to do without something by choice, i.e., to refuse something.

paste *n.* a heavy blow—*v.t.* 1. to overcome a competitor conclusively 2. to hit someone; especially used in the constructions "paste someone one" or "paste someone in the mouth."

pasteboard *n.* something made of pasteboard, as a playing card, ticket, etc.

pasties *n.* [ENTERTAINMENT] decorated

discs worn pasted over the nipples by striptease dancers.

past post *v.* [GAMBLING] to place a bet after a horse race has begun and the winner seems evident.

pat, stand *See* stand pat.

patootie *n.* a beloved. Usually, "sweet patootie."

patron saint *n.* [CRIME] an important criminal who protects a younger, less experienced one.

patsy *n.* a dupe.

paw *v.* to caress awkwardly.

pay dirt *n.* 1. a goal 2. a successful conclusion. From the miner's search for soil bearing valuable minerals—*v.* "hit pay dirt": to succeed.

pay-off *n.* 1. bribery 2. the culmination—*v.t.* "pay someone off": to bribe someone.

payola *n.* bribe money.

pay one's dues *v.* to perform lowly tasks as an apprentice or underling before professing skill in a particular field of endeavor.

pay through the nose *v.* to pay an excessive amount of money.

PCP *n.* [DRUG CULTURE] phencyclidine, an animal tranquilizer often smoked by drug users.

PDQ *adv.* acronym for pretty damn quick.

pea brain *n.* a stupid person.

pea-brained *adj.* foolish.

peacenik *n.* one opposed to war, particularly used during the American involvement in Vietnam.

peach *n.* 1. an attractive woman 2. anything excellent—*v.* to inform.

peachy-keen *adj.* excellent.

pea coat, pea jacket *n.* a short coat made of heavy woolen fabric worn by sailors.

peahead *n.* a stupid person.

peanut butter in one's ears, have *v.* [TRUCKERS' CB] to be not listening to one's Citizen Band radio.

peanut gallery *n.* the most remote seats in a theater.

peanuts *n.* 1. a small amount of money 2.

a short person 3. anything derisively small.

pearl diver *n.* a dishwasher.

pea soup *n.* a thick fog.

peck *n.* 1. a large quantity 2. a quick kiss—*v.* 1. to eat sparingly 2. to nag.

pecker *n.* the penis.

pecking order *n.* the recognition of a definite hierarchy in a group. From the barnyard example of fowl who permit the strongest and most aggressive to peck up the best bits of food before the others have any.

peddle one's papers *v.* 1. to go away 2. to cease annoying. Often used as a command.

peel *v.* to undress.

peeled, keep one's eyes *v.* to watch carefully.

peeler *n.* [BRITISH SLANG] a policeman.

peel out *v.* to depart.

peep *n.* a small noise.

peepee *n. See* pipi.

peepers *n.* 1. the eyes 2. sunglasses.

peeping Tom *n.* one who looks surreptitiously at another undressing, etc., for prurient gratification. From the story of Lady Godiva's ride through Coventry during which only one resident peeped—Tom.

peep show *n.* a lewd entertainment with scantily-clad performers.

peer group *n.* a means of classifying people with a common trait, such as age, intellect, etc.

peeve *n.* an annoyance—*v.* to annoy.

peewee *n.* 1. a short person 2. anything small.

peg *v.* 1. to classify (someone or something) 2. [SPORTS] to throw a ball hard and fast.

peg a shot at someone *v.* [CRIME] to fire a gun at someone.

peg leg *n.* 1. an artificial limb 2. one who wears an artificial leg.

pen *n.* abbreviation for penitentiary.

pencil *n.* the penis.

pencil pusher *n.* an office worker.

penetrate *v.* [CRIME] to commit the crime

of breaking and entering, i.e., forcing entry into locked premises. Often used to indicate illegal government search.

penny-ante *adj.* [GAMBLING] unimportant. From the initial bet made in a game of poker, the ante.

penny pincher *n.* a miserly person.

pep *n.* vitality.

pepper shaker *n.* [TRUCKERS' CB] a truck used for spreading cinders on icy roads

pepper-upper *n.* anything which stimulates, increases vitality.

pep pill *n.* an amphetamine.

peppy *adj.* 1. vital 2. energetic.

pep rally *n.* a planned gathering before an event designed to stimulate the emotions of participants or spectators.

pep talk *n.* a speech designed to encourage or stimulate the listeners.

pep up *v.* 1. to energize 2. to cheer up (someone).

percentage *n.* value.

percolate *v.* to operate efficiently.

perfecta *n.* [GAMBLING] a form of betting in which the gambler must pick the first and second winners of a race, in the correct order to win.

perk *n.* abbreviation for perquisite, any benefit additional to salary on a job—*v.* abbreviation for percolate, as in "to perk coffee."

persnickety *adj.* overly fastidious.

peso *n.* [SPANISH] a dollar.

pet *v.* to kiss and caress.

peter *n.* the penis.

peter out *v.* to diminish gradually.

petnapper *n.* one who steals pet animals in order to collect the reward subsequently offered by the owners for their return—*v.* petnap.

pet peeve *n.* something especially annoying to someone.

petrified *adj.* drunk.

petticoat *n.* 1. a girl or woman 2. the outer rim of an archery target, where no points are gained when hit.

phase out *v.* to withdraw gradually from use.

phedinkus *n.* nonsense. Also used as an interjection.

Philly, Phillie *n.* abbreviation for Philadelphia.

phony *adj.* 1. artificial 2. insincere. Also used as a noun—*v.* "phony up": 1. to simulate 2. to create something fraudulent, an illusion.

phooey *interj.* nonsense.

photo *n.* abbreviation for photograph.

photo finish *n.* [HORSE RACING] a victory by a narrow margin. From a race in which two or more horses cross the finish line at the same time and only a photograph can show which one was actually slightly ahead, and thus the winner.

pic *n.* a movie.

picker-upper *n.* anything that refreshes or renews.

picket *n.* 1. [LABOR] a worker on strike who walks back and forth in front of the place of employment, carrying a placard stating grievances and discouraging customers from patronizing the employer 2. [FOOTBALL] the line of defensive players shielding a ball carrier. Also used as a verb.

pickle *n.* a predicament.

pickled *adj.* drunk.

pickle puss *n.* an unpleasant-looking, unhappy person.

pick-me-up *n.* anything that refreshes or renews.

pick-off *n.* 1. [BASEBALL] tagging a runner out 2. [FOOTBALL] intercepting a pass—*v.* 1. to shoot someone or something 2. [AUTO RACING] to pass another car in a race 3. [BASEBALL] to tag a runner out 4. [FOOTBALL] to intercept a pass.

pick on *v.* to abuse.

pick up *n.* a person who seeks casual sexual encounters usually by frequenting public places where acquaintanceships are often formed for that purpose, such as bars, certain cinemas, etc. Also used as a verb—*adj.* [SPORTS] with local players added to a team or making up a team.

picnic *n.* 1. any task easy to accomplish 2. any pleasant time.

picture, get the *v.* to understand all the ramifications of something.

picture book *adj.* 1. well-staged 2. planned for aesthetic perfection 3. pleasing visually or emotionally.

piddle *v.* to urinate.

piddling *adj.* insignificant.

pie *n.* any task easy to accomplish.

pie alley *n.* [BOWLING] an alley where strikes are frequently made.

piece *n.* 1. a portion of the profits or an interest in an endeavor 2. an attractive woman 3. a gun 4. [DRUG CULTURE] one ounce of narcotics.

piece of cake *n.* 1. an attractive woman 2. any task easy to accomplish.

piece of the action *n.* 1. a share of profits 2. participation in an event 3. sexual activity.

piece of trade *n.* a prostitute, male or female.

pie-eyed *adj.* drunk.

pie in the sky *n.* any highly desirable but improbable goal.

piffle *interj.* nonsense.

pig *n.* 1. a policeman 2. a sloppy person 3. a lewd person 4. an obese person 5. an ungrateful person.

pig board *n.* a small surfboard used for stunts.

pig boat *n.* [MILITARY] a submarine.

pigeon *n.* 1. a dupe 2. an informer.

piggyback *n.* [BROADCASTING] two products advertised in one commercial.

piggy bank *n.* [TRUCKERS' CB] a toll-taking station.

pigheaded *adj.* stubborn.

pig Latin *n.* a verbal amusement, popular in the 1920s, in which words are formed by displacing the first letter or letter grouping of a word to the end of it and adding the sound "ay," so that bank, for example, becomes ankbay, and strum becomes umstray.

pig out *v.* to eat greedily.

pig's eye, in a *interj.* never.

pigskin *n.* 1. a football 2. a saddle.

piker *n.* a miserly person.

pile *n.* 1. a great quantity 2. a lot of money 3. a euphemistic abbreviation for pile of shit: many lies.

pile driver *n.* [WRESTLING] picking up an opponent upside down and banging his head on the floor.

pile it on *v.* to flatter blatantly.

pile on *v.t.* to supply much, many.

pile-up *n.* an automobile accident involving two or more cars.

pilfered *adj.* drunk.

pill *n.* 1. an obnoxious person 2. [SPORTS] a ball 3. a contraceptive drug taken by women.

pillow talk *n.* intimate conversation.

pill popper *n.* one addicted to narcotics in pill form.

pill pusher *n.* a physician.

pilot *n.* 1. [BROADCASTING] an initial episode of a serialized show shown to test public reaction 2. [SPORTS] a team manager.

pimple *n.* the head.

pimpmobile *n.* a large, expensive, gaudy luxury car, of the type typically favored by pimps.

pin *v.* of a young man, to give his fraternity pin to a girl as a symbol of love.

pinch *v.* 1. to steal 2. to arrest. Also used as a noun.

pinch hitter *n.* one who substitutes for another in an emergency. Most often used as a baseball term—*v.* pinch hit.

pin down *v.t.* 1. to trace something to its true origin 2. to force someone to express an opinion.

pineapple *n.* a hand grenade.

pinga *n.* [SPANISH] the penis.

pinhead *n.* a stupid person.

pink, pinko *n.* [POLITICS] a mild radical.

pink, in the *adv.* in excellent condition.

pink slip *n.* a written notice of dismissal from employment, usually put into the pay envelope of the employee fired. Also used as a verb.

pinky *n.* the smallest finger or toe.

pin money *n.* a small sum of money for personal expenses. From a housewife's allowance to buy pins.

pins *n.* the legs.

pin someone's ears back *v.* to rebuke, to chastise; to get revenge on someone.

pin something on someone *v.* to attempt to prove someone guilty of something.

pin the blame on someone *v.* to accuse someone.

pin-up *n.* a photograph of an attractive woman, usually scantily clad, to be pinned up on a man's wall—*adj.* of a woman, attractive, sexy.

pip *n.* anything excellent.

pipe *n.* [ICE HOCKEY] a goal post.

pipe down *v.* 1. to make less noise 2. to cease talking.

pipe dream *n.* an illusion. An early twentieth-century term from the fanciful dreams induced by smoking opium.

pipi *n.* [BABY TALK] urine.

pipin *n.* [OLD SLANG] a person or thing much admired.

piss *n.* urine—*v.* to urinate.

piss and vinegar *n.* energy and enthusiasm.

piss away *v.t.* to dissipate.

pisser *n.* anything annoying or difficult to accomplish.

piss poor *adj.* extremely inferior.

pitch *n.* 1. a persuasive talk 2. [BASEBALL] a ball thrown to the batter by the pitcher.

pitch around *v.* [BASEBALL] to throw balls to the batter that are purposely not fit to hit.

pitch in *v.* 1. to assist 2. to do one's share of a task.

pitching, to be in there *v.* to do one's best.

pitchman *n.* one who seeks to persuade, often to entice listeners to buy something.

pits, the *n.* the most degraded or the worst in any field.

pitted against *adv.* in the position of adversary. From cockfighting, in which the adversary birds face each other in a pit.

pix *n.* motion picture(s).

pixilated *adj.* 1. eccentric 2. drunk.

pizzazz *n.* 1. flamboyance 2. flair.

PJ's *n.* pajamas.

place *v.* 1. [RACING] in a race, to finish second 3. [GAMBLING] in a race, to finish first or second. A gambler who has bet on a competitor to place wins if the competitor finishes first or second.

places, go *v.* to succeed.

plain wrapper *n.* [TRUCKERS' CB] an unmarked police car.

plank down *v.* to pay.

plant *n.* 1. a person placed in a gathering for the purpose of generating a desired public reaction or to spy 2. a news story supplied to the press by one who most often would benefit by its publication—*v.* 1. to place someone in a given situation in order to generate a desired reaction or to spy 2. to hide something 3. to buy someone 4. to supply a news story, usually for one's own purposes.

plant a punch *v.* to hit a desired target with the fist.

plastered *adj.* drunk.

plastic *adj.* 1. synthetic 2. false.

plate *n.* 1. an attractive or fashionable person 2. [BASEBALL] home base 3. [HORSE RACING] a race horse's horseshoe.

platoon *v.* [SPORTS] to alternate players on a team in a position. Also used as a noun and an adjective.

platter *n.* 1. a phonograph record 2. [BASEBALL] home base.

play around *v.* 1. to lead a profligate life 2. to engage in any endeavor flippantly.

play ball *v.* to cooperate—*interj.* the umpire's call that begins a game of baseball.

play both ends against the middle *v.* to achieve one's goal by inducing one's adversaries to eliminate each other. From the card game faro, in which the dealer can play against two players at the same time.

playboy *n.* a dissipated rich hedonist.

play-by-play *n.* an announcer's description of action during a sports competition. Also used as an adjective.

play checkers v. to move from seat to seat in a movie theater in order to approach other spectators to find a sexual partner for a casual sex act, especially of a homosexual.

play doctor n. [ENTERTAINMENT] an anonymous writer called in to revise a poor script for a stage play—v. of children, to examine each other's genitalia.

play down v.t. to minimize the importance of.

play hooky v. See hooky.

played out adj. 1. finished 2. exhausted 3. inoperative.

player n. a pimp.

play for, make a v.t. 1. to make sexual overtures towards someone 2. [SPORTS] to attempt to attain a goal.

play for keeps v. to engage in any endeavor with great seriousness.

play hard v. to be relentless in the pursuit of a goal.

play it cool v. to be relaxed, composed.

play-off n. [SPORTS] an additional competition to break a tied score between players or teams.

play possum v. to feign somnolence, sleep.

play second fiddle See second fiddle.

play the ball v. [FOOTBALL] to get the ball in one's possession.

play the field v. to have many different romantic interests at the same time.

play-to-play See play-by-play.

play up v.t. 1. to exaggerate the importance of 2. to advertise.

plea bargaining n. [LAW] negotiating a plea of guilty by a defendant to a lesser charge in order to expedite the legal process in a case to be tried in court.

plead the fifth v. [LAW] to invoke the Fifth Amendment to the Constitution, which guarantees one's right to refuse to answer a question when the answer might be self-incriminating.

plebe n. a freshman student at Annapolis or West Point.

pledge n. one who has preliminarily joined a fraternity or sorority.

plenty adv. very, as in "plenty good."

plinking n. target practice using small objects to shoot at.

plot n. [ENTERTAINMENT] a detailed categorized list of all the physical elements in a play, their placement and their function.

plotz v. [YIDDISH] 1. to burst 2. to be overwhelmed.

pluck v. 1. to rob or swindle 2. [BRITISH SLANG] to reject (a candidate) in an examination.

plug n. 1. a slow horse 2. an unpaid advertisement—v.t. 1. to advertise 2. to shoot at 3. to hit.

plugugly n. [OLD SLANG] a city ruffian or gangster; a rowdy.

plug nickel n. a counterfeit five-cent piece, hence something of no value. Usually in the expression "not worth a plug nickel."

plugola n. the paying of a bribe, or a bribe paid, for the underhanded promotion of something or someone on radio or television.

plug, pull the v. to expose a fraud. Often in the expression "pull the plug on someone (or something)."

plum n. 1. any desirable goal 2. [POLITICS] a reward given to a loyal supporter after an election victory, often a highly remunerative appointed office—adv. 1. very 2. completely.

plumbers unit n. a group of men instructed by the Nixon White House to "plug leaks in a suspected national security situation." They were convicted of breaking into the national headquarters of the Democratic party at the Watergate complex in Washington, D.C., and this precipitated a national scandal.

plunger n. [SURFING] a wave that falls suddenly.

plunging neckline n. a neckline on a woman's garment cut low enough to reveal part of the bosom.

plunk down v.t. 1. to pay 2. to spend.

plush, plushy *adj.* luxurious, rich.

PO *n.* acronym for post office.

pocket, have someone in one's *v.* to have someone under one's control.

pocket, out of *See* out of pocket.

pocket money *n.* money to be spent on personal needs, i.e., cash that is readily available.

pocket veto *n.* [POLITICS] the option of the President to veto a bill passed by Congress by withholding his signature.

pod *n.* [DRUG CULTURE] marijuana.

point *n.* 1. the purpose 2. the essential meaning.

pointer *n.* 1. a clue 2. a hint.

pointhead *n.* a stupid person.

points *n.* percentage. One point, one percent.

poison pen letter *n.* an anonymous letter calumniating someone.

poke *n.* a punch—*v.t.* "take a poke at someone."

poke fun *v.* to joke.

poke fun at *v.t.* 1. to tease 2. to mock.

poker face *n.* an expressionless countenance. From the card game poker, in which players must show no emotion in order to keep the actual worth of their cards a secret and be able to bluff in the betting.

pokey *n.* a jail.

pol *n.* abbreviation for politician.

polack *n.* a derogatory term for a Polish person.

pole *v.* to study with diligence.

police up *v.t.* to make a place neat and orderly.

polish *n.* 1. elegance 2. refinement.

polish apples *v.* to attempt to please a superior by flattery and fawning actions—*n.* apple polisher.

polish off *v.t.* 1. to finish 2. to consume 3. to defeat.

polish up *v.t.* to ameliorate.

political football *n.* [POLITICS] a seemingly insignificant act that is used to create a political issue.

political plum *n.* [POLITICS] a special consideration, usually a job appoint-

ment, in return for past or future favors.

political suicide *n.* [POLITICS] an unpopular action by an elected official, drastic enough to prevent re-election.

politician *n.* a clever manipulator.

politico *n.* a politician.

pollster *n.* [POLITICS] one who surveys public opinion, usually to predict the outcome of an election.

polluted *adj.* drunk.

pommy, pommie *n.* [AUSTRALIAN SLANG] a British person.

ponce *n.* a pimp.

pond *n.* the ocean.

pony *n.* 1. a race horse 2. [BRITISH SLANG] the sum of twenty-five pounds.

pony tail *n.* a hairstyle in which the hair is drawn back smoothly from the face and fastened with an elastic at the back of the head; the hairstyle resembles the tail of a pony.

pony up *v.* to pay a debt.

poo *interj.* nonsense.

poobah *n.* one with an exaggerated sense of self-importance. From the character in W.S. Gilbert's operetta *The Mikado.*

pooch *n.* a dog.

pooh-pooh *v.* to belittle, discredit.

poop *n.* 1. the rear of a ship 2. information.

pooped *adj.* tired, exhausted.

pooper scooper *n.* a device used to remove dog excrement from the street in order to maintain cleanliness.

poo-poo *n.* [BABY TALK] excrement.

poop out *v.* 1. to fail 2. to become exhausted.

poop sheet *n.* an information sheet.

poor boy *n.* a large sandwich made with French or Italian bread.

poor fish *n.* an indecisive, foolish person, one to be pitied.

poor man's *adj.* a shoddy substitute for.

poor white trash *See* white trash.

pop *n.* 1. a term of address for one's father; hence 2. a term of address for any older man 3. a business transaction—*v.* 1. to take narcotics in pill form 2. [BASEBALL] of a batter, to hit a ball high in the air 3. to pay.

pop a cap *v*. 1. to shoot a gun 2. [DRUG CULTURE] to take narcotics in capsule form.

pop art *n*. an art style popular in the mid-twentieth century, based on a glorification of common objects and mass media.

pop a vein *v*. [DRUG CULTURE] to inject a narcotic directly into a vein.

pop concert *n*. a concert of semi-classical pieces and popular modern tunes.

pop culture *n*. the mid-twentieth century appreciation of utilitarian objects and examples of mass communications media as art.

pope's nose *n*. the fleshy edible tail of a cooked chicken.

pop fly *n*. [BASEBALL] a ball hit high but not far by the batter.

pop off *v*. 1. to leave 2. to go to sleep 3. to die.

pop one's cork *v*. to become extremely angry.

poppa *n*. a term of address for one's father.

pop party *n*. [DRUG CULTURE] a social gathering for the purpose of taking narcotics.

popper *n*. a drug to heighten one's physical pleasure during coitus.

poppycock *n*. nonsense. From the Dutch *papekak*, soft excrement.

pop quiz *n*. a short written examination that had not been announced beforehand.

pop the question *v*. to propose marriage.

pork *n*. political patronage favors.

pork barrel *n*. [POLITICS] government funds from which politicians take as much as possible to sponsor local projects.

pork-chopper *n*. one given a position with little work or responsibility as a political patronage favor.

porky *adj*. saucy, cocky, presumptuous, etc.

porn *n*. abbreviation for pornography.

porno *adj*. abbreviation for pornographic.

portable parking lot *n*. [TRUCKERS' CB] an automobile carrier.

posh *adj*. rich, luxurious.

postboy *n*. [HORSE RACING] a jockey.

posted *adj*. 1. informed 2. announced—*v*. "keep someone posted": to keep someone informed.

posterior *n*. the buttocks.

post man *n*. [BASKETBALL] a basketball player pivotal to the team.

post position *n*. [HORSE RACING] the position in relation to the other horses that a horse will occupy at the starting gate for a race.

post race *n*. [HORSE RACING] a race for which a stable announces all its possible entrants and only specifies which horse or horses will run at a specified time before the race.

post time *n*. [HORSE RACING] the announced starting time of a horse race.

pot *n*. 1. [DRUG CULTURE] marijuana 2. [GAMBLING] the aggregate of bets as prize money 3. an automobile carburetor.

potato *n*. 1. the head 2. a dollar.

potato, hot See hot potato.

potatohead *n*. a stupid person.

potatoes *n*. money.

potatoes, small *n*. anything insignificant.

potbelly *n*. a protruding abdomen—*adj*. potbellied.

pot boiler *n*. a work of popular literature, cinema, etc., with little or no artistic merit, produced only to make money.

potchger around *v*. [YIDDISH] to waste time performing small, useless tasks.

pothead *n*. [DRUG CULTURE] one who habitually smokes marijuana.

pot limit *n*. [gambling] the right to bet a sum equal to the total of all bets made up to that point in a game of cards or dice.

pot luck *n*. 1. literally, a meal of whatever happens to be cooking in the pot 2. a dinner hastily prepared, often with various leftovers—*v.* "take pot luck": to accept whatever is offered for dinner.

pot luck supper *n.* a communal meal composed of whatever foods are brought by the people who will be eating.

Potomac fever *n.* [POLITICS] the facetious evaluation of a desire for power and prominence in government as an illness common in Washington, D.C., situated on the Potomac River.

pot shot *n.* 1. an unfair criticism 2. a haphazard attempt—*v.* "take a potshot at someone or something."

potted *adj.* drunk.

potter's field *n.* a burial ground for the destitute. From the biblical account of how the chief priests used the thirty silver pieces paid to Judas for the betrayal of Jesus to buy a field for burial of the poor, a field used by potters to find clay.

potty *n.* a toilet—*adj.* slightly crazy.

pot walloper *n.* a kitchen helper, particularly one who cleans the pots and pans.

pound a beat *v.* [POLICE] to patrol the streets on foot.

pound one's ears *v.* to sleep.

pound out *v.t.* 1. to typewrite (something) 2. to play (something) on a piano.

pound the books *v.* to study with diligence.

pound the pavement *v.* to walk, especially from place to place in search of work.

pour it on *v.* to increase in intensity, in quantity.

pour it on thick *v.* to flatter blatantly.

POW *n.* acronym for prisoner of war.

poverty pimp *n.* a government worker who profits from administering grants given to aid the poor.

powder *n.* light, dry snow.

powder, take a *v.* to leave.

powderpuff *n.* 1. a weakling 2. a competitor easily defeated—*adj.* of a sports

competition for women.

power grab *n.* an attempt to take power in business or politics, usually illegitimately.

powerhouse *n.* 1. a vital, energetic, forceful person 2. a strong sports team.

power play *n.* 1. any aggressive action to affirm or gain power 2. [FOOTBALL] a football play in which blockers run ahead to clear a path for the ballcarrier.

power politics *n.* a reliance on military strength to affirm international influence.

pow-wow *n.* [AMERICAN INDIAN] a conference—*v.* to confer.

PR *n.* acronym for 1. Puerto Rico 2. Puerto Rican 3. public relations. Also used as an adjective.

practically *adv.* almost.

prairie oyster *n.* a raw egg seasoned with salt, pepper, and a dash of liquor.

prang *v.* [BRITISH SLANG] to cause an aircraft, vehicle, etc., to crash—*n.* a collision.

prat *n.* the buttocks.

pratfall *n.* 1. a fall on the buttocks 2. a setback.

prayer *n.* a hope.

preachy *adj.* annoyingly didactic.

preem *n.* abbreviation for premiere.

preemie, preemy *n.* an infant born prematurely.

pregnant roller skate *n.* [TRUCKERS' CB] a Volkswagen car.

pre-law *n.* studies undertaken in preparation for law school. Also used as an adjective.

prelim *n.* [SPORTS] a preliminary competition held to eliminate less proficient competitors before a major contest.

pre-med *n.* studies undertaken in preparation for medical school. Also used as an adjective.

prep *n.* [HORSE RACING] a preparatory race to condition a horse for more important competitions.

preppie, preppy *n.* a student in a private high school which emphasizes preparation for college entrance.

prep school *n*. a private high school which emphasizes preparation for college entrance.

pres, prez *n*. abbreviation for president.

preserved *adj*. drunk.

presidential bug *n*. a facetious idea that the desire to run for the Presidency is transmitted by a germ causing "presidential fever."

press the flesh *v*. to shake hands.

pressure cooker *n*. a potentially dangerous situation in which there is much tension, conflict. From the airtight metal pot used to cook foods rapidly under steam pressure.

pressure group *n*. [POLITICS] an organized group of people pressing legislators to act on a bill of legislation, or pressuring an institution to modify its policy.

pretty *adv*. 1. rather 2. slightly.

pretty, sitting *adj*. safe; secure; in a favorable position.

pretty-boy *n*. a man with delicate features and a boyish or almost feminine charm.

prexy *n*. president.

prick *n*. 1. an obnoxious person 2. the penis.

prig [BRITISH SLANG] *v*. to steal—*n*. a thief or pickpocket.

prince *n*. an admirable, generous, kind-hearted person.

private eye *n*. a detective not employed by a police department but undertaking investigations for private clients.

prize fighter *n*. a professional boxer.

pro *n*. abbreviation for professional. Also used as an adjective.

process *n*. [BLACK SLANG] a treatment applied to straighten hair.

prod, on the *adj*. [COWBOY SLANG] angry. From the prod pole, used by cowboys to drive a herd of cattle or to poke cattle being shipped in railway cars to make sure all are alive.

prof *n*. abbreviation for professor.

prom *n*. a formal dance at the end of the school year in high school and college.

promote *v*. to acquire (something) by devious or cunning means.

pronie *n*. one who frequently has mishaps, i.e., one who is accident prone.

pronto *adv*. [SPANISH] quickly.

proofs *n*. [PRINTING] sample copy of printed matter made at various stages of production to be checked for correction or approval.

prop *n*. [ENTERTAINMENT] an object used by an actor in a production.

prop man, prop girl *n*. [ENTERTAINMENT] a worker in charge of props for a production.

proposition *n*. an invitation to sexual activity. Also used as a verb.

prossie *n*. abbreviation for prostitute.

protection *n*. 1. [CRIME] extortion; money paid to avoid retribution exacted for lack of payment 2. any artificial means of birth control.

prune *n*. an unpleasant person.

pruneface *n*. an ugly person.

PSA *n*. [BROADCASTING] acronym for public service announcement.

p's and q's, mind one's *See* mind one's p's and q's.

psych *n*. abbreviation for psychology—*v.t.* to make nervous.

psyched up *adj*. 1. stimulated 2. nervous 3. psychologically prepared.

psycho *n*. a psychopath, i.e., a crazy person.

psych out *v.t.* 1. to astonish 2. to overwhelm 3. to make nervous 4. to render crazy 5. to outwit 6. to successfully analyze the thought patterns of another person.

psych up *v.t.* 1. to stimulate 2. to prepare psychologically.

PU *interj*. an exclamation of distaste, particularly at a foul smell.

puddinghead *n*. a stupid person.

puddle jumper *n*. a small motor vehicle.

pug *n*. abbreviation for pugilist, a boxer.

puke *n*. 1. vomit 2. a despicable person—*v*. to vomit.

pull *n*. influence.

pull a boner *v.* to err embarrassingly.

pull a fast one *v.* to attempt a deception, usually successfully.

pull a punch *v.* [BOXING] of a strong boxer, to withhold the full force of a punch. *See also* pull no punches.

pull a train *v.* of a woman, to coit with many men, one right after another.

pull down *v.t.* to earn.

pull down the house *v.* [ENTERTAINMENT] of a performer or performance, to have a great success, usually marked by loud applause or a standing ovation.

pull hitter *n.* [BASEBALL] a baseball batter who normally hits the ball to the same side in the field as the side of home base on which he is standing.

pull in *v.t.* 1. to arrest 2. to earn.

pull no punches *v.* 1. to use one's full strength 2. to speak candidly, albeit harshly.

pull oars *v.* [POLITICS] to toil for one's interest group.

pull one's belt in *v.* 1. to prepare for a period of hunger 2. to economize.

pull out *v.* 1. to withdraw 2. to extend.

pull someone's leg *v.* 1. to tease 2. to joke 3. to deceive playfully.

pull something off *v.* to make something succeed.

pull something on someone *v.* to deceive someone.

pull strings *v.* 1. to manipulate 2. to seek preferential treatment from acquaintances in important positions.

pull the wool over someone's eyes *v.* to deceive someone.

pump *n.* the heart—*v.* 1. [SPORTS] to deceive an opponent by pretending to throw the ball 2. to attempt to gain information from someone.

pump, on *adv.* on credit.

pump iron *v.* to lift weights in body building.

pumpkin *n.* 1. an affectionate term of address, especially for a child 2. [TRUCKERS' CB] a flat tire 3. the head.

pumpkinhead *n.* a fool.

pump priming *n.* stimulation of the economy by government financial intervention.

punch *n.* power, strength, impact.

punch drunk *adj.* dazed, as if by repeated blows about the head.

punch line *n.* the climax of a joke or story.

punch-up *n.* [BRITISH SLANG] a noisy fist fight; a brawl.

punk *n.* 1. a rowdy 2. a violent and deliberately repulsive style of performing rock music 3. a musician or singer performing punk rock—*adj.* pertaining to the style of dress, manner of speech, and other affectations adopted by singers and musicians known for playing punk rock, and their imitators.

punk rock *n.* a deliberately disgusting style of rock music performed with repulsive acts and gestures, insults to the audience, etc., by performers dressed in outlandish costume.

punt *v.* 1. to strike 2. [FOOTBALL] to kick the football.

pup *n.* an inexperienced youth.

puppy love *n.* infatuation; innocent love.

purey *n.* a clear glass marble in a child's game of marbles.

purple *adj.* lurid.

purple heart *n.* [DRUG CULTURE] a barbiturate or barbiturate combined with morphine. Often used by addicted servicemen, thus its name from the military award (the Purple Heart) given for death during combat.

purse *n.* the prize money awarded in a competition.

push *n.* 1. an effort 2. energy, stamina, drive—*v.* 1. to be overbearing 2. to promote sales or the use of something 3. [DRUG CULTURE] to sell narcotics.

push a pen *v.* to do office work.

pusher *n.* [DRUG CULTURE] a narcotics dealer.

push-in *n.* [CRIME] a robbery perpetrated at the victim's door, often by pushing the victim inside as soon as the door is opened.

pushover *n.* 1. anything easy to accomplish 2. a person easily persuaded. Also used as a verb.

push the panic button *v.* to become excited or nervous about something.

puss *n.* the face.

pussy *n.* 1. the female genitalia 2. a sweet old woman.

pussycat *n.* 1. an appealing, kind person 2. one easy to manipulate.

pussyfoot *v.* to avoid direct confrontation.

pussy posse *n.* [POLICE] a police squad combatting vice, specifically prostitution.

puta *n.* [SPANISH] a prostitute.

put a bug in someone's ear *v.* to excite someone's suspicions.

put a bug (or a kink) in something *v.* 1. to disrupt 2. to ruin a plan.

put across *v.t.* 1. to explain 2. to clarify.

put away *v.t.* 1. to imprison 2. to commit to an insane asylum 3. to kill 4. to consume 5. [BOXING] of a boxer, finally to knock out an adversary who has already received many blows.

put down *n.* an insult—*v.t.* 1. to criticize harshly; to insult 2. [HORSE RACING] to kill an injured or ill race horse.

put in one's two-cents worth *v.* to express one's opinion.

put it away *v.* to gorge oneself on food and drink.

put it on the line *v.* 1. to express something directly, clearly 2. to risk something.

put it over *v.* [BASEBALL] to pitch a ball directly over home plate.

put off *n.* 1. a postponement 2. a delaying tactic—*v.* 1. to delay 2. to annoy.

put on *n.* 1. a hoax 2. a bluff 3. a deception—*v.* "put someone on": to tease or to deceive someone.

put one's cards on the table *v.* 1. to expose one's intentions 2. to express oneself completely and truthfully.

put one's foot in it *v.* to commit an indiscretion.

put out *n.* [BASEBALL] eliminating an opponent and causing the adversary team to have an "out" scored against them—*v.i.* 1. to function at one's maximum potential 2. to accord sexual favors—*v.t.* 1. to inconvenience 2. [SPORTS] to cause an adversary player to be eliminated from a game—*adj.* 1. annoyed 2. inconvenienced.

put out a contract *v.* [CRIME] to pay an assassin to murder someone.

put over *v.t.* 1. to deceive 2. to foster the success of something.

put someone down as something *v.* to classify or identify someone as something.

put something on the backburner *See* backburner, put something on the.

put the arm on *v.t.* to detain someone physically.

put the bite on someone *v.* to request money from someone.

put the chill on someone *See* chill on someone, put the.

put the screws on *v.* to apply psychological pressure.

put the squeeze on *v.* to apply psychological pressure.

put the X on someone *v.* [CRIME] to indicate someone to be killed, i.e., to mark someone for murder.

put through the mill (or wringer) *v.* to subject to harsh treatment.

put to sleep *v.t.* [CRIME] to murder.

putt-putt *n.* 1. a small motor 2. a vehicle propelled by a small motor.

put up *v.t.* to lodge, usually for a short time.

put up job *n.* 1. an entrapment 2. a deception.

put up or shut up *v.* a challenge to substantiate one's opinion. From the betting system in a game of poker, in which a player either "puts up" money, i.e., places a bet, or withdraws.

put up with *v.t.* to tolerate.

putz *n.* [YIDDISH] 1. a stupid or obnoxious person 2. the penis.

putz around *v.* [YIDDISH] to spend time idly or wastefully.

Q

Q and A *n.* acronym for questions and answers.

QT, on the *adv.* in secret.

Q2 *adv.* [HOSPITAL JARGON] every two hours.

quad *n.* 1. abbreviation for quadrangle 2. abbreviation for quadruplet—*adj.* abbreviation for quadraphonic.

quail *n.* an attractive woman.

quarterback *v.* to serve as leader in any group endeavor.

quarterback, Monday morning *See* Monday morning quarterback.

queen *n.* 1. a male homosexual 2. an attractive, strong-willed woman—*v.* "queen it up": of a male, to behave in a blatantly feminine manner.

queer *n.* a homosexual—*v.t.* to ruin—*adj.* 1. homosexual 2. counterfeit.

queer duck *n.* an eccentric person.

quencher, thirst quencher *n.* a drink.

quick buck *n.* money earned easily and speedily.

quickie *n.* 1. anything accomplished quickly 2. a brief act of coitus.

quick one *n.* a small drink of liquor rapidly taken.

quick on the draw *adj.* 1. alert 2. intelligent.

quick on the uptake *adj.* 1. quick-witted 2. comprehending rapidly.

quick over *n.* a rapid, appraising glance.

quiff *n.* a sexually promiscuous woman.

quill *n.* [DRUG CULTURE] a matchbook cover folded and used to hold a narcotic in powder form, which is inhaled—*v.* to attempt to win acceptance, favor.

quinella *n.* [GAMBLING] a form of betting in which the gambler must pick the first two winners in a race to win the money.

quint *n.* abbreviation for quintuplet.

quintet *n.* a basketball team.

quisling *n.* a traitor. From Major Vidkun Quisling, who collaborated with the Nazis in their takeover of Norway in 1940.

quit *v.* 1. to malfunction, of a motor 2. to die.

quits, call it *v.* to cease an activity.

quiz *n.* a short written examination. Also used as a verb.

quiz show *n.* a television or radio program in which participants are asked questions and win prizes for correct answers.

quod *n.* [BRITISH SLANG] jail.

quote *n.* abbreviation for quotation.

quotes *n.* abbreviation for quotation marks.

R

rabbi *n.* [POLITICS] a political protector.

rabbit ball *n.* any ball that is made for rapid propulsion.

rabbit ears *n.* 1. an indoor double antenna on a television set 2. hypersensitivity to criticism.

rabbit food *n.* salad vegetables.

rabbit punch *n.* [BOXING] an illegal punch at the back of an opponent's neck.

race horse *n.* a person who works or acts speedily, often carelessly.

racer's edge *n.* [AUTO RACING] the maximum acceleration at which a racing car can turn a corner with the driver maintaining full control.

racket *n.* 1. a criminal endeavor 2. a facetious term for one's occupation or business.

rack up *v.t.* to win points; to score.

radical chic *n.* [POLITICS] espousing revolutionary causes while remaining rich and comfortable.

radish *n.* a baseball.

raft *n.* a large quantity (of something).

rag *n.* 1. an article of clothing 2. a newspaper or magazine 3. ragtime music 4. a sanitary napkin—*v.* 1. to tease 2. to banter.

rag, chew the *v.* 1. to talk 2. to gossip.

raggedy *adj.* old, worn.

ragtime *n.* a style of music with a ragged, i.e., syncopated, tempo.

rag top *n.* a convertible car.

rag trade *n.* the garment industry.

rah-rah *adj.* pertaining to an exaggerated feeling of school or team spirit on a college campus.

railbird *n.* an avid spectator who watches all the preparations for a horse race, dog race, etc., perched upon the rail.

rail lugger *n.* [HORSE RACING] a horse who habitually runs along the inside rail of a race track.

railroad *v.t.* to coerce.

rain cats and dogs *v.* to rain heavily.

rain check *n.* 1. a ticket issued to a spectator when an outdoor event is cancelled because of inclement weather, permitting the spectator to attend at a future date; hence 2. any postponement—*v.* "take a raincheck": to accept a postponement.

rain locker *n.* [TRUCKERS' CB] a shower stall.

rain out *n.* the cancellation of an outdoor event because of rain. Also used as a verb.

rain pitchforks *v.* to rain heavily.

raise cain *v.* to cause a tumult; to behave riotously.

raise hell *v.* to cause trouble; to behave riotously.

raisin *n.* a black person.

raked *adj.* [ENTERTAINMENT] 1. having an inclined floor surface, of a stage 2. of set pieces, constructed at an angle to facilitate viewing from the audience.

rake-off *n.* a percentage or share of profits.

rake someone over the coals *v.* to punish someone severely.

ral *n.* syphilis.

ramshackle *adj.* dilapidated.

R and R *n.* 1. [MILITARY] acronym for rest and rotation, a military leave to recuperate from the stress of combat 2. rock and roll.

rank out *n.* an insult—*v.* to insult.

rank, pull *v.* [MILITARY] to insist on the prerogatives due one's rank, usually to the disadvantage of others.

rap *n.* 1. a criminal charge 2. an insult 3. a reprimand 4. a blow—*v.i.* 1. to discuss seriously 2. to converse—*v.t.* 1. to censure 2. to insult 3. to strike.

rap, beat the *v.* to be acquitted of a criminal charge.

rap, take the *v.* to accept punishment for a crime.

rap session *n.* a discussion of problems and possible solutions.

rap sheet *n.* [POLICE] a police record of criminal offenses.

rapture of the deep *n.* a drunk-like state caused by inhaling too much nitrogen. Common to deep sea divers who descend to great depths and sometimes inhale too much nitrogen.

raspberry *n.* a noise expressing derision, made by sticking the tongue out between closed lips and blowing air.

rat *n.* 1. a contemptible person 2. an informer 3. [LABOR] a non-union worker who replaces a union worker on strike—*v.* 1. to inform 2. [LABOR] to work in place of a striking union worker.

rate *v.* to be worthy of praise.

rate with someone *v.* to be held in high esteem by someone.

ratface *n.* a contemptible, dishonest person.

ratfink *n.* 1. a despicable person 2. an informer—*v.* to inform.

rat-hole *n.* any place that is unpleasant, dirty, small, etc.

rat on *v.t.* to inform on someone.

ratpack *n.* 1. a gang of criminals 2. a group of loyal friends.

rat race *n.* the hectic, competitive world of business.

rats *interj.* a humorous expression of anger, dismay, etc.

rat tail *n.* 1. a comb with a long thin handle 2. a small scratch made by a figure skater's blade on the ice.

rattle *v.* 1. to talk idly 2. to confuse; to make nervous.

rattlebrain *n.* a stupid or confused person—*adj.* rattlebrained.

rattlesnake *n.* a treacherous person.

rattle trap *n.* a dilapidated car.

rattling *adj.* worrisome—*adv.* very.

ratty *adj.* dilapidated.

raunchy *adj.* 1. indecent 2. dirty, old, worn 3. drunk.

rave *n.* [ENTERTAINMENT] a highly favorable critical review. Also used as an adjective—*v.* to express enthusiasm for something.

rave, what's the *See* what's the rave?

raw *adj.* 1. inexperienced 2. unjust 3. indecent 4. naked.

raw, in the *adj.* naked.

raw deal *n.* an unfair treatment.

razor *v.* to divide something into shares.

razz *v.* to ridicule or tease someone.

razzle-dazzle *n.* 1. confusion; bewilderment 2. glamor; excitement. Also used as an adjective—*v.* to confuse; to bewilder.

razzmatazz *n.* 1. florid, ostentatious behavior 2. excitement.

RBI *n.* [BASEBALL] acronym for runs batted in.

reached *adj.* [POLITICS] corrupted, of an official who has accepted bribes or coercion.

read *v.i.* to appear—*v.t.* to understand.

read between the lines *v.* to infer.

read out *n.* 1. information obtained from a computer 2. a summary of information.

ready, the *n.* money.

real *adv.* very.

real gone *adj.* extremely pleasing. An expression popular in the 1950s.

real McCoy, the *n.* the genuine item as represented. From the turn-of-the-century prize fighter Kid McCoy, who had many imitators who adopted the name McCoy.

ream *v.t.* to cheat someone.

rear, rear end *n.* the buttocks

receiving end *n*. [BASEBALL] the playing position of catcher.

red *n*. a communist. Also used as an adjective.

red, red bird *n*. [DRUG CULTURE] barbiturates contained in red gelatin capsules.

red carpet *adj*. preferential. Usually in the expression "red carpet treatment."

red carpet, roll out the *See* roll out the red carpet.

red devil *n*. [DRUG CULTURE] a barbiturate contained in red gelatin capsules.

red eye *n*. inferior whiskey.

red face, have a *v*. to be embarrassed— *adj*. redfaced.

red herring *n*. a misleading issue that detracts from the main one.

redhot *n*. 1. a frankfurter 2. an extremely spicy cinnamon candy—*adj*. 1. exciting 2. stimulating 3. excellent.

red-hot mama *n*. a sexually attractive woman.

red ink *n*. red wine.

red, in the *adj*. operating at a loss. From the bookkeeper's practice of writing gains in black ink and losses in red.

red letter *adj*. important or special. From church feast days whose dates appear in red print on the calendar where other dates are printed in black.

red-light district *n*. a section of town catering to vice, especially where brothels are found. From the former practice of displaying a red light above the doorway of a brothel.

red line *v*. of a financial institution, to withhold mortgage loans on property located within certain areas regarded as high risk areas, particularly because of racial change and lowering of property values within a district.

redneck *n*. a rural southern white person, usually a bigot and a political conservative.

reds *n*. amphetamines.

redshirt *n*. [SPORTS] a school athletic team member not permitted to participate in games for one year because of injury, poor grades, etc. Also used as a verb.

red tape *n*. involved bureaucratic procedures that delay progress. From the nineteenth-century British practice of tying official documents with red string.

reefer *n*. a marijuana cigarette.

reeler *n*. a drinking bout.

re-enter *v*. [DRUG CULTURE] to lose the euphoric effect of a narcotic—*n*. re-entry.

ref *n*. abbreviation for referee. Also used as a verb.

regular *n*. 1. [POLITICS] the candidate representing a political party in an election 2. a steady customer—*adj*. 1. agreeable, pleasant 2. of coffee, served with cream or milk and sugar.

rehash *v*. to discuss something repeatedly; often, to focus on different aspects of a problem in discussion.

relate *v*. to understand or appreciate.

religion, get *v*. 1. to feel sudden religious fervor 2. to be converted.

remington *n*. a machine gun.

rent party *n*. a party given in order to solicit money to pay one's rent from the sale of tickets of admission.

rent strike *n*. an organized protest by tenants who withhold payment of rent to a landlord, putting it in escrow, until the landlord complies with certain demands.

rep *n*. abbreviation for 1. representative 2. reputation.

repeat *v*. of a substance ingested, to cause stomach gas which is emitted orally.

repeater *n*. 1. an habitual criminal, one who returns to prison 2. a student who fails a course and must take it again.

repeaters *n*. [GAMBLING] weighted dice which will inevitably show the same combinations when thrown repeatedly.

re-take *n*. [FILM] a repeat shot of a filmed sequence done in order to correct or improve any element in it. Also used as a verb.

retard *n*. 1. a fool 2. a socially immature

person. 3. a physically handicapped person.

retread *n*. 1. a used automobile tire reconditioned for re-use 2. anything old and worn which is repaired for re-use. Also used as a verb.

re-up *v*. [MILITARY] to re-enlist.

rev *n*. abbreviation for 1. reverend, as a jocular term of address for a minister 2. revolution, a complete rotation, especially of a vehicle's engine—*v*. 1. to accelerate 2. to energize. Often, "rev up."

revisionism *n*. [POLITICS] in communism, a desire to alter the basic Marxist-Leninist doctrine.

rhine *n*. a fat person.

rhino *n*. [BRITISH SLANG] money, cash.

rhubarb *n*. 1. an angry dispute; a fight 2. nonsense—*interj*. [ENTERTAINMENT] the word traditionally spoken in muted tones by actors participating in crowd scenes and improvising crowd noises.

rhubarbs, the *n*. rural areas.

rib, ribbing *n*. an instance of teasing—*v.t.* to tease.

rib-stickers *n*. beans.

rib-tickler *n*. a joke.

ricky-ticky *adj*. flimsy.

ride *n*. 1. a pleasant experience 2. [DRUG CULTURE] euphoria induced by narcotics—*v.t.* to annoy, to nag someone.

ride, go along for the *v*. to participate passively in an event, sometimes just as a spectator.

ride, take someone for a ride *v*. 1. to deceive someone 2. to kill someone. From the practice of criminals killing victims during a car ride and transporting the body to be left in a secluded area.

rider *n*. special considerations added as a final clause in legal contracts.

ride the bench *v*. [SPORTS] to serve as a substitute in a team sport, thus to spend most of the time seated at the bench.

ride the nose *v*. [SURFING] to ride toward the front of one's surfboard, gripping the edge with one's toes.

ridge runner *n*. a person from a rural mountainous area.

rif *n*. 1. [MILITARY] a demotion of rank 2. a dismissal from employment—*v*. 1. to demote 2. to dismiss from employment.

riff *n*. exaggeration.

riffle *v*. to shuffle a deck of cards.

riffle, make the *v*. to succeed.

rig *n*. clothing—*v*. 1. to pre-arrange an outcome dishonestly, illegally 2. to dress or clothe.

right *n*. 1. a punch made with the right fist 2. [POLITICS] the reactionary or ultraconservative viewpoint.

righteous *adj*. exceptionally good.

right guy *n*. an agreeable, honest, trustworthy person.

right off the bat *adv*. immediately.

right on *interj*. expression of approval. From "right on target": accurate, correct. Also used as an adjective.

right to work *n*. [LABOR] the free choice of a worker to eschew union membership and remain employed.

right up there *adj*. 1. excellent 2. among the best.

righty *n*. a right-handed person.

rigid *adj*. drunk.

rimrock *v*. to thwart someone's chance of success.

rinctum *v*. to harm; to damage.

rind *n*. money.

ring *n*. a telephone call—*v*. to enter a horse illegally in a horse race by using a false name.

ring a bell *v*. to remind someone of something.

ring-a-ding *adj*. wildly exciting—*n*. wild excitement.

ringer *n*. 1. an almost identical match of someone or something 2. [HORSE RACING] an excellent race horse entered in a race under a false name in order to obtain greater betting odds for higher winnings 3. a doorbell.

ring-tail *n*. an irritable person.

ring-tailed snorter *n*. a brave and admirable person.

ring the bell *v*. to succeed.

ring up *v.t.* to telephone

rinky-dink *adj.* 1. inferior 2. cheap 3. unsophisticated.

riot *n.* anything exceptionally amusing.

rip *n.* a treacherous person.

rip-off *n.* 1. [CRIME] a robbery; a swindle 2. an exploitation—*v.* 1. to steal 2. to exploit.

ripped *adj.* 1. [DRUG CULTURE] feeling the euphoric effects of a narcotic 2. drunk.

riproaring *adj.* 1. boisterous 2. exciting.

ripsnorter *n.* 1. an outstanding person or thing 2. a violent person or thing.

rise *n.* an emotional reaction.

rise out of someone, get a *v.* to provoke an emotional reaction in someone.

risk one's neck *v.* to put one's security or one's life in danger.

ritz, put on the *v.* to assume an air of elegance or snobbery. From Cesar Ritz, the proprietor of elegant hotels bearing his name in London, Paris, and New York.

ritzy *adj.* 1. of a person: wealthy, elegant, cultured 2. of a place or thing: luxurious, expensive.

river, up the *adv.* in prison. From the location of Sing Sing prison, in Ossining, New York, up the Hudson River from New York City. Often used in the construction "send someone up the river."

rivets *n.* money.

roach *n.* [DRUG CULTURE] the stub of a marijuana cigarette.

roach clip *n.* [DRUG CULTURE] a holder for the stub of a marijuana cigarette.

road, hit the *v.* to leave.

road, on the *adj.* 1. traveling, wandering; 2. [ENTERTAINMENT] of a company of performers, touring from town to town presenting a show.

road apples *n.* horse excrement found on public roadways.

road hog *n.* a driver who straddles the painted road divider, thus preventing other vehicles from passing safely.

roadie *n.* [ENTERTAINMENT] the road manager for a group of touring performers, whose duties include booking accommodations in advance, arranging publicity, etc.

road jockey *n.* [TRUCKERS' CB] a truck driver.

road people *n.* itinerants, i.e., people who travel from place to place with no specific home. Typically, in the late 1960s, young people alienated from society.

roast *n.* an instance of good-natured ridiculing—*v.* to tease or ridicule someone.

Robin Hood's barn, go around *v.* to accomplish anything in an indirect manner.

Robinson Crusoe *n.* a person who prefers solitude.

rob the cradle *v.* to marry someone much younger than oneself.

rock *n.* 1. a diamond 2. rock-and-roll music—*v.* 1. to play or dance to rock-and-roll music 2. to have an exceptionally good time.

Rock, the *n.* Alcatraz prison, the former federal penitentiary located on a rocky island in California.

rock-and-roll *n.* a type of strong-rhythmed popular music introduced in the 1950s, an outgrowth of jazz.

rock crusher *n.* a prisoner in a penitentiary who is assigned to hard manual labor.

rocker, off one's *adj.* crazy.

rockhead *n.* a stupid or stubborn person.

rockheaded *adj.* stubborn; stupid.

rock-ribbed *adj.* staunch.

rocks *n.* 1. the testicles 2. ice cubes.

rocks, on the *adj.* 1. of a drink, served with ice cubes 2. in trouble 3. destroyed.

Rocks for Jocks *n.* a geology course in college.

rocks in one's head, have *v.* to be crazy.

rocks off, get one's *v.* to coit.

rocksy *n.* a geologist.

rock the cradle *See* rob the cradle.

rocky *adj.* 1. uncertain 2. perilous.

Rocky Mountain canary *n.* a donkey.

rod *n.* 1. a gun 2. the penis.

rodman *n.* a gunman.

rods, grab a handful of, or **hit the,** or **ride the** *v.* to ride a freight train illegally by jumping on unnoticed.

rod up *v.i.* to supply oneself with guns— *v.t.* to supply others with guns.

roger *interj.* 1. [RADIO COMMUNICATIONS] the code word for message received 2. understood 3. agreed.

rogue *v.* to ask. Used initially by sixteenth-century thieves.

Roger Rollerskate *n.* [TRUCKERS' CB] a speeding passenger car.

roll *n.* 1. a wad of dollar bills 2. an act of coitus—*v.* to rob someone who is drunk, drugged, or at any comparable physical disadvantage.

roll back *n.* a reduction of prices, wages, etc., to a former level. Also used as a verb.

roller *n.* a prison guard.

roll in *v.i.* to return, usually at night after having attended an entertainment—*v.t.* to have a great deal of something. Often in the construction "rolling in money."

rolling road block *n.* [TRUCKERS' CB] a slow-moving vehicle.

roll in the hay *n.* a casual act of coitus. Also used as a verb.

roll out *v.* to arise.

roll out the red carpet *v.* to prepare a luxurious welcome.

roll up one's flaps *v.* to cease talking.

roof, raise the *v.* 1. to become very angry 2. to make noise in celebration.

rook *v.* to cheat—*n.* rooking.

rookie *n.* a neophyte.

roost *n.* an abode.

root for *v.t.* 1. to encourage 2. to support in an endeavor by shouting and applauding approval—*n.* rooter.

rootin'-tootin' *adj.* 1. energetic 2. noisy 3. exciting 4. excited.

rooty-toot-toot *interj.* an expression of scorn for someone behaving snobbishly, too fastidiously.

rope *n.* a cigar.

rope in *v.t.* 1. to dupe 2. to entice.

ropes, know the *See* know the ropes.

ropy *adj.* [BRITISH SLANG] bad, poor, inferior.

roscoe *n.* 1. a gun 2. a term of address for any man whose name is not known.

rosebud *n.* the anus.

rosy *adj.* fine, excellent.

rot *n.* nonsense.

rot gut *n.* inferior whiskey.

rotten *adj.* 1. inferior 2. mean.

rotten egg *n.* a despicable person.

rotter *n.* [BRITISH SLANG] a despicable fellow, cad, bounder, etc.

rough *adj.* 1. difficult, challenging 2. obscene.

roughhouse *n.* loud, aggressive behavior. Also used as an adjective and a verb.

roughneck *n.* a loud, aggressive, violent person.

rough stuff *n.* aggressive, violent behavior.

round-heel *n.* [SPORTS] a prize fighter who is easily defeated—*adj.* round-heeled.

roundhouse *n.* [BASEBALL] a curve ball in baseball.

round robin *n.* a contest in which each competitor or team is matched against every other competitor or team.

roundtable *n.* 1. a discussion 2. a meeting. From the Arthurian legend in which King Arthur held meetings with his knights seated at a round table to indicate that, since no one was seated at the head of the table, no one was of greater importance than anyone else.

round the bend *adj.* 1. having accomplished the most exacting part of a task 2. drunk 3. crazy 4. old.

round tripper *n.* [BASEBALL] a home run permitting the batter to run all around the bases and back home again.

round up *n.* a gathering—*v.* to gather, collect.

roust *v.t.* to arrest someone.

routine *n.* 1. [ENTERTAINMENT] a variety performer's or a comedian's act 2. persuasive talk.

rowdy-dow *n.* a brawl.

royal *adj.* 1. the most complete 2. the best.

royal screwing *n.* the most treacherous betrayal.

rozzer *n.* [BRITISH SLANG] a policeman.

rubber *n.* 1. automobile tires 2. a condom 3. a competition in three parts: the winner of two of them is declared winner of the competition 4. [HOCKEY] a hockey puck 5. [BASEBALL] the rubber plate of demarcation at the pitcher's mound beyond which the pitcher may not advance while pitching 6. a balloon—*adj.* pertaining to the last game of a series which determines the winner when both competitors or teams have already won an equal amount of games.

rubber arm *n.* [BASEBALL] an exceedingly strong and resilient pitching arm.

rubber check *n.* a check drawn on a bank account containing insufficient funds.

rubber heel *n.* a detective.

rubber man *n.* [CIRCUS SLANG] a balloon seller.

rubberneck *n.* 1. a curious, prying person 2. a sightseer—*v.* to look around with great curiosity.

rubber sock *n.* a shy person.

rubber stamp *n.* a politician who follows directives from a political boss—*v.* to approve automatically—*adj.* following orders from a superior.

rube *n.* 1. an inexperienced person 2. a dupe. Also used as an adjective. *See also* hey Rube!

rub elbows with *v.t.* 1. to associate with 2. to come in contact with.

rub it in *v.* to tease or mock someone by constant reference to a blunder.

rub joint *n.* an inferior dance hall, where, for the price of a dance ticket, a client can rub against an attractive dance partner.

rub out *v.t.* to kill.

rub someone the wrong way *v.* to antagonize someone.

rub something on one's chest *v.* to ignore something, usually an affront.

ruckus *n.* a loud disturbance.

rug *n.* a toupee.

rugged *adj.* 1. dangerous 2. challenging.

rug joint *n.* a superior place of entertainment.

rule out *v.* to render impossible.

rule the roost *v.* to dominate one's limited territory.

rumble *n.* a gang fight. Also used as a verb.

rum-dum *n.* 1. a drunk 2. a fool—*adj.* 1. drunk 2. foolish.

rum hole *n.* a dilapidated, inferior saloon.

rummy *n.* a drunk.

rumpet *n.* an habitual drunkard.

rum runner *n.* a transporter of illegal liquor.

run *n.* 1. a trip 2. a long straight unraveling of woven cloth, usually nylon, caused by the breakage of a thread—*v.i.* [POLITICS] to seek elected office—*v.t.* to transport.

runaround *n.* 1. an evasion of direct response or action 2. a deception.—*v.* "get (or give someone) the runaround."

run a sandy on someone *v.* to deceive someone.

run a tight board *v.* [BROADCASTING] to use all broadcasting time fully, i.e., with no periods of silence.

runaway *n.* an easy victory.

rundown *n.* 1. a summary 2. a thorough explanation.

rung up *adj.* disturbed.

run-in *n.* a confrontation—*v.t.* "run in": to arrest.

run it *v.* to speak.

run it in the hole *v.* to repeat constantly.

runner-up *n.* a contestant not winning, but coming close to it.

running mate *n.* [POLITICS] a candidate for a political office of secondary importance sponsored by the same political party that sponsors the candidate for major office in an election.

running part *n.* [ENTERTAINMENT] a role which is featured in several or all episodes of a serialized show on television or radio.

running shoes, give someone his or her *v.* to reject or dismiss someone.

run off *n.* a final competition to determine a winner when previous competitions resulted in tied scores. Also used as an adjective—*v.t.* 1. to rid oneself of an undesired thing by running 2. to photocopy 3. to print.

run off at the mouth *v.* to talk excessively.

run-of-the-mill *adj.* ordinary; average.

run scared *v.* [POLITICS] to seek office vigorously, as if afraid of losing. Also used in reference to any want or endeavor.

run someone in *v.* to arrest someone.

runt *n.* 1. a person of short stature 2. a contemptible person.

run-through *n.* [ENTERTAINMENT] a rehearsal. Also used as a verb.

rush *n.* 1. [DRUG CULTURE] the sudden pleasurable feeling induced by taking a narcotic 2. in college, choosing candidates for membership in a fraternity or sorority 3. [FOOTBALL] running to prevent the opposing team from keeping control of the ball—*v.* 1. to impose romantic attentions upon someone 2. to seek members for a fraternity or sorority 3. [FOOTBALL] to run at the player carrying the ball.

rush act, the *n.* any aggressive romantic tactics used to attract attention and gain the favor of a beloved.

rushes *n.* [FILM] the initial picture results of a day's filming.

rush hour *n.* the time when most workers travel to and from their place of employment, when roads and public transportation are most congested, generally between 8 and 9 a.m. and 5 and 6 p.m.

Russian roulette *n.* 1. a macabre game in which one bullet is placed in the chamber of a revolver, the player spins the chamber, points the gun at his or her head, and pulls the trigger 2. any dangerous activity.

rust bucket *n.* a dilapidated old ship.

rustle up *v.t.* to gather, collect.

rusty *adj.* no longer proficient because of lack of practice.

rutabaga *n.* a dollar.

S

SA *n*. acronym for sex appeal, i.e., great attractiveness and personal magnetism of the person in question felt by members of the opposite sex.

sachem *n*. [AMERICAN INDIAN] chief, leader. Often used in politics to indicate a party leader or in business to indicate someone of importance.

sack *n*. [SPORTS] 1. in baseball, a base 2. in football, the tackling of a quarterback carrying the ball before he can throw a pass—*v.t.* 1. to discharge from employment 2. [FOOTBALL] to tackle a quarterback before he can throw a pass.

sacker *n*. [BASEBALL] a player guarding a base.

sack, get (or give) the *v*. to be dismissed (or to dismiss) from employment.

sack, hit the *v*. to go to bed.

sack out *v*. to go to sleep; particularly, to fall quickly into a profound sleep.

sack time *n*. 1. bedtime 2. any period of time during which one sleeps.

sack up *v*. to go to bed. Often, "sack up with someone," meaning to go to bed with someone or to spend the night at someone's residence.

sacrifice *n*. [BASEBALL] a play deliberately done which may be a disadvantage to the player in question, but is of help to the team. Also used as a verb and an adjective.

sad apple *n*. 1. an unhappy person, usually one beset by misfortune 2. beer.

saddle shoes *n*. white-laced shoes with a band of leather of a different color across the instep, especially popular among students in the 1950s.

sadie-maisie *n*. or *adj*. sado-masochistic practices in sexual relations, involving inflicting and suffering pain for pleasure.

sad sack *n*. a melancholic person, usually one who depresses others.

safecracker *n*. a criminal who breaks into locked safes to steal the contents.

safety *n*. a condom.

safety valve *n*. 1. any means by which emotions may be vented with no lasting ill-effects 2. [FOOTBALL] a short pass made by the quarterback to the fullback in order to avoid being tackled while in possession of the ball.

sag wagon *n*. [BICYCLE RACING] the motor vehicle which follows the racers and picks up any that cannot complete the race.

sailboats *n*. the feet.

sailor *n*. any man who seeks to please or does please women.

sail through *v.t.* to accomplish with ease.

salad days *n*. one's youth. *See* green.

salmagundi *n*. a dish made of minced meat, egg, anchovies, etc.; hence, a combination or mixture of many diverse elements.

salt *n*. [DRUG CULTURE] heroin.

salt, with a grain (or pinch) of *See* with a grain (or pinch) of salt.

salt, worth one's *See* worth one's salt.

salt and pepper *n*. [DRUG CULTURE] low-grade marijuana—*adj*. of hair, dark hair turning white, thus giving an appearance similar to that of grains of salt and black pepper mixed.

salt away *v.t.* 1. to save 2. to hide for future use.

135

salt horse *n.* salted and dried beef.

salt mines, the *n.* one's place of employment. A humorous comparison between one's job and the arduous task of mining salt supposedly meted out as punishment to dissenters in the Soviet Union.

salt shaker *n.* [TRUCKERS' CB] a truck used to spread salt to melt ice on roads.

salve *n.* money.

Sammy *n.* a mildly derogatory term for a Jewish male.

sand *n.* 1. sugar 2. salt 3. courage.

sandbag *v.i.* to perform with little energy or expertise at the beginning of a contest in order to surprise and overtake the opponent later in the competition—*v.t.* to ambush someone.

sandie *n.* [GOLF] a shot in which a ball is hit out of a sandtrap in one stroke and scores on the next shot.

sandwich board *n.* two flat rectangular boards connected at two corners by straps and painted with advertisement, worn over the body by people paid to walk the streets and display the advertisement.

sandwich man *n.* a man who earns a living by wearing a sandwich board.

San Quentin quail *n.* a sexually attractive young girl. *See* jailbait.

sap *n.* a fool; a dupe.

saphead *n.* 1. a stupid person 2. a fool.

sappy *adj.* foolish.

Saratoga *n.* [POST OFFICE JARGON] a mail satchel.

sarge *n.* [MILITARY] abbreviation for sergeant. Often used humorously for anyone in command in any field.

sash *n.* [DRUG CULTURE] the improvised tourniquet used by addicts to make the veins protrude for an injection of heroin.

sass *n.* impudence—*adj.* sassy.

satch *n.* a person with a large mouth.

Saturday night special *n.* a small handgun readily available through the mail or at certain shops, used by unlicensed persons, usually for perpetrating crimes. So called because of the frequency of crimes committed with them on Saturday nights.

sauce *n.* 1. impertinence 2. liquor—*v.t.* to treat impertinently.

sauce, off the *adj.* abstaining from alcoholic beverages.

sauce, on the *adj.* drinking alcoholic beverages habitually.

sausage *n.* [BROADCASTING] a rapidly-produced commercial.

sausage grinder *n.* [TRUCKERS' CB] an ambulance.

savage *adj.* excellent.

save it *v.* to remain silent. Often used as a command.

savvy *n.* [SPANISH] knowledge or acumen. From the Spanish *saber*, to know. Often used in business or politics.

saw *n.* an old joke or story.

sawbones *n.* a doctor.

sawbuck *n.* a ten-dollar bill. From the Roman numeral X, meaning ten, which resembles in form a carpenter's sawbuck.

sawdust *n.* sugar.

sawdust eater *n.* a lumberjack.

sawdust parlor *n.* a cheap or inferior place of entertainment. From the practice of spreading sawdust on the floor in such places.

sawed-off *adj.* short of stature.

saw wood *v.* 1. to sleep 2. to snore. From the noise of a snore resembling that of a saw on wood.

sax *n.* abbreviation for saxophone, a brass instrument widely used in jazz music and invented by A.J. Sax.

say a mouthful *v.* to say something of importance.

say-so *n.* 1. an opinion 2. a command 3. the right to have an opinion in any given area.

says who? *interj.* a challenge to cite the authority by which certain claims are made or actions taken.

says you *interj.* a sarcastic exclamation of disbelief or disdain.

say uncle *v.* to admit defeat.

scab *n*. [LABOR] a worker who refuses to strike during a labor dispute or who replaces a striking union worker at such a time.

scads *n*. a large quantity.

scag *n*. [DRUG CULTURE] heroin.

scairdy cat *n*. a timorous person.

scale *n*. the standard minimum wage for any given job.

scalp *v*. to purchase tickets to an event at a normal or minimal price to resell at great profit—*n*. scalper.

scam *n*. a dishonest game of chance at a carnival, amusement park, etc.; hence, any swindle. Also used as a verb.

scammer *n*. a swindler.

scamp *v*. 1. to spend time idly 2. to eschew labor.

scandahoovian, scandinoovian *n*. a mildly derogatory term for a Scandinavian person.

scandal sheet *n*. a newspaper, magazine, etc., that features sensationalism, gossip, etc.

scared shitless *adj*. very frightened.

scare up *v*. 1. to find 2. to gather. From the practice of routing game from its hiding place to catch it.

scarf up *v.t.* to eat voraciously.

scat *v*. 1. to leave quickly; 2. [MUSIC] in jazz singing, to sing syllables imitative of the sounds produced by musical instruments. In this sense, also used as a noun and an adjective.

scatback *n*. [FOOTBALL] a clever and speedy ball carrier.

scatter *n*. a secret refuge used to escape detection or capture.

scatter arm *n*. [SPORTS] the tendency to be inconsistent at throwing.

scatter brain *n*. a frivolous person—*adj*. scatter-brained.

scatter gun *n*. a machine gun.

scene *n*. a place where alert, knowledgeable people meet.

scene, make the *v*. to be present among alert, knowledgeable people.

schiz *n*. abbreviation for schizophrenic. Also used as an adjective.

schlang *n*. [YIDDISH] the penis.

schlep *n*. [YIDDISH] 1. an unkempt or ineffectual person 2. a boring or difficult task—*v.i.* to loiter aimlessly. Often, "schlep around"—*v.t.* to carry, drag.

schlimozzl *n*. [YIDDISH] an unfortunate bungler.

schlock *n*. [YIDDISH] worthless merchandise.

schlock joint, schlock shop *n*. a store which carries only cheap, inferior merchandise.

schlub *n*. [YIDDISH] a boorish, inept person—*adj*. inferior, cheap, faulty.

schlump *n*. [YIDDISH] a boor.

schmaltz *n*. [YIDDISH] sentimentality—*adj*. schmaltzy.

schmattah *n*. [YIDDISH] a rag. Often used to indicate any garment which does not please.

schmear *n*. [YIDDISH] 1. a complete defeat 2. a bribe—*v.t.* 1. to abuse someone physically 2. to bribe.

schmegeggie *n*. [YIDDISH] 1. a complainer 2. an eccentric.

schmendrick *n*. [YIDDISH] 1. a weakling 2. a poor fool.

schmo *n*. [YIDDISH] a foolish, boorish person.

schmooze *v*. [YIDDISH] 1. to gossip 2. to chat.

schmuck *n*. [YIDDISH] 1. a nasty fool 2. the penis.

schneider *v*. to defeat decisively.

schnook *n*. [YIDDISH] a fool.

schnorrer *n*. [YIDDISH] a beggar.

schnozz, schnozzle, schnozzola *n*. [YIDDISH] the nose.

schvartzer, schvartzeh *n*. [YIDDISH] a black man or woman.

sci-fi *n*. or *adj*. science-fiction.

scissorbill *n*. one easily duped.

scoff *v*. to eat.

scofflaw *n*. one who ignores the dictates of the law.

scollops on, put the *v*. to adapt oneself to the customs and habits of another culture.

scooch *v*. to move. Usually, to move a bit

to the side to permit another to pass or occupy an adjacent spot (scooch over), or to squeeze into a small spot oneself (scooch in).

scoop n. 1. [JOURNALISM] a news story which is covered exclusively or first by one reporter 2. [BASKETBALL] an underhand shot at the basket made with a scooping motion—v.t. [JOURNALISM] to be the first or only reporter to cover a major news story, especially in competition with others.

scope n. abbreviation for periscope.

scorcher n. 1. an exceptionally hot day 2. a caustic remark 3. an exceptional person.

score n. 1. a success 2. money earned in a criminal way 3. a victim of a crime 4. a partner in coitus—v. 1. to succeed 2. to earn money in a criminal way 3. to be appreciated 4. to succeed in finding a sex partner.

score, know the v. to be aware of a situation in all its aspects and implications.

Scotch coffee n. a humorous term for a cheap substitute for coffee; burnt biscuit used to flavor boiling water. Based on the reputation of the Scottish as a thrifty people.

scotchman n. one who is miserly.

scot free adj. completely free. From the Old English *scot*, a tax or share of a cost.

scouse n. inexpensive, unsavory food.

scout, scoutmaster n. one who is excessively proper, diligent, righteous.

scow n. an unattractive woman.

scrag n. the neck.

scram v. to leave.

scram-bag n. a valise kept packed for a sudden departure.

scramble v. to leave hastily.

scrambled eggs n. [MILITARY] the gold-colored braid decoration on an officer's cap.

scram money n. money kept ready for a sudden departure.

scrape n. 1. a shave 2. a fight.

scrape the bottom of the barrel v. to settle for the least desirable element because none other is available.

scrap heap n. an old, dilapidated vehicle.

scratch n. 1. money 2. a loan 3. the devil 4. [RACING] a contestant removed from competition just before it is to begin—v. to remove from competition just before the beginning of a contest.

scratch around for something v. to look for something.

scratch sheet n. an information sheet for horse racing.

scraunched adj. drunk.

scream n. anything that is extremely funny.

screaming meemies n. a state of nervousness and fright. Originally, the onomatopoeic term for German artillery fire during World War I, then a nervous state resulting from pressure of combat.

screaming queen n. a blatant male homosexual.

screech n. an ill-tempered, nagging woman.

screw n. 1. coitus 2. [PRISON] a prison guard—v. 1. to coit 2. to cheat, swindle.

screwball n. 1. an eccentric 2. [BASEBALL] a ball pitched deliberately to swerve to the side—adj. 1. foolish 2. eccentric 3. erratic.

screw loose, have a v. to be crazy.

screw-up n. 1. an incompetent 2. a mistake—v.t. 1. to ruin 2. to frustrate.

screwy adj. 1. crazy 2. eccentric.

scrip n. 1. a dollar bill 2. money.

scrounge v. 1. to take things from the discards of others 2. to steal. Often in the construction "scrounge around."

scroungy adj. dirty, unkempt, inferior.

scrub n. [SPORTS] a member of a team only allowed to play when victory is certain—v.t. 1. to cancel a thing 2. to dismiss a person.

scruff v. to earn a meager living, usually at odd jobs.

scruffy adj. dirty, unkempt, inferior.

scrumptious adj. 1. delicious 2. excellent.

scud *n.* boring work.

scuffle *v.* to earn a living at an average job.

scumbag *n.* 1. a condom 2. a despicable person.

scupper *n.* a prostitute.

scut *n.* an obnoxious, unlikable person.

scuttlebutt *n.* 1. rumor 2. gossip. Originally, the fresh water barrel on a ship where sailors often gathered to talk.

scuzzy *adj.* dirty, repulsive, inferior.

sea, at *adj.* bewildered.

seabee *n.* a member of a construction battalion of the United States Navy.

sea dust *n.* salt.

seagoing bellhops *n.* a humorous Navy term for members of the United States Marines whose uniforms are reputed to resemble that of bellhops.

sea gull *n.* a woman who pursues a sailor or sailors.

sea lawyer *n.* one who professes to have vast knowledge and seeks to display it.

sea legs *n.* acclimation to being on board a ship.

search me *interj.* an exclamation of puzzlement.

seat *n.* the buttocks.

seat of one's pants, by the *adv.* 1. instinctively 2. without thinking.

seat-of-the-pants *adj.* of knowledge or performance, instinctive, intuitive.

seaweed *n.* spinach.

sec *n.* 1. abbreviation for secretary 2. abbreviation for second.

second banana *n.* 1. [ENTERTAINMENT] a performer in show business, especially burlesque, who plays a subordinate role to the star comedian by serving as straightman 2. anyone in a subordinate position. *See* straightman.

second childhood *n.* a state of mild senility.

second class citizen *n.* one who is treated with low regard and is deprived of certain rights.

second fiddle *n.* one of lesser importance, i.e., a subordinate. Often used in the expression "to play second fiddle."

From the orchestral function of playing harmony as opposed to playing the showier part on the violin, the melody.

seconds *n.* 1. a second portion of food taken after the first 2. merchandise in which there is a slight defect and which is sold at a reduced price.

second string *adj.* 1. [SPORTS] of a player who substitutes for a regular player on a team; hence 2. anyone of secondary qualifications in a given field. Also used as a noun.

second wind *n.* a spurt of suddenly renewed energy after exhaustion.

section eight *n.* [MILITARY] 1. a release from the armed services for psychological reasons; hence 2. a crazy person.

section out *v.* of an ocean wave, to break unevenly, in sections. Especially used by surfers to judge the surfing quality of a wave.

see a man about a horse, have to the humorous excuse given to substitute for a real reason to leave the presence of others. It is understood that the real reason is usually to go to the lavatory.

seed *v.* [SPORTS] to arrange the season's schedule for sports teams so that those known to be the best in their sport do not play against each other early in the season.

seeded *adj.* [SPORTS] ranked in one's field on the basis of one's performance. The highest rank: top seeded.

see each other [STUDENT SLANG] *v.* date each other, but not consistently.

seep *n.* a jeep that can be used in water as well as on land.

see red *v.* to become infuriated.

see you *interj.* a casual farewell with the hope or promise to see each other again.

sell *v.* of merchandise, to be popular on the market.

sell like hotcakes *v.* to be extremely popular and sell rapidly.

sell oneself short *v.* to underestimate one's own worth.

sell someone on something *v.* to convince someone of something.

sell one's saddles *v.* to have no money. From the last item a cowboy would sell, and only when in extreme poverty.

sellout *n.* 1. [ENTERTAINMENT] a performance for which all the tickets have been sold 2. a betrayal of trust—*v.* sell out: 1. to sell all the tickets for a performance 2. to betray.

send *v.t.* to excite emotionally. Especially popular in the late 1950s.

sender *n.* anything that excites or pleases.

send-off *n.* a celebration to wish someone well on a new endeavor or a journey.

send someone to the cleaners *v.* to swindle someone of all their assets.

send someone to the showers *v.* [SPORTS] to dismiss someone from the major action. From the practice of sending a player to shower upon removal from a sports competition.

send up *v.t.* to sentence someone to prison.

send up a trial balloon *v.* to test public reaction to an idea, a new product, etc. Originally, trial balloons were launched to test wind strength and direction before a manned balloon flight.

sensaysh *adj.* sensational.

serious about someone *adj.* interested in establishing a permanent romantic relationship with someone.

serious headache *n.* [CRIME] a bullet in the head.

serious trouble, in *adj.* [CRIME] marked for murder.

serum *n.* liquor.

set *n.* 1. the musical pieces played by musicians at one performance 2. the scenery establishing the setting of a play.

setback *n.* a reversal.

set down *v.t.* to defeat.

set of threads *n.* clothing.

set someone back (a sum) *v.t.* to cost someone (a sum).

set someone up *v.* 1. [CRIME] to expose someone to retribution 2. to pressure

someone psychologically in order to persuade to render service.

settle, settle the score *v.* to exact revenge.

settle someone's hash *v.* 1. to exact revenge 2. to rebuke someone.

set up *n.* 1. a pre-arranged plan 2. an arrangement to predetermine the results of a competition 3. a dupe 4. all necessary implements and ingredients to mix alcoholic beverages.

seventy-eight *n.* a phonograph record that plays at seventy-eight revolutions per minute.

seventh heaven *n.* euphoria. From the term in astronomy indicating the highest ring of stars.

sew up *v.* 1. to complete 2. to assure final success.

sex job *n.* a sexually attractive person.

sex kitten *n.* a sexually attractive young woman.

sexpert *n.* a sex therapist; one well versed in all aspects of human sexuality.

sexploitation *adj.* pornographic. Usually in reference to films which exploit prurient interests.

sexpot *n.* a sexually attractive person.

shack up *v.* 1. to spend the night 2. to cohabit (with someone).

shade *n.* 1. a person who deals in stolen goods 2. a black person.

shades *n.* sunglasses.

shadow *n.* 1. a detective 2. one who follows another persistently and in secret to gain information—*v.* to follow another secretly and persistently.

shady *adj.* 1. dishonest 2. illegal.

shaft *v.t.* to cheat or take advantage of someone. Also in the construction "to get (or give someone) the shaft": to be cheated (or to cheat someone).

shag *v.* [BASEBALL] to catch batted balls in baseball practice.

shake *n.* 1. a drink made with ice cream, milk, and syrup 2. a moment 3. a chance, often in the expression "to give someone a fair shake."

shake, fair *n.* an equal opportunity.

shake, on the *adj.* involved in anything criminal.

shake, put someone on the *v.* to coerce someone to pay money.

shake a leg *v.* to hurry. Often used as a command.

shake a wicked leg *v.* to dance well.

shakedown *n.* [CRIME] extortion.

shake down *v.t.* to force payment from a victim.

shake it up *v.* to hurry. Often used as a command.

shakes, the *n.* convulsive quivering from fear, nervousness, alcoholism, withdrawal from drugs, etc.

shakes, no great *adj.* 1. inferior 2. without excellence.

shake the lead out *v.* to hurry. An abbreviated form of "shake the lead out of one's pants." Often used as an interjection.

shake-up *n.* 1. a shock 2. a redistribution, especially of tasks within the staff of an organization—*v.t.* shake up: to upset emotionally.

sham *n.* a policeman.

shampoo *n.* champagne.

shamrock *n.* a person of Irish heritage.

shamus *n.* 1. a detective 2. a policeman.

shanghai *v.* to force or coerce someone to do something against their will.

Shangri La *n.* any peaceful retreat. From the imaginary city of peace and beauty high in the Himalayas in James Hilton's novel *Lost Horizon.*

shank *n.* [CRIME] a knife.

shanks' pony *n.* the legs—*v.* "ride on shanks' pony": to walk.

shanty Irish *n.* a derogatory term for poor people of Irish birth or heritage, especially used right after the great immigration in the nineteenth century.

shanty town *n.* an impoverished area or town.

shape *n.* a woman's attractive physique.

shape, in *adj.* in a state of good health and strength.

shape up *v.* 1. to come to fruition 2. to develop well.

shark *n.* one with great expertise or cunning; often one who uses skill to cheat others.

sharp *n.* one with great expertise or cunning.

sharpie *n.* one who exhibits intelligence, style, or expertise.

shave, a close *See* close shave.

shaver *n.* a young boy. Usually "little shaver."

shavetail *n.* 1. [MILITARY] a newly appointed second lieutenant 2. anyone who is inexperienced. Originally, the term for an unbroken mule.

shebang *n.* 1. a shack or hut 2. uproar.

sheeny *n.* a derogatory term for a Jewish person.

sheepskin *n.* a diploma. From the parchment made of sheep skin on which diplomas were traditionally written.

sheet *n.* a newspaper.

sheik, sheikh *n.* a man to whom women are irresistibly attracted.

shekel *n.* [YIDDISH] 1. a coin. Usually used in the plural, shekels, meaning money 2. a one-dollar bill.

shelf *v.t.* 1. to discontinue an activity 2. to postpone a project.

shelf, on the *adj.* or *adv.* in a state of disuse.

shellac *v.t.* 1. to defeat conclusively 2. to thrash someone.

shellacking *n.* a beating.

shell out *v.* to pay out money.

shenanigan *n.* a trick. Usually used in the plural, shenanigans, mischievous behavior.

shh *interj.* a request for silence.

shiever *n.* one who cheats, deceives.

shifter *n.* [CRIME] one who deals in stolen goods.

shift for oneself *v.* to take care of one's own needs.

shifty, shifty-eyed *adj.* untrustworthy.

shikker *n.* [YIDDISH] a drunk.

shikker, on the *adj.* drunk.

shiksa *n.* [YIDDISH] a non-Jewish girl.

shill *n.* [GAMBLING] 1. one who entices bettors in a game of chance 2. a carnival employee who encourages people to come inside a tent, stand, etc., for entertainment.

shindig n. a dance; a social gathering; a party.

shine n. 1. homemade liquor 2. a disturbance.

shiner n. a black eye.

shine to, take a v.t. to become fond of.

shine up to someone v. to attempt to win recognition or friendship from someone.

shingle n. a framed diploma.

shingle, hang out one's v. to open one's practice, of a doctor, lawyer, etc.

shinny v. to climb, gripping the climbing surface with one's shins.

shiny n. liquor.

ship comes in, when one's n. when one's aspirations are realized.

ship out v. to leave.

shirt, lose one's v. to lose all one's money.

shirt on, keep one's v. to relax and be patient.

shirtsleeve diplomacy n. [POLITICS] active and informal international dealings with less regard for traditional form than for content.

shirttail n. [JOURNALISM] an editorial column.

shirttail kin n. distant relatives.

shirty adj. [BRITISH SLANG] 1. ill-tempered 2. angry.

shit n. 1. excrement 2. lies, deception 3. [DRUG CULTURE] heroin—v. 1. to defecate 2. to deceive.

shit ass n. a stupid, despicable person.

shit bullets v. 1. to defecate with difficulty because of constipation 2. to perform an arduous task.

shit hits the fan, when the n. anticipation of embarrassment or punishment when one's misdeeds become known.

shit stain n. a stupid, despicable person.

shiv n. [CRIME] a knife—v. to stab.

shivaree, shivee n. a celebration or social gathering for entertainment.

shiv artist n. one who uses a knife as a weapon.

shlemiel n. [YIDDISH] an ineffectual, foolish, or clumsy person.

shlep, shlepp See schlep.

shnook n. [YIDDISH] 1. a shy, ineffectual person 2. a dupe.

shoe n. an automobile tire.

shoe is on the other foot, the an expression indicating a complete reversal of a situation.

shoestring, on a adv. with little financial resources.

shoestring catch n. [SPORTS] catching the ball at the last possible moment before it hits the ground by a great physical maneuver.

shoofly n. a member of the police force who spies on fellow officers and monitors dishonesty in the ranks.

shoo-in n. [HORSE RACING] a sure winner. Often used in politics to indicate a candidate sure to win.

shook, shook up adj. emotionally upset.

shoot v. 1. to take a photograph 2. to pass, i.e., to send something to someone—interj. 1. a euphemism for shit 2. a command to tell, to relate rapidly and succinctly 3. a command to proceed immediately.

shoot a line v. to exaggerate.

shoot from the hip v. to be nervously aggressive, bellicose. Originally, a cowboy who did not bother to remove his gun from its holster shot directly from the hip.

shooting gallery n. a place where drug addicts can go to inject themselves with narcotics.

shooting iron n. a gun.

shooting match, the whole n. anything in its entirety.

shoot off one's mouth, shoot off one's trap v. to speak tactlessly, indiscreetly.

shoot one's cookies v. to vomit.

shoot one's wad v. 1. to spend one's total amount of money 2. to reveal one's position completely on any given issue.

shootout n. a gun battle.

shoot the breeze *v.* to talk idly.

shoot the bull *v.* to talk idly.

shoot the works *v.* to wager or spend everything.

shoot up *n.* an assault involving wanton use of firearms—*v.* 1. to grow rapidly 2. to fire one's gun freely, wantonly 3. [DRUG CULTURE] to inject oneself with narcotics.

shop, set up *v.* to open a business.

shoptalk *n.* conversation pertaining exclusively to one's job—*v.* talk shop.

short *adj.* lacking money—*v.* [DRUG CULTURE] to inhale a narcotic.

short and sweet *adj.* brief.

short arm *v.* [BASEBALL] to throw a ball with one's arm not fully extended.

short arm inspection *n.* medical inspection of the penis.

shortchange *v.* to cheat another, especially of money.

shortchange artist *n.* an expert at cheating others of money, usually in business transactions.

short end of the stick *n.* the worst part of anything.

short eyes *n.* [PRISON] a child molester.

short hairs, have someone by the *v.* 1. to have an opponent in a vulnerable position 2. to control someone.

short heist *n.* [CRIME] pornography.

shortie *n.* anyone or anything small in size.

short man *n.* [BASEBALL] a pitcher put into play towards the end of a game to maintain the team's lead when the initial pitcher tires.

short of hat size *adj.* stupid.

short one *n.* a quick drink of liquor.

short pint *n.* a person short in stature.

short sheet *v.* 1. to play a practical joke 2. to take advantage of someone.

short snort *n.* a small drink of liquor.

shorts, the *n.* the state of being without money.

shot *n.* 1. a blow 2. a drink of liquor 3. a photograph 4. a chance; a try 5. an injection of drug with a hypodermic needle 6. [GAMBLING] a ratio of a competitor's chance of winning compared with that of the other competitors 7. [SPORTS] the impulsion of a ball with an implement—*adj.* 1. drunk 2. tired 3. ruined.

shot at something, a *n.* an opportunity to do something. *See* take a shot.

shotgun quiz *n.* a surprise examination.

shotgun wedding *n.* a wedding which takes place because the bridegroom is pressured by the bride's father.

shot in the arm *n.* a stimulus, i.e., anything which serves to give energy, enthusiasm.

shoulder, straight from the *adv.* directly, honestly, frankly.

shovel *n.* 1. a spoon 2. the front part of a ski, which is bent upward like a shovel.

shovel, put to bed with a *adj.* extremely drunk.

shove off *v.* to leave.

shove off (out) for *v.t.* to depart for (a particular destination).

show *v.* to appear.

showboat *v.* [SPORTS] to play in a showy manner for the benefit of the spectators. Also used as a verb or an adjective.

showcase *n.* [ENTERTAINMENT] a production in which the actors are not paid but have an opportunity to perform before an audience, thus displaying their talents in the hope of being seen by someone who will provide paid employment. Also used as verb and an adjective.

show down *n.* a final reckoning. From the card game poker, in which after the betting is completed, the players must show their cards by putting them down on the table face up to determine the winner.

shower-stick *n.* an umbrella.

show-off *n.* a person who seeks to attract attention—*v.* to behave in a showy manner, i.e., to display one's merits ostentatiously.

show up *v.* 1. to appear 2. to expose the shortcomings of someone or something.

shrewd dude *n*. one who is alert, knowledgeable, well-dressed.

shrimp *n*. a short person.

shrink *n*. a psychiatrist; abbreviation for head-shrinker.

shtik *n*. [YIDDISH] 1. a characteristic attention-getting movement, grimace, act, etc., of a given performer 2. less than admirable activity.

shuck *n*. deception—*v*. 1. to hoax 2. to undress.

shush *v*. to become quiet. Often used as an interjection.

shush up *v*. to silence. Usually used as a command.

shut down *v.t.* to defeat.

shut-eye *n*. sleep.

shut-in *n*. a person who is unable to go outside because of illness, infirmity, fear, etc.

shut one's trap *v*. to cease talking.

shut-out *n*. 1. [LABOR] a tactic of management to refuse work to laborers by locking them out of the place of employment 2. [SPORTS] any game in which the loser has scored no points.

shutterbug *n*. a photography enthusiast.

shutters *n*. the eyelids.

shut up *v*. 1. to cease talking 2. to keep silent. Usually used as a crude command for silence.

shylock *n*. [CRIME] a usurer. From Shakespeare's usurer in *The Merchant of Venice*.

shyster *n*. a dishonest and cunning person, especially a lawyer known for unethical behavior.

sick *adj*. 1. perverted 2. mentally ill.

sickie *n*. 1. a pervert 2. a psychologically maladjusted person.

sick out *n*. [LABOR] a concerted effort by workers to protest management's policies by having many workers absent themselves from their jobs at the same time, giving illness as an excuse.

side, go over the *v*. to absent oneself without permission. Specifically, in the Navy, to leave one's ship without a pass.

side, on the *adv*. in addition.

side bar *adj*. additional.

sidekick *n*. a partner or companion who is always at one's side.

sidetrack *v.t.* to arrest.

sidewalks, hit the *v*. 1. to walk 2. to look for a new job, especially by walking from place to place.

sidewalk superintendent *n*. one who observes construction workers; hence, one with no official authority who seeks to direct, guide, supervise others in their work.

side-wheeler *n*. a left-handed person.

sidewinder *n*. a treacherous person. Actually, the term for a rattlesnake.

sieve *n*. anything which requires constant expense, attention, etc.

signal zero *n*. or *adj*. [POLICE] an emergency. From the police radio code.

sign in *v*. to sign one's name when entering.

sign off *n*. 1. [BROADCASTING] a signal that broadcasting is temporarily ceasing 2. a farewell—*v*. 1. to end a broadcast 2. to cease communication 3. to leave.

sign on *v*. 1. to hire oneself out 2. to join a group, specifically of workers.

sign out *v.i.* to sign one's name when leaving—*v.t.* to take something as a loan and register one's responsibility for its safekeeping with a signature.

sign up *v*. 1. to volunteer 2. to show an interest by signing one's name—*adj*. pertaining to a list, etc., used for signatures.

silk, hit the *v*. to jump from an airplane using a parachute.

silks *n*. [HORSE RACING] a jockey's uniform; specifically, the color and design of uniform used by a specific stable as means of instant identification of a rider and horse on the track during a race.

silk stocking *adj*. rich. Often used to designate a wealthy neighborhood.

silver *n*. coins.

silver jeff *n*. a twenty-five cent piece.

silver wing *n.* a fifty-cent piece.

simmer down *v.* to become calm. Often used as a command.

simoleon *n.* a one-dollar bill.

Simon Legree *n.* a cruel taskmaster. From the character, an evil slave driver, in Harriet Beecher Stowe's novel *Uncle Tom's Cabin.*

simp *n.* a fool.

simpatico *adj.* [ITALIAN] 1. compatible 2. pleasant.

simple Simon *n.* a fool.

sin bin *n.* [ICE HOCKEY] the bench reserved for players out of the game because of a penalty.

sing *v.* to inform.

single *n.* 1. a one-dollar bill 2. an unmarried person 3. [BASEBALL] a hit that permits a runner to run from one base to the next 4. [SPORTS] a competition involving only one person competing against one other person—*v.* [BASEBALL] to hit a ball permitting a runner to run one base.

single-o *adj.* unmarried.

singles *adj.* 1. [SPORTS] of a competition in which one person plays against one person 2. pertaining to anything specifically for unmarried adults.

sink *v.t.* [SPORTS] to cause (a ball) to land in a hole or basket.

sinker *n.* 1. a doughnut 2. [BASEBALL] a pitched ball which drops slightly as it nears home plate.

sinkers *n.* the feet.

sis *n.* 1. abbreviation for sister 2. an effeminate male.

sissy *n.* 1. a coward 2. an effeminate male. Also used as an adjective.

sissybar *n.* a metal bar shaped like an inverted U, attached behind the seat of a motorcycle or bicycle to prevent a rider from sliding backward.

sissypants *n.* 1. a coward 2. an overly fastidious male.

sister *n.* 1. any female 2. [BLACK SLANG] abbreviation for soul sister, a black female. Often used to indicate solidarity.

sit *v.* to care for a child during the absence of its parents.

sit-com *n.* [TELEVISION] abbreviation for situation comedy, a type of amusing show, usually broadcast weekly, based on a limited group of people dealing with life situations.

sitdown *n.* a meeting.

sit-down strike *n.* [LABOR] a protest characterized by workers occupying their normal positions at their place of employment but refusing to work or to leave.

sit-in *n.* a protest characterized by passive resistance. Coined in 1960 to describe the technique used by black protestors to integrate the Woolworth's lunch counter in Raleigh, N.C. They sat there even when no one would serve them.

sit in *v.* to join a group activity.

sit on a lead *v.* [SPORTS] to play cautiously in order to maintain a winning score in competition.

sit on it *interj.* a mildly derisive command to keep silent, to stop annoying, to be patient. Popularized by the character The Fonz in the television situation comedy *Happy Days.*

sit on one's hands *v.* 1. to do nothing 2. [ENTERTAINMENT] of an audience, to withhold applause.

sit on the ball *v.* [SPORTS] to retain possession of the ball to prevent the other team from scoring in competition.

sit out *v.t.* to refrain from participation, often hoping for a better opportunity in the near future.

sitter *n.* one who cares for a child in the absence of its parents.

sit tight *v.* 1. to remain calm 2. to wait patiently.

sitting duck *n.* a vulnerable, potential victim.

sitting pretty *adj.* in a favorable position.

situash *n.* a situation.

sitzbein *n.* the buttocks.

six-bits *n.* seventy-five cents.

sixer *n.* [PRISON SLANG] a sentence of six months in prison.

six-gun, six-shooter *n.* a pistol from which six bullets can be shot before reloading.

six ways to Sunday *adv.* by many and various means.

size up *v.* 1. to judge at a glance 2. to estimate.

sizzle *v.* 1. to be very hot 2. to be exciting 3. to die in the electric chair.

sizzler *n.* 1. an extremely hot day 2. anything exciting, titillating, or sexually suggestive.

sizz-water *n.* carbonated water.

skag *n.* a fool.

skate, good *n.* a pleasant, honest person. Originally, *skite,* meaning fellow. *See also* cheapskate.

skate on thin ice *v.* to be in a tenuous situation.

skaty-eight *n.* a large number (without having taken an exact count).

skedaddle *v.* to leave quickly.

skee *n.* whiskey.

skeeter *n.* a mosquito.

skeleton set *n.* [ENTERTAINMENT] a framework of scenery made to remain in place for an entire play, but so constructed as to allow certain interchangeable flats to be placed in position for various scenes.

skid row *n.* a dilapidated area with many cheap bars and dirty hotels usually populated by derelicts. Originally, to get logs from the forest to the mill at lumbering camps in the Northwest, they were skidded along a road. Soon brothels and bars were built along the road (later, row) to serve the men's needs.

skids, hit the *v.* 1. to become unlucky 2. to fail.

skids, on the *adv.* in a state of decline.

skids to (on) someone, put the *v.* to cause someone's failure or ruin.

skillet *n.* a mildly derogatory term for a black person.

skillion *n.* an incredibly large number of something.

skim *v.* to take money for oneself illegally, and systematically, from monies set aside for any purpose, or from a subordinate's salary, usually in return for the promise of continued employment.

skimmer *n.* a wide-brimmed hat with a shallow crown.

skin *n.* 1. a dollar bill 2. nudity—*v.t.* to cheat someone.

skin alive *v.t.* 1. to chastise someone severely 2. to defeat someone conclusively.

skin flick *n.* a pornographic movie.

skinflint *n.* a miserly person.

skin game *n.* any situation in which there is no chance of success. Originally, any game of chance in which the victim had no possibility of winning.

skin, get under someone's *v.* to annoy someone.

skin, give someone some *v.* to shake hands with someone.

skin-head *n.* a bald person. In the late 1960s and early 1970s some rowdy British working class youths with shaved heads or very short hair were known as skin-heads.

skinner *n.* a mule driver.

skinny dip *v.* to swim in the nude. Also used as a noun.

skin off someone's back, no *n.* no sacrifice, i.e., something done without difficulty.

skin of one's teeth, by the *adv.* barely.

skin pop *v.* [DRUG CULTURE] to inject a narcotic subcutaneously, but not directly into a vein or artery.

skins *n.* drums.

skip *v.* to leave quickly. Often in the expression "skip town."

skip it *interj.* an admonition to forget something of little importance.

skirt *n.* any female, especially an attractive young woman.

skivvies *n.* underwear.

skull *n.* an intellectual.

skull-buster *n.* 1. a challenging problem 2. a violent person.

skullduggery *n.* deception, trickery.

skuller *n.* [BASEBALL] the heavy plastic cap used by a batter.

skull session *n.* a meeting at which strategies are planned and discussed. Often used in reference to football teams.

skunk *n.* a mean, despicable person.—*v.* 1. to ruin a plan or project 2. to cheat 3. to betray.

skunk someone out of something *v.* to cheat someone out of something.

sky cap *n.* an airport porter.

sky jack *v.* to hijack an aircraft. Also used as a noun, but more commonly in the form "sky jacking."

sky pilot *n.* [LUMBERJACK SLANG] a member of the clergy.

sky rocket *v.* to increase rapidly in scope or size.

slab *n.* 1. a town 2. [BASEBALL] the rectangular plate on the pitcher's mound 3. a table used to hold a corpse 4. a tombstone.

slack it down *v.* [BLACK SLANG] to comb one's hair.

slack season *n.* a prolonged period during which sales in any specific business are predictably slow.

slam *n.* a caustic criticism; an unpleasant remark. Also used as a verb.

slam-bang *adj.* or *adv.* rough, violent; roughly, violently.

slammer *n.* a prison.

slant *n.* 1. a point of view 2. a bias—*v.t.* to express with bias.

slap *adv.* directly or abruptly. Often in the expression "slap in the middle (of something)."

slap-bang *adj.* or *adv.* careless, rough; carelessly, roughly.

slap-happy *adj.* silly.

slap in the face *n.* an insult.

slap one's gums *v.* to talk idly.

slap someone's wrist *v.* to chastise someone.

slate *n.* [POLITICS] the list of candidates sponsored by a party in an election.

slate, a clean *n.* an unblemished record. Often, a new beginning discounting any past misdeed.

slave driver *n.* a demanding employer or superior at work.

slay *v.t.* to affect strongly; usually to astonish, surprise, or overwhelm.

sleazy *adj.* 1. inferior; of poor quality 2. garish.

sleep around *v.* to engage in many casual sexual relationships.

sleeper *n.* 1. anything that achieves an unexpected success 2. [HORSE RACING] a horse whose running ability has been hidden, often in order to raise betting odds, before it is pushed to win a surprise victory in a race 3. [GAMBLING] an uncollected winning bet in the game of faro 4. [POLITICS] a clause within a bill of legislation that changes or negates its apparent intention 5. [BOWLING] a pin left standing behind another after the first ball of a frame is played.

sleep-in *n.* a domestic employee who lives in the residence of the employer. Also used as a verb and an adjective.

sleep off *v.* to rid oneself of an undesired physical condition or mental state by sleeping, such as drunkenness, unhappiness, anxiety, etc.

sleep out *v.* to work in domestic employ but maintain one's own separate residence. Also used as an adjective.

sleep with *v.t.* to coit with.

sleeve, something up one's *See* something up one's sleeve, have.

sleeve, wear one's heart on one's *See* wear one's heart on one's sleeve.

sleeve on someone, put the *v.* to arrest someone.

sleighride *n.* 1. any pleasant occasion 2. a swindle 3. [DRUG CULTURE] a dose of cocaine, which is known as snow—*v.* to take cocaine.

sleuth *n.* a detective.

slew *n.* a large number of something.

slewfoot *n.* a policeman; a detective.

slice *n.* 1. a percentage or share 2. [BASEBALL] a pitcher's movement impelling a ball to curve to the right (for a right-handed batter) or to the left (for a left-handed batter). Also used as a verb.

slick *adj*. 1. superficially attractive 2. excellent; enjoyable 3. clever 4. skillful but superficial.

slick chick *n*. an attractive, stylish, clever woman.

slime *n*. 1. an obnoxious, despicable person 2. unpleasant or obscene talk or deeds.

sling a nasty (or **wicked foot**) *v*. to dance with expertise.

slinger *n*. a waiter or waitress.

sling hash *v*. to be employed as a waiter or waitress.

sling it *v*. to exaggerate.

sling the bull *v*. 1. to exaggerate 2. to talk idly.

slinky *adj*. 1. sleek 2. graceful.

slip *n*. 1. a mistake 2. [PRINTING] an initial sheet printed to verify the correctness of type setting before more copies are printed.

slip, get (or **give someone**) **the** *v*. 1. to lose track of someone during a pursuit 2. to evade a pursuer.

slip off *v*. to leave unnoticed.

slip one's trolley *v*. to lose one's sanity.

slip out *v*. to leave unnoticed.

slippery *adj*. crafty; deceitful.

slip someone five *v*. to shake someone's hand.

slip up *n*. an error, mistake, blunder—*v*. to err; to fail.

slob *n*. a clumsy, boorish person. Often, one to be pitied, in the expression "poor slob."

slop *n*. 1. unappetizing food 2. sentimentality.

slop-chute *n*. a cheap saloon.

slope *n*. a derogatory term for a Vietnamese.

sloppy *adj*. 1. untidy 2. careless 3. sentimental.

sloppy Joe *n*. a sandwich filled with ground beef in a spiced tomato-based sauce.

sloppy Joe's *n*. any small, cheap restaurant.

slosh, slosh around *v*. 1. to agitate liquid 2. to move something about in liquid 3. to wade, especially in dirty water.

slosh down *v*. to ingest quickly and carelessly.

slot *n*. 1. the means of systematically classifying a person by social status, job function, philosophy, etc. 2. [FOOTBALL] an open area between the offensive end and the tackle.

slot, in the *adj*. ready to perform or to be used next.

slot machine *n*. a mechanical gambling or vending device which is activated by a coin inserted in the slot.

slough off *v*. [BASKETBALL] of a basketball player, to abandon guard of an opponent in order to help a teammate elsewhere.

slough up *v*. to arrest.

slow burn *n*. a progressively worsening anger.

slowdown *n*. [LABOR] a decrease in production or productivity.

slow on the draw *adj*. stupid.

slow on the uptake *adj*. 1. insensitive 2. slow-witted.

slowpoke *n*. 1. a procrastinator 2. a lazy person.

slow, take it *v*. to be careful.

slug *n*. 1. a bullet 2. a drink 3. a blow; a punch 4. a counterfeit coin—*v*. 1. to strike, to punch 2. [PRINTING] to proofread a page of printed matter, usually by checking the end words of lines against a master copy to be sure that a line was not deleted or transposed accidentally.

slug-fest *n*. an exciting fight; hence, an exciting competition. Often used to describe a baseball game with high scores.

slugger *n*. [SPORTS] 1. a strong, aggressive boxer 2. a baseball player adept at batting.

slug-nutty *adj*. dazed from physical or psychological abuse. *See also* punch drunk.

slug on someone, put the *v.* to attack someone physically or verbally.

sluice the worries *v.* to drink alcoholic beverages to forget one's problems.

slum *v.* 1. to seek entertainment in a dilapidated area 2. to associate with people beneath one's social rank, used sarcastically or humorously.

slumber party *n.* a social gathering of adolescent or pre-adolescent girls at which the guests remain over-night.

slumgudgeon, slumgullion *n.* a stew made from scraps of meat and vegetables.

slumlord *n.* an owner of dilapidated dwellings who collects rents but makes no attempt to maintain the buildings.

slumming *n.* 1. going to dilapidated areas for entertainment 2. associating with people of inferior social position, used sarcastically or humorously.

slurp *v.* to eat or drink noisily.

slurpy *adj.* pertaining to food which is often eaten with a great deal of noise.

slush *n.* 1. sentimentality 2. nonsense.

slush fund *n.* 1. contributed money which is used by a politician for any personal use and is not accounted for 2. any money set aside for illegal purposes, such as bribery. From the practice of selling slush—waste grease—from aboard ship for the sailors' personal benefit.

SM *n.* acronym for sado-masochism. *See also* sadie-maisie.

smack *n.* 1. a slap 2. a loud kiss 3. the sound made by a hit or a kiss 4. [DRUG CULTURE] heroin—*v.* 1. to hit 2. to kiss—*adv.* directly. Often in the expression "smack in the middle."

smack-dab *adv.* directly.

smack down *v.* 1. to chastise severely 2. to discredit.

smacker *n.* 1. the mouth 2. a loud kiss 3. a hard blow 4. a dollar.

smackeroo *n.* 1. a defeat 2. a collision 3. a very hard blow 4. a dollar.

small beer *n.* anything insignificant or unimportant. Literally, beer of low alcoholic content.

small bread *n.* an insignificant amount of money.

small fry *n.* children. From fry, the term for baby salmon.

small game *n.* an unambitious goal.

small one *n.* a small quantity of an alcoholic beverage.

small potatoes *n.* anything insignificant or unworthy. Specifically, a small amount of money.

small time *adj.* minor; insignificant.

smart bomb *n.* [MILITARY] a bomb directed to its target by a self-contained guidance system, which responds to a laser beam or television signals, as from an aircraft.

smart alec, smart guy *n.* one who behaves impudently.

smart money *n.* money invested by an expert or by someone with privileged information.

smarty, smarty pants *n.* one who behaves impudently because of an exaggerated feeling of self-importance.

smash *n.* a great success—*adj.* extraordinarily successful.

smashed *adj.* drunk.

smear *n.* 1. calumny 2. a complete defeat—*v.* 1. to slander 2. to defeat conclusively—*adj.* pertaining to calumny. Often in the expression "smear tactics," to ruin an opponent's reputation by calumny.

smell a rat *v.* to sense or suspect deception or a conspiracy.

smeller *n.* the nose.

smidgen *n.* a small amount.

smoke *n.* 1. a cigarette 2. [BASEBALL] a ball thrown so hard and fast that it seems to leave behind a trail of smoke.

smoke eater *n.* a fire fighter.

smoke-filled room *n.* [POLITICS] the proverbial setting for major political deals and decisions.

smoke out *v.t.* to induce a revelation of something hidden. From the process of forcing bees from their nests in hollow trees by making a smoky fire beneath them.

smoke screen *n.* diversionary tactics used to create a misleading impression. From the naval tactic of creating a dense cloud of black smoke to mask ship maneuvers from the enemy.

Smokey, Smokey-the-Bear *n.* [TRUCKERS' CB] a policeman. From the resemblance between Smokey-the-Bear pictured on a forest ranger's hat and the hat worn by many state policemen.

Smokey two-wheeler *n.* [TRUCKERS' CB] a policeman on a motorcycle.

smokin' *adj.* of clothing, having fecal stains.

smooch *n.* a kiss—*v.* to kiss.

smoocher *n.* 1. the mouth 2. one who kisses frequently.

smooth *adj.* clever and appealing.

smooth article, smoothie *n.* 1. a clever person with a pleasant, easy manner 2. a suave, glib, attractive person; usually, a man.

smush *n.* the mouth—*v.* to crush.

snafu *n.* [MILITARY] Army slang, the acronym for situation normal, all fucked up—i.e., a state of confusion, disorder.

snake eyes *n.* [GAMBLING] a throw of the dice resulting in one dot showing on each of the two dice.

snake-in-the-grass *n.* a treacherous person.

snap *n.* 1. energy; enthusiasm 2. an easy task—*v.* to suffer a mental breakdown.

snap course *n.* a course of study, especially in college, which requires little effort to receive a good grade.

snap it up *v.* to hurry. Often used as a command to increase speed.

snap out of it *v.* 1. to recover one's wits quickly after a state of depression or inattention 2. to recover one's strength quickly after an illness.

snapper *n.* a climactic remark at the end of a speech.

snappers *n.* the teeth.

snappy *adj.* 1. lively; energetic 2. attractive.

snappy, make it *v.* to hurry.

snap to it *v.* to begin immediately. Often used as a command to work quickly and well.

snap up *v.t.* to purchase quickly and greedily.

snatch *n.* 1. [CRIME] a robbery 2. a kidnapping 3. a vagina—*v.t.* to steal.

snazzy *adj.* 1. attractive 2. fashionable 3. ostentatious.

sneaky Pete *n.* 1. homemade liquor 2. a clever, deceptive person.

snide *n.* an untrustworthy person.

sniffer *n.* 1. the nose 2. a handkerchief.

sniffy *adj.* haughty; disdainful.

snifter *n.* 1. a small portion of liquor 2. [DRUG CULTURE] one who uses or is addicted to cocaine.

snip *n.* anything easily accomplished.

snipe *n.* a cigarette butt.

snippety *adj.* impertinent.

snitch *v.* 1. to steal 2. to inform. Often, "to snitch on someone": to inform on someone.

snag *v.* [BRITISH SLANG] to kiss, embrace, etc.

snooker *v.* 1. to deceive 2. to swindle. From the billiard game snooker, in which one player can force another to play even when the shot will obviously only result in a foul.

snoot *n.* 1. the nose 2. [BROADCASTING] a funnel-like attachment placed on a light to focus the beam.

snoot full, have a *v.* 1. to be surfeited with anything 2. to be drunk.

snooty *adj.* 1. haughty 2. disdainful.

snooze *n.* a nap—*v.* to sleep.

snop *n.* [DRUG CULTURE] marijuana.

snort *n.* 1. a small drink of liquor 2. [DRUG CULTURE] a quantity of narcotic inhaled through the nose—*v.* [DRUG CULTURE] to inhale a narcotic through the nose.

snot *n.* 1. mucus secreted from the nose 2. an impudent, obnoxious person.

snot-nose *n.* an impudent, haughty person.

snotty *adj.* impertinent; rude.

snow *n.* 1. [DRUG CULTURE] cocaine 2. small white blotches on a televised image owing to poor reception—*v.* to deceive, usually by overwhelming with insincere talk.

snowball *v.* to increase rapidly in speed, size, or scope.

snowball chance *n.* little or no chance at all. Abbreviated form of "as much chance as a snowball in hell (or in July)."

snowbird *n.* [DRUG CULTURE] a cocaine addict.

snowdrop *n.* [MILITARY] a military policeman in the United States Army.

snow job *n.* a deception.

snowshoe *n.* a detective.

snow under *v.t.* to overwhelm with work.

snub out *v.* to crush the lighted end of a cigarette.

snuff *v.* to kill—*adj.* pertaining to sadistic sexual acts during which a person is deliberately killed.

snuff, up to *adj.* 1. of good quality 2. feeling fine.

snuff out *v.t.* to kill.

snug *n.* a small gun.

snurge *v.* to avoid any unpleasant task, person, or situation.

so *interj.* an expression of disdain, disbelief, or disinterest.

soak *v.* 1. to charge exhorbitant prices 2. to drink liquor—*n.* 1. a drinking spree 2. a drunk.

soaked *adj.* drunk.

soaker *n.* a diaper cover.

soak yourself, go *interj.* an expression of irritation at another's actions, attitudes, etc.

so-and-so *n.* a despicable person. A euphemism for any stronger words to describe a dreadful person.

soap *n.* money—*v.* to seek advantage by flattery.

soap box, on one's *adv.* vociferously expounding one's opinion on an issue. Originally, wooden crates made to package soap were used as makeshift platforms to elevate a speaker (a soap box orator) before a crowd, usually for making political speeches.

soap box derby *n.* a race of cars made at home by children.

soap opera *n.* [BROADCASTING] a serialized daily radio or television drama dealing with the tribulations of a group of people. Originally, most such dramas were sponsored by companies selling a variety of soaps and detergents.

soaring *adj.* rapidly increasing.

sob sister *n.* [JOURNALISM] a newspaper columnist who writes excessively sentimental human interest stories; hence, anyone who relishes relating sad tales.

SOB *n.* acronym for son-of-a-bitch.

sob story, sob stuff *n.* a story related to elicit sympathy.

sock *v.* to hit with the fist. Also used as a noun.

sock away *v.t.* to save, especially money, as if hiding it in a sock.

sockeroo *n.* anything that is a great success.

sock it to someone *v.* to tell something to someone plainly, brutally.

socko *adj.* 1. powerful 2. impressive.

soda back *adj.* of whiskey, served with soda in a separate glass.

soda jerk *See* jerk, soda or beer.

sod widow *n.* a woman whose husband has died. *See* grass widow.

sofa lizard *n.* a man who avoids expense by courting a woman at her own residence instead of taking her to places of entertainment.

soft *n.* money that is earned with little effort.

soft, the *n.* money.

soft core *adj.* pertaining to pornography in which sex acts are simulated.

soft drug *n.* [DRUG CULTURE] any nonaddictive narcotic.

softie *n.* a sentimentalist; one easily swayed by an emotional appeal.

soft landing *n.* an easy accomplishment. From the astronaut's landing on the moon, which was accomplished smoothly and carefully.

soft money *n.* 1. paper money 2. money in an inflated economy.

soft pedal *v.t.* to understate the importance of.

soft-sell *n.* the technique of presenting a product or idea in a subtle way—*v.* to promote a product or idea subtly. Also used as an adjective.

soft shell *adv.* 1. not entirely committed (to an idea) 2. pretentiously posturing as.

soft-soap *n.* flattery—*v.* to flatter.

soft touch *n.* 1. a generous person susceptible to emotional appeals 2. one who freely lends money or grants favors 3. one easily deceived.

software *n.* [MILITARY] strategy, as opposed to weapons (hardware).

Sol *n.* the sun.

solar plexus *n.* the upper abdominal region.

soldier *n.* [CRIME] a low-ranking member of organized crime.

solid *adj.* 1. excellent 2. dependable.

solid, Jackson *interj.* excellent.

solitaire *n.* suicide.

solo *v.* to act or live alone.

solo home run *n.* [BASEBALL] a home run hit when no other player is on base.

so long *interj.* a farewell.

some *adj.* 1. excellent 2. superior 3. attractive.

somebody *n.* a person of importance.

some pumpkins *n.* an important person or thing.

something *n.* 1. a person or thing of excellence 2. anything astonishing.

something doing *n.* an interesting or unusual happening.

something else *n.* anything excellent, remarkable, or astonishing.

something going for oneself, have *v.* to have a special skill, talent, etc., which places one at an advantage.

something on the ball, have *v.* to be alert intelligent, or aggressive.

something up one's sleeve, have *v.* [GAMBLING] to have a surprise element that could be decisive in a strategy. From the game of poker, in which dishonest gamblers have been known to keep cards hidden on their person to add to their hand of cards during the game to assure a win.

song *n.* 1. a confession 2. an inexpensive price.

song and dance *n.* evasive speech; excuses, lies, exaggeration. Often used in the construction "give someone a (real) song and dance."

songbird *n.* 1. a female singer 2. an informant.

son-of-a-bitch *n.* a despicable person—*interj.* an exclamation of surprise.

son-of-a-gun *n.* 1. a scoundrel 2. a naughty child—*interj.* an exclamation of surprise.

sooner *n.* 1. one who begins before an official starting time 2. specifically, a settler who claims land before the designated date of settling 3. an Oklahoman 4. an Australian.

SOP *n.* acronym for standard operating procedure.

sop *n.* a drunk.

soph *n.* abbreviation for sophomore, a second year student in high school or college.

soppy *n.* a drunk—*adj.* sentimental.

sore *adj.* angry.

sorehead *n.* 1. one easily angered 2. [POLITICS] one who leaves one political party for another, especially after an imagined offense.

SOS *n.* a request for aid in danger or trouble.

so-so *adj.* mediocre.

so's your old man *interj.* an expression of derision and sarcasm, particularly popular in the 1920s.

soul *n.* 1. deep feeling 2. understanding—*adj.* pertaining to black culture.

soul brother *n.* [BLACK SLANG] a fellow black male.

Soul City *n.* Harlem, the major black community in New York.

soul food *n.* [BLACK SLANG] food typical

of southern black cuisine.

soul kiss *n.* a long, intimate kiss during which the partners' tongues touch.

soul sister *n.* [BLACK SLANG] a fellow black female.

sound *v.t.* 1. to antagonize someone 2. to provoke a fight.

sounding board *n.* a trusted person used to advise on the viability of an idea.

sound off *v.* 1. to call out in response to a roll call 2. to speak loudly, abusively 3. to verbalize one's opinions strongly.

soup *n.* 1. speed 2. nitroglycerin.

soup, in the *adj.* in trouble.

souped up *adj.* 1. of a motor vehicle, adjusted to reach greater speeds than originally intended 2. excited.

soup house *n.* a cheap, low quality restaurant.

soup strainer *n.* a moustache.

soup to nuts, from *adv.* completely; all-inclusive.

soup up *v.t.* to alter the structure of a vehicle or in any way increase its capacity for speed.

soupy *adj.* excessively sentimental.

sour *adj.* 1. unpleasant 2. cantankerous—*v.* 1. to fall into disfavor 2. to go awry 3. to make unpleasant.

sour, go *v.* to spoil.

sour apples, for *adj.* incapable (of doing something) despite the desire, necessity, etc.

sourball *n.* a person who continually complains.

sour grapes *n.* a disparagement of anything desirable but unattainable. From the Aesop fable of the fox who tried to reach some beautiful grapes but found them beyond his reach and consoled himself with the thought that they must have been sour.

sourpuss *n.* a gloomy, unpleasant person.

souse, souse pot *n.* a drunk.

soused *adj.* drunk.

soused to the gills *adj.* extremely drunk.

southpaw *n.* a left-handed person.

south with something, go *v.* to abscond

with something.

sow *n.* an unattractive woman.

sow-belly *n.* bacon.

so what *interj.* an exclamation of indifference, defiance.

sozzled *adj.* drunk.

space cadet *n.* [STUDENT SLANG] a foolish person.

spaced, spaced out, spacey *adj.* 1. [DRUG CULTURE] under the influence of drugs 2. dazed, incoherent, crazy.

space out *v.i.* 1. [DRUG CULTURE] to experience the effects of a narcotic 2. to daydream—*v.t.* to astonish or overwhelm.

spade *n.* a black person.

spade a spade, call a *See* call a spade a spade.

spades, in *See* in spades.

spaghetti Western *n.* a cowboy movie made on a low budget in Italy in imitation of American Westerns.

Spanish fly *n.* an aphrodisiac.

Spanish walk *n.* a forcible ejection, usually by grabbing someone by the collar and pushing him or her all the way out—*v.* walk Spanish.

spank *v.t.* to defeat.

spanker *n.* 1. a swift horse 2. anything outstanding.

spanking new *adj.* 1. just acquired 2. completely unused.

spanking, take a *v.* 1. to be defeated 2. to suffer the consequences of one's acts.

spare *n.* [BOWLING] knocking down all ten pins with the two balls accorded one player in a frame. Also used as a verb.

spare tire *n.* 1. excessive fat around one's waistline or abdomen 2. an extra or unnecessary person 3. a boor.

spark *v.* to woo, especially to kiss and caress.

sparkler *n.* 1. a firework that burns slowly and gives off sparks 2. a diamond.

sparklers *n.* bright eyes.

sparkplug *n.* an energetic person, especially a group member who motivates or activates others.

spas, spastic *n.* a clumsy, unattractive

person—*adj.* weird, demented, foolish.

speak *v.* of a thing, to be expressive, touching.

speakeasy *n.* a public establishment in which illegal liquor is sold. From the era of Prohibition, during which many clandestine drinking places were established to serve the public demand.

speak one's mind *v.* to express oneself forthrightly.

speak one's piece *v.* 1. to orate, i.e., to deliver a speech 2. to express one's opinion on a particular issue.

speak to *v.t.* to rebuke.

spear *n.* a fork—*v.* [SPORTS] to attack an opponent with one's stick (as in hockey) or one's head (as in football) thrust like a spear.

spec, on *adv.* abbreviation for on speculation. Often used to indicate a conditional acceptance for a job, etc.

specs *n.* 1. eyeglasses 2. specifications.

spectacular *n.* an extraordinary show, either (a) a televised variety show featuring many famous performers, or (b) a work of cinema featuring many famous performers, a large cast and beautiful locations, or stunning filming techniques.

speed *n.* 1. [DRUG CULTURE] an amphetamine, especially Methedrine 2. one's usual level of performance, capacity, or taste.

speedball *n.* a rapid and energetic worker.

speed freak *n.* [DRUG CULTURE] an habitual user of amphetamines.

speed merchant *n.* an athlete known for speed in performance.

speed shop *n.* a store specializing in automotive equipment used to customize cars and make them capable of achieving great speed.

speed trap *n.* an area of a public road specially monitored by the police to catch people driving above the speed limit.

speed-up *n.* an acceleration.

speed up *v.* to accelerate.

spellbind *v.* 1. to hypnotize 2. to fascinate.

spellbinder *n.* anything which fascinates. Often used to describe a work of mystery in popular fiction, cinema, etc., or a gifted political orator.

spell out *v.t.* to explain in great detail.

spic, spick *n.* a derogatory term for an Hispanic person.

spic and span *adj.* sparkling clean and neat.

spider *n.* 1. a deceptive or treacherous person 2. a frying pan, especially one with attached legs to facilitate cooking over an open fire.

spiel *n.* 1. a long, involved story 2. a tale of misfortune 3. a vendor's enticing remarks—*v.* to orate.

spiffed out *adj.* dressed elegantly.

spifflicated *adj.* drunk.

spiffy *adj.* 1. stylish 2. attractive 3. well dressed.

spike *n.* 1. [DRUG CULTURE] a homemade hypodermic needle 2. (plural) nails attached to the bottom of shoes to prevent slipping, especially used in sports 3. [ENTERTAINMENT] a mark made on the floor of a stage to indicate placement of set pieces—*v.* 1. to add liquor to a non-alcoholic drink 2. [SPORTS] to injure another player with the spikes on one's sport shoes 3. [ENTERTAINMENT] to mark the floor of a stage to indicate placement of set pieces.

spiked beer *n.* beer with whiskey added.

spikes *n.* 1. women's shoes with high, thin heels 2. athletic shoes with spikes attached to prevent slipping.

spike someone's gun *v.* to prevent someone from accomplishing something.

spill *n.* a fall—*v.* 1. to inform 2. to divulge.

spill, take a *v.* to fall.

spiller *n.* [SURFING] a wave that crests and breaks evenly.

spill one's guts *v.* 1. to express one's emotions freely 2. to relate everything one knows about a particular subject.

spill the beans *v.* to reveal a secret.

spinach *n.* 1. money 2. nonsense.

spindle shanks *n.* 1. thin legs 2. a person with thin legs.

spine *n.* 1. resilience 2. courage.

spinoff *n.* [ENTERTAINMENT] a secondary treatment of a subject based on an earlier successful treatment thereof in a play, television show, novel, etc.; any creative work conceived to exploit the success of an earlier similar work.

spinout *n.* [AUTO RACING] loss of steering control in an auto, causing it to skid and spin.

spit and image, spittin' image *n.* the exact resemblance.

spit ball, spitter *n.* 1. a small wad of paper placed in the mouth and impelled by a sharp breath of air to hit any target 2. [BASEBALL] a ball illegally moistened with saliva by a pitcher in order to cause it to lose altitude abruptly before reaching home plate.

spit box *n.* 1. a cuspidor 2. [RACING] the sample of urine taken from a horse or dog to test for drugs in the system before a race.

spit cotton *v.* to have a parched mouth.

spitting image *n.* the exact resemblance.

spizzerinktum *n.* energy; vitality.

splash *n.* 1. a spectacular event 2. great success 3. a body of water.

splash, make a *v.* to attract attention.

splashy *adj.* ostentatious.

splat *interj.* the sound of something viscous hitting a hard surface, of something being squashed.

splendiferous *adj.* splendid and lush.

splice *v.* to marry.

splice the main brace *v.* to drink liquor.

spliff *n.* [DRUG CULTURE] a marijuana cigarette.

splinter group *n.* a faction that separates itself from a group to become a separate entity.

split *n.* 1. a share; a portion 2. a small bottle of wine, soda water, etc., enough for one serving 3. [BOWLING] the resulting arrangement of pins after the first ball of a frame has been played and leaves two or more pins standing far enough apart to prevent all from being knocked down by the next ball—*v.i.* to leave; to leave quickly—*v.t.* to divide.

split a double *v.* [BASEBALL] to win one game of a double-header. *See* double-header.

split a gut *v.* 1. to expend a great deal of energy 2. to work very diligently.

split end *n.* 1. [FOOTBALL] a player placed far to the side of the rest of the formation to receive passes 2. the bottom of a shaft of hair which becomes damaged and splits.

split hairs *v.* to insist on inordinate precision and fine distinction in an argument or discussion.

split one's sides *v.* to laugh uproariously.

split the uprights *v.* [FOOTBALL] to score an additional point after a touchdown.

split ticket *n.* [POLITICS] in an election, votes cast for candidates from different political parties by one voter—*v.* split one's ticket.

split-up *n.* 1. a separation from someone with whom one was intimate 2. a divorce.

split up *v.* 1. to separate 2. to divorce.

spoiler *n.* 1. a contestant who cannot win but whose presence or performance lessens the chances of another contestant 2. [AVIATION] a flap in the wing of an airplane which can be lifted to increase wind resistance and reduce speed.

spoilsport *n.* one who mitigates another's pleasure.

spoils system *n.* [POLITICS] the distribution of favors by the winning political party in an election.

spondulix *n.* money; coins.

sponge, sponger *n.* 1. a parasitic person 2. a drunk—*v.* 1. to obtain favors, goods, etc., by borrowing or begging 2. to live by depending on the generosity of others.

sponge, throw in the *v.* to admit defeat

From the fighters' practice of throwing an object in the boxing ring to admit defeat.

spoof *n.* 1. a joke 2. a hoax 3. a parody—*v.* 1. to tease 2. to trick.

spook *n.* 1. a derogatory term for a black person 2. a ghostwriter. *See* ghostwriter—*v.* to frighten.

spoon *n.* 1. a fool 2. [DRUG CULTURE] two grams of heroin—*v.* to kiss and caress.

spoony *adj.* foolishly sentimental.

sport *n.* 1. a carefree, fun-loving person 2. a gambler.

sporterize *v.* [SPORTS] to transform an army rifle into a hunting rifle by changing certain parts.

sporting house *n.* 1. a gambling den 2. a brothel.

sporty *adj.* jaunty, carefree, gay.

spot *n.* 1. a small portion of something 2. a place, especially a place of entertainment 3. one's position at work 4. a difficult position 5. [ENTERTAINMENT] abbreviation for spotlight 6. a radio or television commercial—*v.* [SPORTS] to accord an opponent a lead, either as a handicap or by error.

spot, hit the *v.* to be appropriate and satisfying.

spot, in a *adv.* in a difficult situation.

spot, on the *adv.* in an embarrassing situation.

spot breaker *n.* [BROADCASTING] a short commentary, announcement, etc., separating two commercials.

spotlight, in the *adv.* at the center of attention.

spot pass *n.* [SPORTS] throwing the ball to an area of the field or court to be caught by any teammate arriving there first.

spot starter *n.* [BASEBALL] a pitcher who starts a game but does not pitch regularly.

spout *n.* [BRITISH SLANG] a pawn shop.

spray hitter *n.* [BASEBALL] a batter who hits to any area of the field.

spread *n.* 1. a generous assortment and attractive arrangement of food 2. a feature article in a newspaper or magazine 3. [PRINTING] a pair of facing pages containing matter which runs across both pages and is regarded as a single page.

spread it on thick *v.* 1. to exaggerate 2. to flatter excessively.

spread oneself thin *v.* to assume many tasks simultaneously.

spring *v.t.* 1. to free from prison 2. to pay another's expenses.

spring chicken *n.* 1. a young woman 2. an inexperienced person.

spring fever *n.* restlessness experienced with the coming of spring.

spring something on someone *v.* to surprise someone with something.

sprout *n.* a young person.

sprout wings *v.* to die.

spruce up *v.* 1. to groom oneself carefully and dress attractively 2. to clean or renovate a place.

spud *n.* a potato.

spudge around *v.* to be active.

spuds *n.* money.

spur of the moment, on the *adv.* abruptly; quickly.

spurs, win one's *See* win one's spurs.

squab *n.* an attractive woman.

square *adj.* 1. honest; straightforward; trustworthy 2. stodgy; old-fashioned; naive. Also used as a noun.

square a beef *v.* to settle a complaint.

square around *v.* [BASEBALL] of a baseball batter, to stand facing the pitcher.

square deal *n.* a fair treatment.

squarehead *n.* 1. a stupid person 2. a derogatory term for a German or Scandinavian.

square off *v.* to prepare for combat by facing one's opponent.

square oneself *v.* to make amends.

square peg, square peg in a round hole *n.* a misfit.

square shooter *n.* a trustworthy person.

square up *v.* 1. to liquidate one's debts 2. to assume a combative stance.

squash *n.* the face.

squaw *n.* a wife.

squawk *n.* a complaint—*v.* to complain.

squawk box *n.* a public address system.

squeak *v.* to inform.

squeaker *n.* a narrow escape.

squeal *v.* to inform.

squealer *n.* an informer.

squeegee *n.* a boor.

squeeze *n.* 1. a blatant male homosexual 2. [ECONOMICS] a period of attrition 3. pressure to influence another's actions—*v.* to pressure someone.

squeeze box *n.* an accordion.

squeeze on someone, put the *v.* to pressure someone to do something.

squeeze play *n.* [BASEBALL] an attempt by the runner at third base to reach home plate as soon as the pitcher throws the ball to be batted.

squib *n.* a short advertisement.

squib kick *n.* [FOOTBALL] a kick impelling the ball to bounce a relatively short distance.

squiff *v.* to eat voraciously.

squiggle *n.* a short wavy line—*v.* to squirm.

squirrel *n.* a crazy or eccentric person.

squirrelly *adj.* crazy or eccentric.

squirt *n.* 1. a person of short stature 2. a person of little importance.

stab *n.* an attempt.

stab in the back *n.* 1. a betrayal 2. an act of treachery—*v.t.* to betray.

stable *n.* 1. a dirty, messy place 2. a group of individuals in the employ of one person. Used in politics, entertainment, sports.

stable push *n.* inside information.

stack, stacks *n.* a large quantity.

stacked *adj.* of a woman, having a body with large breasts.

stacked deck *n.* 1. [GAMBLING] cards deliberately pre-arranged in order to give a dishonest gambler an assured win; hence 2. any situation with a preordained outcome. Used in the expression "play with a stacked deck."

stack up *v.* 1. to add up; to total 2. to compare.

stag *n.* 1. a male who attends a social gathering without a female companion

2. [BUSINESS] a stock broker not registered with a stock exchange. Also used as a verb.

stag, go *v.* of a male, to go alone to a social function at which both men and women are present.

stage door Johnny *n.* [ENTERTAINMENT] an admirer who waits for a performer at the stage door. Usually a man seeking to woo a chorus girl.

stagefright *n.* [ENTERTAINMENT] nervousness at appearing before an audience.

stagehand *n.* [ENTERTAINMENT] one who works at a theater moving scenery, props, doing lighting, etc.

stage whisper *n.* [ENTERTAINMENT] a whisper made loud enough for the audience to hear.

stag party *n.* a party for men only. Often, a party given for a groom just before his wedding to give him one last taste of bachelorhood.

stag line *n.* the men at a social gathering, a dance, etc., who did not bring female companions and who stand clustered together.

stake *n.* 1. a share in a business venture 2. a wager—*v.* 1. to lend money for a business venture 2. to pay someone's way 3. to wager a certain amount of money on something.

stake, at *adv.* 1. being risked 2. to be gained with the success of a venture.

stake-out *n.* a group, usually of police, hidden in strategic spots to watch the actions of a suspect.

stake out *v.* to spy on the actions of someone from a hidden vantage point.

stakes, pull up *v.* 1. to move 2. to leave a residence, a business, etc.

stall *n.* a delaying tactic—*v.* 1. to delay 2. to procrastinate.

stall off *v.t.* to evade something.

stampede *v.* [POLITICS] to rush to the support of a candidate in an election. Also used as a noun.

stamping ground *n.* a place usually frequented by a specific person or group.

stanch *v.* to begin.

stand a chance *v.* to have a possibility of success.

standard bearer *n.* [POLITICS] the candidate chosen by a political party to lead it to victory.

stand-by *n.* a substitute player in sports or entertainment.

stand by *v.* 1. to wait 2. to act as a substitute player—*interj.* a warning to prepare for an imminent action.

standee *n.* one who stands because no seats are available.

stand for *v.t.* 1. to represent 2. to tolerate.

stand-in *n.* 1. one who substitutes for another 2. [ENTERTAINMENT] an actor who takes the place of a featured player for the setting of lights, etc. Also used as a verb.

standing *n.* in New York City, parking a vehicle for a short time, leaving at least one person in it.

stand in good stead *v.* to be acceptable.

stand-off *n.* a contest with no definitive result, a tied score.

stand off *v.t.* to keep (someone or something) at a distance.

stand-out *n.* anything remarkable.

stand out *v.* to be remarkable.

stand pat *v.* 1. to assume a position and resist change 2. [GAMBLING] to keep the cards dealt instead of exchanging them for others in a game of poker.

stand someone's guts, can't an expression of the intense dislike of another person.

stand someone to something *v.* to pay someone's way.

stand someone up *v.* to fail to appear for an appointment.

stand-up comedian *n.* a performer who entertains by telling jokes, stories, etc., while standing at a microphone.

stand up for *v.t.* 1. to defend (someone or something) 2. to serve as the groom's attendant at a wedding.

stand up with someone *v.* to act as a witness at a wedding.

stanza *n.* [SPORTS] any time division in a sports competition. Used in sportswriting.

star *n.* 1. a celebrity 2. the most important person in a group—*v.* [ENTERTAINMENT] to be the leading actor in a play or movie—*adj.* the most outstanding.

starboard *n.* the right side of a ship.

star boarder *n.* a voracious eater. From the habits of lodgers in boarding houses who often eat greedily.

starch *n.* courage.

stardust *n.* a romantic atmosphere.

stargazer *n.* 1. an astrologist 2. an impractical person, one given to reverie instead of action.

starkers *adj.* naked.

stash *n.* 1. a hiding place 2. [DRUG CULTURE] a hidden supply of narcotics—*v.t.* to hide. Also, stash away.

stat *interj.* [HOSPITAL JARGON] a warning of an emergency requiring immediate response.

static *n.* contention, dissension, or discord.

stay-at-homes *n.* [POLITICS] eligible voters who choose not to vote.

stay bought *v.* to remain loyal to one's source of corruption. Used in politics, business, etc., where bribery is common.

steady *n.* one's exclusive romantic involvement at any given time.

steady, go *v.* to date one person exclusively.

steal *n.* 1. a bargain 2. [BASEBALL] the successful advance of a player from one base to the next when there is no hit—*v.t.* [BASEBALL] steal a base, e.g., first, second, third, or home.

steam, let off (some) *v.* to express anger, as if to relieve oneself of steam pressure.

steamed up *adj.* 1. angry 2. excited.

steam roller *n.* harsh acts or pressure tactics used to destroy any opposition. Also used as a verb and an adjective.

steam up *v.t.* 1. to stimulate; to excite 2. to provoke; to anger.

steel elbow *n.* the ability to use one's

elbow forcefully to push through a crowd.

steep *adj.* extreme.

steer *n.* advice—*v.* advise.

steer, a bum *n.* bad advice.

stems *n.* the legs.

stem to stern, from *adv.* throughout. Literally, from the front to the back of a ship.

step, out of *adj.* old-fashioned.

step, watch one's *v.* to behave circumspectly.

step off the carpet *v.* to wed.

step off the deep end *v.* 1. to involve oneself inadvertently in a complicated problem, situation, etc. 2. to become insane.

step on it *v.* to hurry. Often used as a command. From the use of the accelerator pedal in a vehicle which must be pressed with the foot to increase speed.

step on someone's lines *v.* [ENTERTAINMENT] of a performer, to speak at the wrong time during a production, thus interrupting another performer.

step on the gas *v.* 1. to increase speed in a motor vehicle 2. to hurry. From the accelerator pedal of a motor vehicle which regulates the release of gasoline to the engine.

step on the vocal *v.* [BROADCASTING] of an announcer, to speak over part of a vocal recording.

step out *v.* to seek entertainment away from one's residence, in social engagements, clubs, theaters, etc.

step out of line *v.* to misbehave.

step up *v.i.* to approach—*v.t.* to increase.

stern *n.* the buttocks.

stew *n.* 1. a troublesome situation 2. a confused situation. Often used in the expression "be in a stew"—*v.* 1. to harbor negative feelings 2. to worry 3. to be angry.

stew bum *n.* a drunk.

stewed, stewed to the gills *adj.* drunk.

stew in one's own juice *v.* 1. to harbor negative feelings to one's own detriment 2. to bear the adverse results of

one's acts.

stick *n.* 1. a dull, boring, or emotionless person 2. [DRUG CULTURE] a marijuana cigarette—*v.t.* to entrap someone.

stick around *v.* to remain in a place.

sticker *n.* a knife used as a weapon.

stick in one's craw *v.* of speech, to be inexpressible because of a state of excitement or emotional upset.

stick-in-the-mud *n.* 1. a reactionary 2. a bore.

stick it to someone *v.* 1. to punish someone 2. to exact retribution.

stick it up *v.* a euphemism for "stick it up one's ass," an expression of disdain, annoyance, anger, etc. Often used as an interjection.

stickman *n.* [GAMBLING] an employee at a gambling house, who oversees the play, especially at a dice table, raking in the chips and dice, as with a stick.

stick of gage *n.* [DRUG CULTURE] a marijuana cigarette.

stick of tea *n.* [DRUG CULTURE] a marijuana cigarette.

stick one's neck out *v.* to risk one's safety or comfort. From the practice of chopping off the heads of barnyard fowl; a person is thought to be in the same position of disadvantage when taking a risk.

stick out like a sore thumb *v.* to be obtrusive.

sticks, the *n.* any rural area.

sticktoitiveness *n.* tenacity.

stick to the ribs *v.* of food, to be nourishing or filling.

stickum *n.* glue; any sticky substance.

stick up *n.* an armed robbery—*v.t.* to rob with use of a weapon, usually a gun.

stick up for *v.t.* to defend someone or something.

stick with *v.t.* 1. to remain faithful to 2. to provide with an undesirable thing.

sticky *adj.* 1. humid 2. tenuous.

sticky end of the stick *n.* the least desirable element.

sticky-fingered *adj.* prone to steal.

sticky wicket *n.* a person or situation

which must be handled with patience and intelligence in order to derive a desired result. From the game of cricket.

stiff *n.* 1. a corpse 2. a victim of a swindle; hence, a dupe, a fool 3. a person lacking emotion—*v.t.* to swindle someone—*adj.* 1. ill-at-ease 2. drunk 3. extreme.

stiffneck *n.* a prude.

stiff upper lip, keep a *v.* 1. to be resilient 2. to keep courage.

sting *n.* a swindle—*v.t.* to cheat, swindle.

stinger *n.* 1. an electric heating coil used to warm liquids 2. [BROADCASTING] the final bit of music or sound effects in a commercial.

stingo *n.* [BRITISH SLANG] strong beer or ale.

stink *n.* 1. a noisy argument 2. a clamor—*v.* to be despicable.

stinker *n.* 1. an obnoxious person 2. a difficult task.

stinkeroo *n.* anything inferior, distasteful, or disgusting.

stinking *adj.* 1. obnoxious 2. mean 3. drunk—*adv.* extremely.

stinko *n.* an obnoxious person. Also used as a humorous pet name—*adj.* 1. drunk 2. obnoxious.

stinkpot *n.* an obnoxious person.

stinky *adj.* 1. a malodorous 2. inferior 3. unpleasant. Also used as a humorous pet name.

stir *n.* a jail.

stir crazy *adj.* psychologically disturbed from having spent too much time in prison.

stitches, in *adv.* laughing boisterously.

stomach *v.* to tolerate.

stone *adj.* staunch; firmly committed—*adv.* completely.

stone blind *adj.* drunk.

stone broke *adj.* completely impoverished.

stone cold *adj.* 1. extremely cold 2. dead.

stoned *adj.* 1. drunk 2. [DRUG CULTURE] under the influence of drugs.

stonewall *v.* 1. to pose formidable obstacles in an investigation 2. to obfuscate a matter.

stood in bed, should have a humorous expression of frustration at the futility of one's efforts on a particular day when it might have been better to remain in bed.

stood up *adj.* abandoned or ignored without explanation by one with whom one had a social engagement.

stooge *n.* 1. [ENTERTAINMENT] the member of a team of comedians who is the perpetual victim of the other partner's pranks 2. a dupe; a fool 3. a submissive underling.

stoolie *n.* an informer. Abbreviation for stool pigeon.

stool pigeon *n.* an informer.

stoopnagel *n.* a clumsy, boorish person.

storm *n.* a violent outburst of emotion or excitement.

storm, in a *adv.* 1. angrily 2. excitedly.

storm out *v.* to leave in great anger.

story *n.* a lie.

story teller *n.* a liar.

stow *v.t.* to stop.

stowaway *n.* one who hides in a ship, airplane, etc., in order to obtain free passage—*v.i.* stow away: to hide in a ship, airplane, etc., in order to obtain free passage—*v.t.* stow something away: to eat something, usually voraciously.

stow it *interj.* a command to cease talking.

stow the gab *v.* to cease talking.

STP *n.* [DRUG CULTURE] an hallucinogenic drug. From STP motor oil, supposed to improve the performance of a car's motor.

straddle *v.* to hesitate between alternatives, never fully choosing one.

straight *n.* 1. a heterosexual 2. a non-criminal—*adj.* 1. heterosexual 2. non-criminal 3. trustworthy 4. of whiskey, undiluted—*adv.* 1. truthfully 2. directly.

straight arrow *adj.* 1. trustworthy; honest 2. stodgy; prim. Also used as a noun.

straight face *n.* a countenance displaying no emotion.

straight from the horse's mouth *See* horse's mouth, straight from the.

straight from the shoulder *adv.* directly; honestly.

straight goods *n.* the truth.

straightman *n.* 1. [ENTERTAINMENT] a member of a team of comedians acting as a foil for the comedian who delivers the laugh lines; hence 2. anyone who serves in a secondary position.

straight out *adv.* directly; abruptly.

straight talk *n.* direct and truthful talk.

straight up *adj.* of whiskey, served undiluted by soda, water, or ice.

strange bedfellows *n.* unlikely allies usually brought together by transitory mutual needs. Originally used in politics.

straphanger *n.* a commuter using mass transportation. From the leather straps (or the more modern metal equivalent thereof) found in commuter vehicles to be held by those standing to steady themselves during the ride.

strapped *adj.* without money.

strapped for something *adj.* in need of something.

strapping *adj.* 1. strong 2. large.

straw boss *n.* [LABOR] a supervisor with no real power.

straw hat *adj.* [ENTERTAINMENT] pertaining to theaters located outside of urban centers, usually to summer theaters in small communities.

straw in the wind *n.* an indication of future possibilities.

straw man *n.* 1. a person with no power 2. [POLITICS] an elected official or candidate for office who slavishly follows the directives of a party boss or other hidden power.

straw poll *n.* [POLITICS] a random sample of opinion taken to determine the needs and desires of a constituency.

straws, grasp at *v.* to try desperately to find a solution to a problem.

streak *n.* a period of time marked by a specific characteristic, such as a streak of good luck, a winning streak, etc.

streak *v.* to run naked through a public place—*n.* streaker.

streamer *n.* [JOURNALISM] a headline on a newspaper which runs across the entire width of the page.

street, the *n.* 1. the general area of vice in an impoverished urban setting 2. [BUSINESS] the location of a stock exchange 3. that group of people working in the vicinity of the stock exchange and dealing in stocks.

street Arab *n.* a homeless person, usually a child left to wander the streets.

street fair *n.* an urban festival where stands are set up in the street to sell goods, foods, etc., i.e., an urban carnival.

street life *n.* modern urban existence in impoverished areas where many people congregate in the street for recreation, social contact, etc., and often indulge in or become victims of criminal activities.

street people *n.* homeless people who congregate in the streets and public places of cities. Especially during the late 1960s and early 1970s, the many young people who, feeling alienated from society, took to living in the streets.

street smarts *n.* the ability to live by one's wits in a complicated urban environment.

street theater *n.* a group of performers acting in various public places around the city, using a portable stage or improvising a stage at each playing site in order to bring theater to people who would not normally seek it out.

streetwalker *n.* a prostitute.

streetwise *adj.* clever and assertive in dealing with the problems of modern urban street life.

stretch *n.* a term of imprisonment—*v.t.* 1. to knock down 2. to kill 3. to hang.

strike *n.* 1. [LABOR] a cessation of work in protest 2. [ENTERTAINMENT] removal of set pieces and scenery from a stage at the termination of a production—*v.i.* 1.

[LABOR] to cease work in protest 2. [ENTERTAINMENT] to take apart the scenery after a production is finished—*v.t.* to appear; to seem to someone.

strike a happy medium *v.* to reach a successful compromise.

strike a sour note *v.* 1. to cause unhappiness 2. to make a social blunder 3. to be awkward.

strike home *v.* 1. to deliver an effective remark 2. to deliver an effective blow.

strike it rich *v.* 1. to obtain sudden wealth fortuitously 2. to have sudden good fortune. First applied to miners who struck a vein of gold in their search for precious metals.

strike oil *v.* to have a great and unexpected success.

strike out *v.* 1. [BASEBALL] of a batter, to swing three times at acceptably pitched balls without being able to hit them; hence 2. to fail. Also used as a noun.

string *n.* 1. [SPORTS] players on a team grouped according to their ability: first string are the most proficient 2. [HORSE RACING] the group of horses owned by one stable.

string, on a *adv.* 1. in a state of suspense 2. at someone's mercy.

string along *v.i.* 1. to follow 2. to join— *v.t.* to deceive someone, especially with an implicit promise of reward if certain conditions are met.

string along with someone *v.* to follow someone's lead.

string band *n.* a group of musicians playing together on stringed instruments.

stringbean *n.* a tall, thin person.

strings *n.* an implicit condition that must be fulfilled in order to actualize a contract, an agreement. Often in the expression "no strings attached": a straightforward agreement with no hidden conditions.

strings, pull *v.* to use one's influence to affect a situation.

string up *v.t.* to hang someone.

strip *n.* 1. a street, especially one which is a center of entertainment, of night life 2. a dance during which the performer removes one article of clothing at a time to the rhythm of the music; abbreviation for striptease—*adj.* pertaining to striptease.

strip cell *n.* [PRISON] an empty prison cell.

striper *n.* [MILITARY] one accorded a rank in the armed services, permitting an appropriate stripe to be worn on the uniform sleeve. Usually used with the number of stripes representing the rank: two-striper, four-striper.

stripper *n.* one who performs a striptease dance.

striptease *n.* a burlesque entertainment in which one or more performers remove one article of clothing at a time to the rhythm of music.

strong arm *v.* to use physical force against someone—*adj.* pertaining to violence, aggression.

strong-arm man *n.* [CRIME] one who uses violence to impose his will.

strung out *adj.* 1. crazy 2. dazed 3. [DRUG CULTURE] under the influence of drugs.

strut one's stuff *v.* to display one's proficiency at something.

stub *n.* a short person.

stuck *adj.* incapable of extricating oneself from a difficult situation.

stuck on someone *adj.* enamored of someone.

stuck up *adj.* haughty; self-satisfied; snobbish.

stuck with *adv.* forced to accept.

stud *n.* a sexually attractive and active male.

student *n.* a neophyte, i.e., an inexperienced person.

stuff *n.* money.

stuff, know one's *v.* to be well versed in a particular specialty.

stuff, that's the *interj.* an exclamation of encouragement and support.

stuffed shirt *n.* a pompous person.

stuffy *adj.* 1. ponderous; pretentious; stodgy 2. lacking fresh air.

stumblebum *n.* 1. a clumsy person 2. a derelict.

stump *v.* 1. to baffle 2. [POLITICS] to campaign. From rural campaigns during which a candidate would often stand on a tree stump and address a crowd.

stumper *n.* 1. a baffling problem 2. a politician who travels about making speeches.

stump it *v.* 1. to run away; to escape 2. to travel around the country making political speeches.

stump-jumper *n.* a country dweller.

stung *adj.* swindled

stunned *adj.* drunk.

stunner *n.* 1. an exceptionally attractive person 2. anything extraordinary.

stunning *adj.* 1. remarkable 2. attractive.

stupe *n.* a stupid person.

sub *n.* abbreviation for substitute or submarine—*v.* to substitute for someone.

submarine *n.* 1. a large sandwich made with French or Italian bread 2. [FOOTBALL] a play in which the defensive lineman ducks past the offensive lineman to reach the ball carrier 3. [SURFING] a surfboard too small for its rider—*v.* to execute a submarine play in the game of football.

such-and-such *n.* a rascal.

suck *v.* 1. to commit fellatio 2. to be disgusting, insufficient, stupid, etc.

suck around *v.* to attempt to gain favor by flattery.

sucker *n.* a fool; a dupe.

sucker list *n.* a compilation of names of people easily persuaded to purchase something or donate money.

sucker play *n.* 1. a foolish move 2. [SPORTS] a deceptive act to entrap an opponent or an inadvertent, foolish play.

suck in *v.t.* to deceive.

suck off *v.t.* to perform fellatio on.

suck up to someone *v.* to attempt to gain favor by flattery.

suck wheels *v.* [BICYCLE RACING] to ride directly behind another bicyclist in order to profit from the reduced air pressure and expend less effort to maintain speed.

sudden death *n.* [SPORTS] an additional playing period added to a game ending in a tied score in order to break the tie and accord the win to the first player or team to score.

suds *n.* beer.

sugar *n.* 1. money 2. an affectionate term of address 3. a display of affection 4. [DRUG CULTURE] LSD soaked in a sugar cube.

sugarcoat *v.t.* to render something more acceptable or appealing.

sugarcoated *adj.* appearing initially more pleasant than something actually is.

sugarcoating *n.* a palliative.

sugar daddy *n.* a rich male, usually an older one, who supports his mistress and lavishes expensive gifts on her.

suicide caro, suicide load *n.* [TRUCKERS' CB] a potentially dangerous shipment, such as dynamite, nerve gas, etc.

suicide squad *n.* [FOOTBALL] the group of players used for the most dangerous plays.

suit up *v.* [SPORTS] to don the team uniform just before going to play.

sun belt *n.* that area of the United States noted for its warm climate.

Sunday best *n.* one's finest clothes. Also called Sunday clothes.

Sunday driver *n.* an incompetent driver.

Sunday punch *n.* [BOXING] a prize fighter's most effective punch.

sundowner *n.* 1. a drink of liquor in the evening 2. a strict person, one who would retire early in the evening instead of seeking entertainment.

sunk *adj.* doomed.

sunny *adj.* cheerful; genial.

sunny-side up *adj.* 1. of eggs, fried on one side, leaving the yellow intact and looking like the sun 2. a prone position with the buttocks exposed.

sunshine *n.* [DRUG CULTURE] LSD.

sunshine law *n.* a law against making secret decisions at the government level.

suntan *n.* [BLACK SLANG] a light complexion of a black person.

super *n.* a building superintendent—*adj.* wonderful.

super-duper *adj.* excellent; extraordinary.

superfecta *n.* [GAMBLING] a form of betting in which the gambler wins by picking the four winners of a race in the proper order.

super power *n.* a rich, well-armed nation whose influence is felt worldwide.

superstar *n.* the most prominent celebrity. Coined by Andy Warhol.

supersub *n.* [SPORTS] a substitute player as proficient as the player replaced.

sure-fire *adj.* certain of success.

sure thing *n.* anything that is certain—*interj.* certainly.

surfari *n.* a group of surfboard riders looking for a beach suitable for surfing.

-sville *suffix* the most startling example of whatever adjective is used as the root word, as in "dullsville," meaning extremely dull.

swab *n.* 1. a boor 2. an epaulet; a humorous comment on its resemblance to a mop.

swabbie *n.* a sailor: one who must swab, i.e., mop, the deck of a ship.

swag *n.* booty, i.e., stolen goods.

swagger stick *n.* [MILITARY] a short cane or stick carried by army officers.

swagging *n.* taking business or government property for personal use.

SWAK *adj.* acronym for "sealed with a kiss," of a letter.

swallow *v.* 1. to believe 2. to accept gullibly as the truth.

swallow the anchor *v.* [NAUTICAL] to go ashore.

swank *n.* 1. luxury 2. elegance. Also used as an adjective.

swankily *adv.* 1. with style 2. with assurance.

swankiness *n.* luxury or elegance.

swanky *adj.* 1. luxurious 2. elegant 3. elite.

swan song *n.* a last great work or performance, usually one of great beauty. The swan, a bird normally without song, was thought to burst into song when death was near.

swat *n.* a hard blow—*v.* to strike.

swazzled *adj.* drunk.

swear off *v.t.* to renounce.

sweat *n.* difficulty—*v.i.* 1. to work very hard 2. to worry; to suffer 3. to give information under duress.

sweat, no *interj.* an exclamation that a task can be performed with no difficulty.

sweat blood *v.* to exert oneself strenuously.

sweat box *n.* [PRISON] a small cell used when questioning a suspect.

sweat bullets *v.* to exert oneself strenuously.

sweater girl *n.* a woman with an attractive bosom, who displays it by wearing tight sweaters. A 1950s term.

sweat it *v.* 1. to be apprehensive 2. to endure.

sweat it out *v.* 1. to wait nervously and apprehensively for something to happen 2. to endure hardship to arrive at a goal 3. to obtain information by duress.

sweatshop *n.* [LABOR] a place of employment where management abuses workers with long hours, substandard pay, etc.

swede *n.* a clumsy or awkward person.

sweep *n.* 1. a great victory 2. [BROADCASTING] several recordings played one after the other without interrupting commentary—*v.* 1. to win an overwhelming victory 2. [POST OFFICE JARGON] to remove mail from the shelves for delivery.

sweep, a clean *n.* a great victory in an election, a sports competition, etc.

sweet *adj.* 1. pleasant; charming 2. effeminate.

sweeten *v.* 1. [BROADCASTING] to add pre-recorded laughter to a sound track to accentuate comedic moments 2. [GAMBLING] to add money to the pot before the actual betting begins in a game of poker 3. [BUSINESS] to add valuable securities to one's collateral for a loan.

sweeten up someone *v.* to flatter someone by words or actions in order to win favor, and usually to obtain actual recompense.

sweetheart *n.* 1. a lover 2. a cooperative person 3. anything which is pleasing.

sweetheart contract *n.* [LABOR] a negotiated contract which benefits management and the union but does not benefit the workers.

sweetie *n.* abbreviation for sweetheart; a term of endearment.

sweetie-pie *n.* a diminutive of sweetheart; a term of endearment.

sweet mama *n.* [BLACK SLANG] a female lover.

sweet man, sweet papa *n.* [BLACK SLANG] a male lover.

sweet on someone, be *v.* to be enamored of someone.

sweet pea *n.* a term of endearment; a sweetheart.

sweets *n.* a term of endearment; a sweetheart.

sweet-talk *n.* flattery—*v.* to use flattery to convince someone of something.

sweet tooth *n.* a proclivity or desire for sweet foods.

swell *n.* 1. a fashionably dressed person 2. a member of elite society—*adj.* wonderful, exciting, excellent, stylish, etc.

swelldom *n.* the aggregate group of the stylish and elite.

swelled head, have a *v.* to be extremely proud of oneself.

swellhead *n.* an egotist.

swig *n.* a drink; a gulp—*v.* to drink in gulps.

swim, in the *adj.* successful; knowledgeable; alert to current styles.

swing *n.* 1. a trip; a tour 2. an attempt 3. a style of jazz music played by the big bands of the 1930s 4. [ENTERTAINMENT] an understudy, particularly a dancer covering several roles in a musical production—*v.i.* 1. to be hanged 2. to lead a profligate life 3. [SPORTS] to play two positions equally well on a team—*v.t.* to accomplish something successfully.

swing, in full *adv.* at a maximum; at an apogee.

swing both ways *v.* to be bisexual.

swinger *n.* 1. one leading a profligate life 2. one alert to current customs 3. [SPORTS] a team member who covers two positions.

swinging *adj.* lively, sophisticated, ultrafashionable, etc.

swingles *n.* a contraction of "swinging singles," unmarried people leading a profligate life. Also used as an adjective.

swing man *n.* 1. [SPORTS] a player who plays two positions equally well, especially in basketball 2. [DRUG CULTURE] a drug dealer.

swing room *n.* [POST OFFICE JARGON] a lunch room.

swing voter *n.* [POLITICS] a voter who does not strictly adhere to one party's choice of candidates and who is more influenced by issue or personality than party affiliation. This voter often swings (changes the determination of) an election.

swipe *v.* to steal; to pilfer.

swish *n.* an effeminate male homosexual. Also used as an adjective.

swisher *n.* [BASKETBALL] a ball which passes through the basket without touching the rim.

swishy *adj.* effeminate.

switcher *n.* [POLITICS] a voter registered with one party who votes for candidates from another party.

switcheroo *n.* a sudden and surprising reversal.

switch hitter *n.* 1. [BASEBALL] a baseball player who can bat either left- or right-handed 2. a bisexual.

sync, in (or **out of**) *adj.* synchronized (or not properly synchronized). Usually of a soundtrack and image which must be properly coordinated for a movie.

syph *n.* abbreviation for syphilis.

T

T *n.* 1. [BASKETBALL] abbreviation for a technical foul, a violation of the rules not involving personal contact or injury to an opponent 2. [FOOTBALL] a formation of players on the offensive in the approximate form of a letter T.

tab *n.* 1. a bill, i.e., a tabulation of cost 2. [DRUG CULTURE] a capsule containing LSD.

table-hop *v.* to move from table to table at a private social gathering or a public restaurant or night club in order to socialize with acquaintances.

tackhead *n.* a stupid person.

tacky *adj.* 1. inferior 2. garish 3. dishonorable.

tad *n.* a child.

tail *n.* 1. the buttocks 2. a sexually attractive person 3. a person who follows another in secret—*v.t.* to follow in secret.

tail, have something by the *v.* to have something fully under control.

tail bone *n.* the buttocks.

tail female *n.* [HORSE RACING] a race horse's female lineage.

tailgate *v.* of a driver of a motor vehicle, to follow another vehicle too closely.

tail male *n.* [HORSE RACING] a race horse's male lineage.

tailor-made *adj.* perfectly suitable.

tail piece *n.* [PRINTING] a small line ornament used at the end of a chapter.

take *n.* 1. the sum of money earned in any endeavor 2. an individual share in profits 3. bribe money 4. [BROADCASTING/FILM] the taping or filming of a scene—*v.t.* to cheat someone.

take, on the *adj.* receiving bribes.

take a bath *v.* to be wiped out financially.

take a crap *v.* to defecate.

take a dive *v.* [BOXING] to feign injury, thus to lose a fight on purpose.

take a gander *v.* to look.

take a leak *v.* to urinate.

take a powder *v.* to leave rapidly.

take a raincheck *v.* to accept a postponement.

take a shot *v.* to take a risk. Often used as a command to give something a try.

take a walk *v.* [POLITICS] to give support to a candidate of an adversary party.

take down a peg or two *v.t.* to humiliate. From the practice of the British Navy in the eighteenth century to raise or lower a flag to signal a ceremony for a change in rank—to raise for a promotion, to lower for a demotion.

take five *v.* to take a brief rest period, one lasting five minutes.

take gas *v.* [SURFING] to lose control of one's surfboard.

take in *v.* 1. to dupe 2. to see and understand 3. of a garment, to make smaller.

take it *v.* to withstand something unpleasant.

take it away *v.* to begin.

take it lying down *v.* to accept meekly.

take it on the chin *v.* 1. to receive a hard blow 2. to withstand misfortune with courage.

take it on the lam *v.* 1. to leave quickly 2. to escape.

take off *n.* 1. a parody 2. a beginning—*v.* 1. to leave 2. to go on a short holiday 3. [DRUG CULTURE] to feel the effects of a narcotic.

take off the gloves *v.* 1. to concede a loss 2.

166

to give up. From the boxer's gesture of removing his gloves at the end of a match.

take on *v.t.* 1. to assume responsibility for 2. to engage in an argument, a fight.

take-out *adj.* pertaining to food prepared in a restaurant and taken home to be eaten.

take someone for *v.t.* 1. to swindle someone out of 2. to cheat someone.

take someone to the cleaners *v.* to swindle someone of all of their money.

take something with a grain (or **a pinch**) **of salt** *v.* to deem something to be of little consequence.

take ten *v.* to take a brief rest period, one lasting ten minutes.

take the bull by the horns *v.* 1. to confront an adversary 2. to face a problem.

take the cake *v.* to be extraordinary, remarkable.

take the count *v.* [BOXING] of a boxer, after having been knocked down, to be unable to rise while the referee counts to ten and then declares the opponent to be the winner by a knockout.

take the rap *v.* to accept guilt and any punishment imposed for a crime.

talk big *v.* to brag.

talkies *n.* motion pictures with sound. Used especially in the 1930s to distinguish them from silent pictures.

talk shop *v.* to discuss business, especially during one's free time—*n.* shoptalk.

talk someone's ear (or **head**) **off** *v.* to talk excessively.

talk through one's hat *v.* 1. to talk idly 2. to exaggerate 3. to lie.

talk turkey *v.* to speak forthrightly and seriously about something.

T and A *n.* 1. an acronym for tits and ass 2. [BROADCASTING] sex in television shows.

tangle *n.* an argument; a fight—*v.* to argue; to fight.

tank *n.* a jail cell.

tank *v.* to lose a contest or competition on purpose—*n.* tank job.

tanked, tanked up *adj.* drunk.

tank town *n.* a very small town.

tank up *v.* to become drunk.

tap *v.t.* to request a loan from someone.

tape measure job *n.* [BASEBALL] a particularly far flying ball batted for a home run.

tapped out *adj.* without any money.

tar *n.* 1. coffee 2. a sailor.

tar beach *n.* the rooftop of a city building used by residents for sun bathing. Often the roof is covered with tar for waterproofing.

tarp *n.* a tarpaulin.

tart *n.* a prostitute.

task force *n.* [MILITARY] 1. a group of soldiers selected for assignment to combat 2. a euphemism for committee, used in business and politics.

taste *n.* a small amount.

ta-ta *interj.* a parting salutation.

tattletale *n.* one who reveals the misdeeds of others, i.e., an informer—*v.* to tell of another's misdeeds.

taxi dancer *n.* a woman employed by a dance hall to partner paying customers in a dance.

taxi squad *n.* [FOOTBALL] football players hired in excess of the number permitted a team, who practice with the regular players but do not play in games, waiting to replace regular players in the future. From the practice of Arthur McBride of the Cleveland Browns who, in the 1940s, hired more football players than permitted for a team and used them to drive taxis for his taxi-cab company to justify their salaries.

T-bone *n.* [AUTO RACING] a collision in which a car hits the side of another car at a perpendicular angle or hits any object at such an angle.

TD *n.* [FOOTBALL] a touchdown.

tea *n.* [DRUG CULTURE] marijuana.

tead up *adj.* [DRUG CULTURE] experiencing the effects of marijuana.

tea kettle *n.* [BROADCASTING] a small commercial radio station that reaches only a small audience.

tear at *v.* to attack (someone).

tear-jerker *n.* 1. a work of popular literature, cinema, etc., which is designed to move the reader or spectator to tears 2. an explanation used to evoke sympathy.

tear off *v.* 1. to take 2. to receive.

tear off a piece *v.* to coit.

tear up the peapatch *v.* to behave obstreperously.

teaser *n.* 1. one who excites sexually, but ultimately offers no gratification 2. [ENTERTAINMENT] the scenery piece hung just behind the proscenium arch to demarcate the upper limits of an audience's view of a stage.

tea-stick *n.* [DRUG CULTURE] a marijuana cigarette.

tech *n.* abbreviation for 1. technology 2. a school of technology—*adj.* technical.

technocrat *n.* [POLITICS] one who wields power in policy-making through scientific knowledge.

tee off *v.t.* to anger.

teed off *adj.* angry.

teed up *adj.* drunk.

teen *n.* an adolescent.

teeny bop drive *n.* [BROADCASTING] the evening hours when teenagers driving with friends form the major car radio listening audience.

teenybopper *n.* a young adolescent devotee of the currently popular music.

telegraph *v.* to communicate subtly by physical gesture, often to indicate a reaction inadvertently.

telephone numbers *n.* [CRIME] bribery payments in five figure numbers.

tell it to the Marines *interj.* an exclamation of disbelief. From the British Navy's traditional belief that the Marines are gullible.

tell off *v.* to chastise.

tell someone where to get off *v.* to establish clearly one's limits of tolerance of another's annoying, angering behavior.

ten, tenner, ten spot *n.* a ten-dollar bill.

ten, take *See* take ten.

tenderfoot *n.* a neophyte. Originally, a seventeenth-century term for a young horse.

Tenderloin *n.* 1. a district in midtown New York at the turn-of-the-century which was a center of vice and corruption. Named for the choicest cut of meat by the police who received excellent bribes from criminals wishing to continue their illegal pursuits in the area 2. now, any area that is the center of vice in a city.

10-4 *interj.* [THE CB or POLICE 10 CODE] message received, understood.

tennis elbow *n.* an inflammation of the muscles of the arm often resulting from vigorous play at tennis by one not in the proper physical shape, or from any similar exertion.

tennis shoes *n.* [TRUCKERS' CB] tires for trucks.

ten-percenter *n.* an agent who receives a ten percent commission from a client's wages.

ten spot *n.* a ten-dollar bill.

ten-vee *adj.* the worst; the most inferior.

terrific *adj.* wonderful; exciting; admirable.

Texas leaguer *n.* [BASEBALL] a fly ball which lands between the infield and the outfield and is not caught before hitting the ground.

that ain't hay *interj.* an expression of admiration, often for a large sum of money.

that-a-way *adj.* pregnant.

that kills it *interj.* an expression of resignation, disappointment, frustration, anger, at any element which ruins a plan, a situation, etc.

that rings a bell *interj.* an expression of recognition, remembrance.

that's all she wrote *interj.* an expression of finality: there is no further information beyond that which was just stated.

that's the boy, that's the girl *interj.* *See* attaboy, attagirl.

that's the ticket *interj.* an expression of

encouragement, admiration, etc., at an apt gesture, word, observation, etc.

that's the way the ball bounces, the cards are stacked, the cookie crumbles, etc. *interj.* a humorous expression of resignation to life's vagaries.

that way *adj.* 1. enamored of someone 2. pregnant.

there, not all *adj.* 1. crazy 2. stupid.

there you go *interj.* an expression of encouragement when someone has begun doing or saying the right thing.

there you go again *interj.* an expression of annoyance at repeated verbiage or bad behavior.

thermos bottle *n.* [TRUCKERS' CB] a truck carrying a liquid cargo.

thick *adj.* stupid.

thick, in *adj.* closely associated (with someone) 2. deeply involved (in something).

thick as thieves *adj.* 1. involved in a plot 2. closely associated.

thick-skinned *adj.* insensitive.

thin *adj.* 1. having little money 2. insubstantial 3. [SPORTS] of a team, lacking a core of excellent players.

thinclad *n.* [RACING] a member of a track racing team.

thin dime *n.* a very small amount of money.

thin dime, not have a *v.* to have no money.

thin dime, not worth a *adj.* inferior; worthless.

thing *n.* 1. one's field of interest or expertise 2. the penis.

thing, do one's own *v.* to behave entirely in accordance with one's own wishes.

thing about, have a *v.t.* 1. to have a predilection for 2. to have an aversion to.

thingamabob, thingamajig *n.* any object for which the proper name is not known.

think box *n.* the brain.

thinker *n.* the brain.

think piece *n.* an article, column, etc., in a newspaper, magazine, etc.

think tank *n.* 1. [POLITICS] a group of highly-qualified advisers to the President, usually at the vanguard of national defense; hence 2. any group of highly-skilled, intelligent people determining policy.

thin one *n.* a dime.

third degree *n.* intensive questioning, often involving torture, to learn desired information.

third rate *adj.* inferior.

third sex, the *n.* homosexuals.

third wheel *n.* anyone extraneous, unnecessary, or unwanted.

third world *n.* [POLITICS] 1. the newly formed or traditionally poor nations of the world 2. any poor, uneducated, or politically weak group within a country. Also used as an adjective.

thirty-three *n.* a phonograph record which plays at thirty-three revolutions per minute.

thou *n.* a thousand dollars.

threads *n.* clothing.

thread the needle *v.* [SPORTS] 1. to throw a ball within a very specific limited area 2. to run through a well-guarded area of a playing field, avoiding all opposing players.

three bagger, three-base hit *n.* [BASEBALL] a hit permitting the batter to run a total of three bases.

three-dollar bill *n.* an eccentric.

three-letter man *n.* a homosexual.

three-point landing *n.* 1. [AVIATION] a perfect landing of an airplane; hence 2. any successful culmination.

three-point stance *n.* [FOOTBALL] a body position in which both feet remain on the ground slightly apart, legs are bent at the knees, the body is bent forward, and one hand touches the ground, often in preparation for passing the ball.

three-ring circus *n.* 1. confusion 2. anything chaotic.

three sheets to the wind *adj.* drunk.

throat, cut one's own *v.* to behave in a self-destructive manner.

throat, cut someone's *v.* to behave

treacherously.

throat, jump down someone's *v.* to chasten severely.

through the mill, put *See* put through the mill.

through the wicket *adv.* [SPORTS] of a ball, passing between the outspread legs of a player.

through thick and thin *adv.* under all circumstances.

throw *v.* to lose a contest deliberately.

throw a fit *v.* to become furious or extremely upset about something.

throw a party *v.* to plan and host a social gathering.

throw in the towel, the sponge *v.* [SPORTS] to concede a loss. From the practice in boxing of tossing an object in the ring when a fighter can no longer fight in a match.

throw someone's name around *v.* to mention the name of an important person as a friend in order to gain some advantage.

throw the book at someone *v.* 1. to prosecute someone to the fullest extent of the law 2. to punish or chastise someone to a serious extent.

throw the bull *v.* to talk idly, gossip, exaggerate, or lie.

throw the hooks into *v.* 1. to cheat someone 2. to manipulate someone.

thruput *n.* 1. the state of a problem in the process of being resolved 2. a situation as it stands at any given moment.

thrust *n.* 1. import 2. meaning.

thumb, thumb a ride *v.* to signal with one's thumb the direction in which one hopes to travel in order to attract a driver to stop his or her vehicle and take on a passenger.

thumb, on the *adv.* traveling by thumbing a ride.

thumb one's nose at *v.t.* 1. to scorn 2. to mock.

thumbprint n. 1. one's identifying predilections 2. one's personality.

thumbs down *n.* a sign of rejection. From ancient Rome, the gesture supposed to indicate the fate of a gladiator whom the spectators condemned to death.

thumbsucker *n.* [JOURNALISM] a political analysis written to provoke thought.

thusly *adv.* thus.

ticked off *adj.* angry.

ticker *n.* the heart.

ticket *n.* [POLITICS] the candidates representing one political party in an election.

ticket, that's the *See* that's the ticket.

tick, full as a *adj.* drunk.

ticketyboo *adj.* fine, excellent, in working order, etc.

tickled pink *adj.* extremely pleased.

tickler *n.* a moustache.

tickle the ivories *v.* to play the piano.

tickling *n.* [FISHING] catching fish with one's hands, usually by grabbing the fish at the gills.

tick tock *n.* [JOURNALISM] the chronological background of a major event or decision.

tidbits *n.* 1. small pieces 2. bits of gossip.

tiddly *adj.* drunk.

tied *adj.* married.

tied down *adj.* occupied; busy.

tied up *adj.* 1. of a person, occupied 2. of a situation, completed to one's satisfaction.

tie-in *n.* 1. a connection 2. a relation.

tie into *v.t.* to attack someone physically or verbally.

tie it up *v.* 1. to complete successfully 2. to resolve a problem.

tie one on *v.* to get drunk.

tie out *v.* [POST OFFICE JARGON] to bundle and dispatch mail from the post office.

tiger *n.* an energetic, aggressive person.

tiger, paper *See* paper tiger.

tight *adj.* 1. drunk 2. penurious.

tight as a tick *adj.* drunk.

tight-ass *n.* a prudish, rigid person—*adj.* tight-assed.

tight money *n.* an economically depressed situation in which it is difficult to earn money.

tight spot *n.* a difficult situation.

tightwad *n.* a miserly person.

Tijuana taxi *n.* [TRUCKERS' CB] a police vehicle with flashing lights and decorated with the local insignia.

tilt at windmills *v.* to engage in futile efforts. From Cervantes' *Don Quixote*, in which the self-styled knight-errant sees windmills as wicked giants to combat.

timber *interj.* 1. a warning to beware of imminent physical danger 2. a cry of triumph at the successful completion of anything.

time, have oneself a *v.* to enjoy oneself.

time of day, not give someone the *v.* 1. to ignore someone 2. to refuse to acknowledge someone in any way.

time of one's life, have the *v.* to enjoy oneself immensely.

tin *n.* 1. a police badge 2. a member of a police force.

tin can *n.* an old, dilapidated ship.

tin cow *n.* canned milk.

tin-horn *n.* a braggart—*adj.* inferior, cheap, tawdry.

tinker's dam *n.* 1. anything insignificant 2. nothing. Often used in the expressions "not worth a tinker's dam," and "not give a tinker's dam." From the small lumps of putty-like substance used by tinkers in former times to repair cracked pots and pans.

tin lizzie *n.* 1. a Model-T Ford 2. an old, dilapidated automobile. "Lizzie," an abbreviation for limousine.

Tin Pan Alley *n.* the area of a city associated with the popular music business.

tinsel teeth *n.* 1. teeth with metal braces 2. a derogatory term for one who wears orthodontic braces.

tinsel town *n.* Hollywood.

tin star *n.* a detective.

tip *n.* advice.

tip off *n.* 1. a warning 2. a hint—*v.* to warn.

tip one's elbow *v.* to become drunk.

tip one's mitt *v.* to betray oneself.

tip over *v.* to rob.

tipster *n.* one who gives advice, who informs.

tipsy *adj.* slightly drunk.

tip-top *adj.* the best; excellent.

tired *adj.* trite, as in "a tired idea."

tit for tat *n.* petty retaliation to equalize offenses.

tits *n.* a woman's breasts.

tits, how are your *interj.* a rude or casual greeting, the equivalent of "how are you?"

tizzy *n.* 1. emotional confusion 2. distress.

TKO *n.* acronym for technical knockout, a decision rendered by the official judges of a boxing match in which neither fighter has been knocked out, but one seems severely weakened and would not be able to continue the fight without incurring great injury.

TLC *n.* acronym for tender, loving care.

toad *n.* a despicable person.

toady *v.* to attempt to gain favor by flattery and by performing services for those in a position of power. Also, "toady up to someone." Also used as a noun.

to a T *adv.* precisely, exactly, perfectly. Possibly from "to a tittle," an expression with the same meaning popular in sixteenth-century England.

to boot 1. in excess of something 2. in addition to.

toff *n.* [BRITISH SLANG] a fashionable, upper-class person.

together *adj.* 1. calm 2. self-assured 3. alert.

together, get it *v.* 1. to organize one's thoughts or actions in pursuit of a goal 2. to become self-assured, relaxed, alert.

together, get one's act *v.* to organize one's thoughts or actions in pursuit of a goal.

together, go *v.* to date someone regularly.

togs *n.* clothing.

toke *n.* an inhalation of smoke from a tobacco or a marijuana cigarette—*v.* to smoke.

tokus *n.* [YIDDISH] the buttocks.

tomato *n.* a sexually attractive woman.

tomboy *n.* a girl who enjoys or excels at pursuits formerly assumed to be of interest only to boys.

tombstone *adj.* pertaining to the dead.

tombstone loans *n.* [CRIME] bank loans made under the names of dead people by underworld figures who then use the money for illegal enterprises, such as usury.

tombstone votes *n.* [CRIME] votes cast illegally by using the names of dead people at the polls in order to assure a candidate's victory.

tomcat *n.* a man in search of a sexual partner—*v.* to seek a sexual partner.

tommy *n.* a British soldier.

tommy gun *n.* a machine gun.

tongue *n.* one who speaks for another.

tongue-in-cheek *adv.* facetiously.

ton of bricks, hit someone like a *v.* to surprise or overwhelm someone.

Tony *n.* any of the awards given annually in the United States for special achievement in the theater.

tony *adj.* 1. luxurious 2. stylish 3. ironic.

too big for one's breeches See breeches, too big for one's.

toodle-oo *interj.* a parting greeting.

tool *n.* 1. one who is easily duped 2. a student who studies too diligently 3. the penis—*v.* to drive an automobile.

too much *adj.* outstanding; overwhelming. Also used as an interjection of admiration.

toot *n.* a drinking spree—*v.* [DRUG CULTURE] to sniff cocaine.

toot, on a *adv.* indulging in a drinking spree.

toothpick *n.* a tall, thin person.

too-too *adv.* excessively.

toots, tootsy *n.* a beloved; often an affectionate term of address.

tootsies *n.* the feet.

top *n.* 1. the first part 2. the beginning—*v.t.* to improve on another's performance—*adj.* best.

top, blow one's *v.* to become angry.

top banana *n.* the most important comedian in a vaudeville show.

top dog *n.* the most important person in any organization—*adj.* 1. the best 2. the most important.

top drawer *adj.* 1. the most important 2. the best.

top hole *adj.* [BRITISH SLANG] first rate.

topic A *n.* [JOURNALISM] the most important news story.

top notch *adj.* 1. the best 2. the most skillful.

topper *n.* a remark, joke, etc., that tops or surpasses all preceding ones.

tops *n.* the best. Also used as an adjective.

top seeded *adj.* [SPORTS] the best in a category.

top story *n.* the head.

torch *n.* [CRIME] an arsonist—*v.* to commit arson.

torch (for someone), carry a *v.* to be enamored (of someone).

torch song *n.* a sentimental song treating unrequited love or lost love.

tormentor *n.* [ENTERTAINMENT] the curtains or pieces of scenery placed at the extreme right and left at the front of a stage to mask the extreme sides from the audience's view.

torpedo *n.* 1. a large sandwich made on Italian or French bread or a roll 2. [CRIME] a paid assassin.

toss a party *v.* to plan and host a social gathering.

toss one's cookies *v.* to vomit.

toss up *n.* an arbitrary choice. From the practice in basketball of tossing a ball up between two opposing players who each try to tap it to their team's side to determine which team should gain possession of the ball.

total *v.* 1. to destroy completely 2. to kill.

totem pole, high man on the *n.* a person of authority and importance.

totem pole, low man on the *n.* a person of little authority and importance.

touch *n.* 1. one who lends money freely 2. a request for a loan—*v.* to ask for a loan.

touché *interj.* an exclamation of triumph over an opponent's confusion and momentary inability to respond to a challenge or insult. From the fencing term indicating that one has been touched by an opponent's foil.

touch-up *n.* [PRINTING] handwork on a negative, positive, or artwork.

touch up *v.* to remove spots or unwanted lines, or to improve the reproduction characteristics of a picture.

tough *adj.* 1. excellent 2. unfortunate.

tough buck *n.* money that was difficult to earn.

toughie *n.* anything difficult or tough.

tough it out *adj.* to remain firm or unyielding in the face of difficulty, adversity, etc., often in a brazen or defiant way.

tough shit *interj.* an expression of disdain, annoyance.

tough something through *v.* to face an unpleasant situation boldly or stoically.

tout *n.* [GAMBLING] one who encourages betting, especially by selling privileged information about a race, a contest. Also used as a verb.

town, go to *v.* to do anything with great enthusiasm.

town, on the *adv.* seeking entertainment at various public places around town, such as night clubs, dances, etc.

townie *n.* a native of a town, especially as opposed to a student attending college in the town.

track record *n.* 1. [RACING] the tabulation of a racer's speeds and distances covered 2. anticipated successes of a person or an organization based on past record of success.

tracks *n.* [DRUG CULTURE] marks on the body of an addict caused by repeated injections of narcotics.

tracks, make *v.* to leave rapidly.

trade-off *n.* 1. a compromise in a political bargain 2. any compromise. Also used as a verb.

traffic *n.* [SPORTS] the concentration of players in one area of a playing field.

tragic magic *n.* [DRUG CULTURE] heroin.

trailer *n.* a short film which serves as an advertisement for a feature motion picture.

train *n.* 1. coitus with a succession of different partners 2. [SURFING] a series of waves—*v.* "pull a train": of a woman, to coit with several different partners, one right after the other.

tramp *n.* 1. an immoral woman 2. a prostitute.

trap *n.* the mouth.

traps *n.* drums.

trash *n.* 1. nonsense 2. poor, uneducated people—*v.* 1. to vandalize; to destroy 2. to thrash 3. to search through trash to salvage any usable objects.

trashy *adj.* 2. inferior 2. sensational 3. gaudy, garish.

trembler *n.* [PRISON] a prisoner who appears afraid of other prisoners.

trendy *adj.* currently popular.

trey *n.* 1. a three in a deck of cards. 2. [DRUG CULTURE] a three-dollar quantity of cocaine.

trial balloon *n.* 1. anything used to test public reaction before committing oneself to a plan, an idea, etc. 2. [POLITICS] an idea offered by a politician anonymously to test public reaction. Originally, trial balloons were launched to test wind strength and direction before a manned balloon flight.

trick *n.* 1. a prostitute's customer 2. a sexual partner.

trifecta *n.* [GAMBLING] a gambling game in which the bettor must correctly indicate the three winners of a race in the correct order in which they finish in order to win.

trigger *v.* to serve as a catalyst. Also, "trigger off."

triggerhappy *adj.* eager to shoot.

trim *v.t.* to defeat soundly.

trip *n.* 1. [DRUG CULTURE] a period of hallucination caused by a drug 2. any exciting experience—*v.* [DRUG CULTURE] to experience the effects of an hallucinogenic drug.

trip, bad *n.* 1. a frightening or distressing experience caused by taking an hallucinogenic drug 2. any distressing or frightening experience.

tripe *n.* nonsense.

triple bogey *n.* [GOLF] a score of three strokes over par made on one hole.

Triple Crown *n.* 1. [HORSE RACING] the distinction of one horse winning the three major horse races of the year in the United States: the Preakness, the Kentucky Derby, and the Belmont Stakes 2. [SPORTS] the distinction of a baseball player who leads the league in a given year in batting average, home runs, and runs batted in.

triple header *n.* a sporting event consisting of three scheduled competitions.

triple play *n.* [BASEBALL] one play resulting in three players being put out.

triple threat *n.* 1. [FOOTBALL] a football player proficient in kicking, running, and passing the ball 2. anyone adept in three fields or areas of pursuit.

trip up *v.t.* 1. to confuse 2. to entrap.

trolley, off one's *adj.* crazy.

trom *n.* abbreviation for trombone.

troops *n.* 1. [POLITICS] the supporters working for a candidate's election 2. any group of supporters.

trot out the ghosts *v.* [POLITICS] to call to mind past great statespersons belonging to one's own political party, in order to profit from the reflected glory and to remind of the failures and mediocre politicians of the opposing party in order to discredit it.

trots *n.* 1. [HORSE RACING] harness racing 2. diarrhea.

truck *v.* 1. to transport something 2. to live casually.

trull *n.* [THIEVES' slang] a prostitute or trollop.

trump up *v.* to falsify.

trumped up *adj.* artificial; false.

try-out *n.* 1. an experiment; a test 2. a test of one's ability, especially in a sport 3. an audition.

try out *v.i.* to be tested for membership on a team, for suitability for a role in a play, etc.—*v.t.* to experiment; to test.

TS *interj.* acronym for tough shit, an expression of scorn.

tsuris *n.* [YIDDISH] 1. misfortune 2. misery.

tub *n.* 1. a boat 2. a fat person 3. a large quantity of something.

tube, the *n.* a television set.

tub of lard *n.* a fat person.

tuchus, tukkis *n.* [YIDDISH] the buttocks.

tucker *n.* [AUSTRALIAN SLANG] food.

tuck shop *n.* [BRITISH SLANG] a bakery or confectionery, especially near a school.

tumble *n.* a chance—*v.* "give someone a tumble": to give someone a chance, an opportunity.

tumble *v.* to comprehend.

tummy *n.* the abdomen; the stomach.

tuneout *n.* [BROADCASTING] any element that displeases a listener and is responsible for the loss of listeners to a particular broadcast—*v.* to cease listening.

tune-up *n.* a general repair to insure proper operation of a mechanical device.

tune up *v.* to put in proper running order.

turf *n.* a neighborhood area regarded by someone, especially a street gang, as its own territory or domain.

Turk *See* young Turk.

turkey *n.* 1. [ENTERTAINMENT] a failure 2. [BLACK SLANG] a fool 3. a coward 4. [DRUG CULTURE] a capsule purported to contain drugs, but actually containing only a placebo 5. [BOWLING] three strikes scored one right after the other.

turkey-shoot *n.* anything easy to accomplish or perform.

turn *v.* to earn money.

turn a deaf ear *v.* 1. to ignore 2. to disdain.

turn blue *interj.* an abrupt, rude dismissal.

turncoat *n.* a traitor. Literally, one who turns a coat inside out to hide a uniform associated with the losing side in a battle.

turn down *v.* to reject.

Turner *n.* a German.

turn in *v.* 1. to go to bed 2. [CRIME] to surrender, as to the police.

turnip *n.* [OLD SLANG] a pocket watch.

turn off *n.* anything depressing, repulsive, or boring.

turn off *v.i.* to feel repelled or bored—*v.t.* to create feelings of depression or disgust.

turn-on *n.* anything exciting, stimulating, or pleasing.

turn on *v.i.* [DRUG CULTURE] to feel the pleasant effects of a narcotic; to take drugs for the pleasurable effects they bring—*v.t.* 1. [DRUG CULTURE] to administer or supply a narcotic to someone 2. to create feelings of excitement, pleasure.

turn on the heat *v.* 1. to make uncomfortable, as by applying moral pressure 2. to expend as much energy as possible to achieve a goal.

turnout *n.* 1. the audience for any event 2. [DANCE] the angle at which a dancer's legs are positioned, placing the feet, as nearly as possible, at a 180-degree angle 3. [POLITICS] the number of voters participating in an election.

turn out *v.* 1. to be present 2. [DANCE] to place one's feet at an angle approaching 180 degrees 3. to vote in an election.

turn the tables *v.* to reverse a situation, usually to place an adversary at a disadvantage one has experienced oneself.

turn turtle *v.* 1. to become helpless 2. [SURFING] to lie on one's surfboard and grasp it with hands and legs, turning over with the board on top to avoid injury from a particularly dangerous wave.

turn up *v.* 1. to appear 2. to arrive 3. to be found.

turn up one's nose at something *v.* to scorn something.

turn up one's toes *v.* to die.

turtle doves *n.* lovers showing great affection for each other.

tux *n.* abbreviation for tuxedo.

twat *n.* 1. the vagina 2. a woman viewed as a sex object 3. a stupid woman.

twenty *n.* a twenty-dollar bill.

twenty-three skidoo *interj.* a nonsense expression popular in the 1920s.

twerp *n.* a foolish, obnoxious person.

twi-night double-header *n.* [BASEBALL] two successive baseball games played by the same two opposing teams on the same day, with the first game held in late afternoon and the second lasting into the night.

twink *n.* a homosexual.

twist someone around one's little finger *v.* to control someone.

twisted *adj.* 1. insane 2. perverted.

two-bit *adj.* 1. shoddy 2. inferior 3. of little value.

two-bits *n.* twenty-five cents.

two-by-four *adj.* small; insignificant.

twofer *n.* a ticket which admits two people to an event for the price of one.

two shakes of a lamb's tail *n.* 1. a short period of time 2. a moment.

two-shot *n.* [BROADCASTING] a scene with two actors.

two-spot *n.* a two-dollar bill; two dollars.

two-time *v.* to behave unfaithfully towards one's spouse or lover—*n.* two-timer.

two-time loser *n.* 1. a criminal sent to prison for the second time 2. a twice-divorced person.

two-way street *n.* a situation requiring reciprocal actions.

type cast *v.* [ENTERTAINMENT] to judge an actor only on past portrayals of one type of character or on looks alone, and to hire that actor only for similar roles.

typing pool *n.* [BUSINESS] a group of typists employed by a company to be at the disposal of all the executives.

U

ubble-gubble *n.* nonsense.

ugly *adj.* 1. obnoxious; despicable 2. [BLACK SLANG] having negroid features.

ump *n.* abbreviation for umpire.

umpteen *n.* a large number—*adj.* umpteenth.

unanswered *adj.* [SPORTS] of points scored by a player or a team in competition, not matched by the opposing player or team.

unattached *adj.* 1. not married 2. [SPORTS] not contracted to a specific team.

unc *n.* abbreviation for uncle.

Uncle Charlie *n.* [TRUCKERS' CB] the Federal Communications Commission or any of its representatives.

Uncle Dudley *n.* oneself. Usually in the expression "Now, tell your Uncle Dudley."

Uncle Sam *n.* the personification of the United States of America.

Uncle Sugar *n.* [CRIME] the Federal Bureau of Investigation.

Uncle Tom *n.* a black man who appears to other blacks to be subservient to whites. Often used by black radicals against black moderate leaders who advocate non-violence. From the novel *Uncle Tom's Cabin,* by Harriet Beecher Stowe (1852), and used originally to mean a long-suffering, kind and stoical black man, like the hero of the book.

uncool *adj.* unsophisticated; boorish; unpleasant.

under, get out from *v.* to extricate oneself from a troublesome situation.

undercover *adj.* clandestine.

underdog *n.* 1. an habitual victim 2. a weakling 3. one not likely to win.

undergrad *n.* or *adj.* abbreviation for undergraduate.

underground *n.* or *adj.* a clandestine group opposed to the current power structure and working to undermine it.

underhanded *adj.* 1. treacherous 2. sneaky.

under one's belt, get something *v.* 1. to eat something 2. to master knowledge or a skill previously unmastered.

under one's hat, keep something *v.* to keep something secret.

underpinnings *n.* 1. undergarments 2. the legs.

under the counter *adv.* surreptitiously—*adj.* secret.

under the daisies *adj.* dead.

under the table *adj.* drunk—*adv.* 1. secretly 2. illicitly.

under the weather *adj.* 1. ill 2. drunk.

underwraps *adv.* 1. hidden 2. secret.

undies *n.* abbreviation for undergarments.

unflappable *adj.* imperturbable.

ungepotchket *adj.* [YIDDISH] 1. bewildered 2. messy 3. ill-assorted.

unglued *adj.* emotionally upset.

unholy alliance *n.* [POLITICS] the unlikely partnership of natural political adversaries united against a common cause. From the Holy Alliance treaty of 1815 between Russia, Prussia, and Austria.

unisex *adj.* of styles, equally suitable for both men and women.

unmentionables *n.* undergarments.

un poco *n.* [SPANISH] a little.

unreal *adj.* 1. unbelievably excellent 2. surprisingly bad.

unwell *adj.* menstruating.

up *adj.* 1. lively, energetic, or optimistic 2. of eggs, fried on one side.

up anchor *v.* to leave. Often used as a command.

up and about, up and around *adj.* in good health after a period of illness.

up and at 'em *interj.* a call to begin work, activity—*adj.* 1. forceful 2. energetic 3. aggressive.

up and coming *adj.* newly successful and with great promise of future success.

up and down, look (someone or **something)** *v.* to examine summarily but thoroughly.

up-and-up *adj.* 1. honest 2. legitimate.

up-and up, on the *adv.* 1. in an honest manner 2. fairly.

up a tree *adv.* in difficulty.

up a wall, drive someone *v.* to frustrate or infuriate someone.

upbeat *adj.* [MUSIC] lively, energetic, or optimistic.

upchuck *v.* to regurgitate. Also used as a noun.

update *n.* the latest news—*v.* to revise.

up front *adv.* in advance, usually of a payment.

up his (her) alley *adj.* suited to one's tastes or abilities, as in "that's right up his alley."

up mail *n.* [POST OFFICE JARGON] mail ready for a carrier to deliver.

upper *n.* [DRUG CULTURE] any drug which increases the metabolism and induces a feeling of euphoria; an amphetamine.

upper crust *n.* the elite.

upper story *n.* the head, mind, brain.

uppity *adj.* impertinent.

ups and downs *n.* vicissitudes.

upscale *adj.* rich.

upset the apple cart *v.* to spoil someone's carefully laid plans. The Ancient Romans used to "upset a cart" with the same meaning.

up someone's alley, right *adv.* in some-

one's field of specialization.

up someone's ass *interj.* an expression of disdain and anger. An abbreviated form of "shove it or stick it up someone's (usually your) ass."

upstage *n.* [ENTERTAINMENT] the area of a stage farthest from the audience. In the past, stages were built on a slant and the area towards the rear was literally up compared with the area towards the front. *See* downstage *and* raked—*v.* to distract the focus of attention from the principal actor in a scene.

upstairs *n.* the head, mind, brain.

up stakes *v.* to leave. From the stakes driven in the ground to indicate possession of land and its boundaries, especially during the settling of the American frontier.

uptake, quick on the *adj.* 1. quick-witted 2. comprehending rapidly.

up the creek *adj.* in a difficult situation.

up the mark *v.* to raise a standard.

up there *adv.* in one's head, mind, brain.

up the river *adj.* imprisoned.

up the river without a paddle *See* up the creek.

uptight *adj.* 1. nervous 2. tense.

up to *v.* to be engaged in.

up to here *adv.* to the point of satiety.

up to snuff *adj.* 1. in operating order 2. in good health 3. of good quality.

up to the gills *adj.* or *adv.* drunk.

up-to-the-minute *adj.* [BROADCASTING] pertaining to the latest available data.

uptown, the boys *See* boys uptown, the.

up yours *interj.* an expression of belligerence and disdain. A euphemism for "up your ass."

use one's bean, head, noggin, or **noodle** *v.* 1. to use one's intelligence 2. to reason 3. to think.

user *n.* [DRUG CULTURE] one who uses narcotics.

ush *v.* to work as an usher.

utmost, the *n.* the most excellent, satisfying, pleasing.

V

V *n.* a five-dollar bill.

vacation *n.* a term in prison.

vag *n.* 1. a vagrant 2. a charge of vagrancy lodged against someone. Also used as a verb.

vamoose *v.* [SPANISH] to leave, usually quickly. From the Spanish *vamos,* meaning "let's go."

varnish remover *n.* any strong or bad-tasting drink.

varsity *adj.* collegiate. An abbreviated form of university.

vaude *n.* or *adj.* abbreviation for vaudeville.

VC *n.* acronym for Viet Cong.

VD *n.* acronym for venereal disease.

veep *n.* a vice-president.

veggies *n.* vegetables.

veggy *n.* a vegetarian.

velvet *n.* money to be spent frivolously.

verbal diarrhea *n.* verbosity; habitual chatter.

vestibule *n.* the buttocks.

vet *n.* 1. abbreviation for veteran 2. abbreviation for veterinarian.

vibes *n.* abbreviation for vibrations, i.e., feelings, positive or negative emotional responses, sensed but not verbalized.

vic *n.* [PRISON] a convict.

vine, the *n.* wine.

VIP *n.* acronym for very important person.

viper *n.* a treacherous person.

voice over *n.* [BROADCASTING] the spoken elements of a commercial or a show recorded separately from the visual aspect. Also used as a verb.

voodoo ball *n.* [BASEBALL] a baseball stitched in Haiti, a country noted for the practice of voodoo.

vulcanized *adj.* drunk.

W

wack, wackadoo, wacko *n.* an eccentric.

wack, off one's *adj.* crazy.

wacky *adj.* eccentric.

wad *n.* 1. a large amount of money 2. a roll of dollar bills.

wad, blow one's *v.* to spend all one's money.

waffle *v.* [POLITICS] to avoid committing oneself on an issue.

wagon *n.* [ENTERTAINMENT] a low platform on wheels that holds a section of scenery or a set piece so that it can be wheeled on and off stage as necessary.

wag one's chin *v.* to talk idly or excessively.

wagon, fix someone's *v.* 1. to retaliate 2. to do someone harm.

wagon, off the *adj.* drinking alcoholic beverages after a period of abstention.

wagon, on the *adj.* abstaining from use of alcoholic beverages.

wagon to a star, hitch one's *v.* to aspire to an ambitious goal.

wahoo *interj.* a cry of triumph—*n.* a boor.

wail *v.* 1. to play jazz music with great expertise 2. to leave.

walk *n.* [BASEBALL] a batter's privilege to walk to first base when the pitcher has thrown four balls deemed by the umpire to be unfit to hit (out of the strike zone) on that player's turn at bat. Also used as a verb—*v.* to be freed from prison.

walk, cock of the *See* cock-of-the-walk.

walk a flat *v.* [ENTERTAINMENT] to move a piece of scenery by carrying it vertically when manually changing the set during a play.

walk (all) over someone *v.* to take advantage of someone.

walkaway *n.* an easy or assured victory. Usually of a competition in which one competitor is known to be far superior to all the others.

walk heavy *v.* to behave as one of importance.

walkie-talkie *n.* a small portable radio transmitter and receiver.

walking-around money *n.* money that is meant to be spent frivolously.

walking dandruff *n.* body lice.

walking papers *n.* 1. a dismissal from employment 2. a rejection from friendship—*v.* "get (or give someone his or her) walking papers."

walk off *v.i.* to leave—*v.t.* to rid oneself of an undesired thing by walking. Often used concerning excess weight, drunkenness, anxiety, etc.

walk off with *v.t.* 1. to win (something) 2. to steal (something).

walk-on *n.* [ENTERTAINMENT] a small acting role that requires no dialogue. Also used as a verb.

walk out *n.* [LABOR] a strike by unionized workers, who leave their place of employment and collectively refuse to work under present conditions. Also used as a verb.

walk out on *v.t.* to desert.

walkover *n.* 1. an easy or assured victory 2. one easily defeated.

walk soft *v.* to conduct oneself with humility.

walk tall *v.* to conduct oneself with pride, dignity.

walk-up *n.* an apartment building without an elevator. Also used as an adjective.

walk wide *v.* to proceed with caution.

wall, drive someone up a *v.* to confuse, frustrate, or infuriate someone.

wall-eyed *adj.* drunk.

wallflower *n.* one who shyly awaits the attention of others at a social gathering, especially an unattractive or introverted girl or woman.

wall, go over the *v.* to escape from prison.

wall, go to the *v.* 1. to be forced into a desperate situation 2. to fall into bankruptcy in business.

wallop *n.* 1. a hard blow 2. a drink of liquor—*v.* 1. to strike; to thrash 2. to defeat.

wallop, pack a *v.* to have great power or strength.

wall, push someone to the *v.* to force someone to act in desperation.

wall-to-wall *adj.* completely filled with; containing as many of or as much as possible.

walrus *n.* a fat person.

wampum *n.* [AMERICAN INDIAN] money.

wangle *v.* 1. to manipulate cleverly 2. to persuade.

want ad *n.* an advertisement in the classified section of a publication indicating a job, residence, commodity, etc., available or desired.

wardheeler *n.* [POLITICS] 1. a politician who follows party policy assiduously 2. an aide who solicits votes and performs minor tasks for the party leaders. A ward in an urban political district. Heeling is a term used in training dogs and means to walk at one's master's heels.

war horse *n.* 1. an old person still active or enthusiastic 2. [POLITICS] an experienced politician. Usually in the expression "old war horse."

warmer upper *n.* 1. anything that creates warmth 2. anything which serves to ingratiate or to induce feelings of sympathy, friendship, etc. 3. anything which causes initial excitement, especially in preparation for something else 4. an exercise that serves to prepare someone for competition.

warm someone's ear *v.* to talk excessively to someone.

warm-up *n.* [SPORTS] a preparatory exercise.

warm up *v.* to exercise oneself in preparation.

war of nerves *n.* a conflict of interests or ideologies characterized by psychological pressure exerted by each side on the opposition.

war paint *n.* make-up.

warpath, on the *adj.* [AMERICAN INDIAN] 1. angry 2. prepared to fight.

warped *adj.* perverted.

wash *v.* [CRIME] to invest ill-gotten money in legitimate business enterprises, paying taxes on it and thus cleaning it of the stigma of its source.

wash, come out in the *v.* to be revealed eventually, after having been hidden.

wash down *v.t.* to drink something after having eaten something.

washed out *adj.* 1. tired 2. wan 3. colorless.

washed up *adj.* 1. finished 2. ending in failure.

wash one's hands of *v.t.* to disclaim responsibility.

washout *n.* a failure.

WASP *n.* acronym for White Anglo-Saxon Protestant, once the ethnic majority in the United States. Also used as an adjective.

waste *v.* to kill.

wasted *adj.* 1. killed 2. having no money.

waster *n.* 1. a killer 2. a gun.

watchdog committee *n.* [POLITICS] a committee that monitors government expenditures to eliminate wasteful spending.

water, above *adj.* out of trouble.

water, first *See* first water, of the.

water, hold *v.* of an idea, to be logical.

water, in deep *adj.* in trouble.

water, in hot *adj.* in trouble.

water, like *adv.* freely.

water at the mouth *v.* 1. to salivate in anticipation; hence 2. to be envious.

waterboy *n.* one who performs minor tasks for a superior.

Watergate *n.* 1. a downfall 2. an embarrassing situation causing ultimate repudiation and defeat. From the scandal following the break-in of Democratic headquarters in the Watergate hotel in Washington, D.C., by the Nixon Republicans in 1972 in order to place eavesdropping devices and to learn certain information. Also used as a verb.

water hole *n.* [TRUCKERS' CB] any rest and refreshment stopping place for truck drivers.

watering hole *n.* a bar.

waterloo *n.* a decisive defeat. From Napoleon's defeat at Waterloo by the forces led by the Duke of Wellington in 1815.

waterworks, turn on the *v.* to cry.

wax *v.* 1. to defeat conclusively 2. to excel.

waxing *n.* a beating.

wax, put on *v.t.* to record.

waxworks *n.* [POLITICS] the honored guests at a political dinner who are characterized as figures in a wax museum because they must appear intelligent and candid at all times.

way, in a big *adv.* 1. enthusiastically 2. fully.

way-out *adj.* 1. excellent 2. unusual 3. esoteric. Also used as an interjection.

weak sister *n.* a coward.

wearies, the *n.* a state of fatigue or depression.

wear more than one hat *v.* to be qualified in several different fields.

wear one's heart on one's sleeve *v.* to make no attempt to conceal one's love interest.

wear out one's welcome *v.* to impose one's presence on others to the point of being no longer welcome.

wear thin *v.* to become tedious, boring, insufficient.

weasel out *v.* to withdraw in a cowardly fashion.

weasel words *n.* misleading statements that disguise a lack of substance to an argument or to a position held. Popularized by President Theodore Roosevelt.

weather, under the *adj.* 1. ill 2. weak 3. drunk.

weed *n.* 1. marijuana 2. a cigarette.

weeds *n.* clothing.

weed tea *n.* marijuana.

weekend warriors *n.* members of the National Guard.

weenie, weinie *n.* 1. a frankfurter 2. the penis.

weeper *n.* a work of popular literature, cinema, theater, etc., geared to incite tears.

weeps, put on the *v.* to cry.

wee-wee *n.* [BABY TALK] urine—*v.* to urinate.

weight *n.* 1. importance 2. influence—*v.* "throw one's weight around": 1. to behave insolently 2. to demonstrate one's importance in an obnoxious fashion.

weirdie, weirdo *n.* an eccentric.

welch, welsh *v.* to fail to fulfill an obligation.

welcome to the NFL *interj.* [SPORTS] a humorous warning of rough confrontations to come. Often used in business. From the National Football League of teams whose activities are often brutal.

well-fixed *adj.* 1. rich 2. secure.

well-heeled *adj.* 1. rich 2. secure.

well, I'll be *interj.* an exclamation of surprise.

well-off *adj.* 1. rich 2. secure.

well-oiled *adj.* drunk.

well-stacked *adj.* 1. of a woman, fully developed, i.e., with large breasts.

well-to-do *adj.* rich.

wench *n.* an attractive woman.

western *n.* 1. a work of popular literature or cinema dealing with the American West 2. an omelet made with ham, onions, and green peppers.

wet *v.* to urinate.

wet, all *adj.* entirely mistaken.

wetback *n.* an illegal immigrant to the United States from Mexico. So called because a chief means of immigration is to swim across the Rio Grande into Texas.

wet behind the ears *adj.* inexperienced. From the last place to dry on a newborn animal.

wet blanket *n.* a depressing, gloomy person.

wet-head *n.* a dull, boring person 2. an inexperienced person.

wet hen, mad as a *adj.* very angry.

wet-nose *n.* an inexperienced person.

wet one's goozle *v.* to drink alcoholic beverages.

wet one's whistle *v.* to drink, especially alcoholic beverages.

whack *n.* 1. a blow 2. a chance; an attempt—*v.* 1. to strike 2. to apportion 3. [DRUG CULTURE] to dilute a drug.

whack, out of *adj.* not functioning properly.

whack at, have a (or **take a**) *v.t.* to attempt something; to take a chance at something.

whacked out *adj.* 1. exhausted 2. crazy, eccentric 3. [DRUG CULTURE] high on drugs.

whack off *v.* to masturbate.

whack out *v.t.* to produce rapidly and automatically.

whack someone out *v.* to kill someone.

whack up *v.* to divide, apportion.

whale *n.* a fat person.

whale of a *adj.* an exceptional specimen of.

wham *v.* to strike.

wham-bam *adj.* 1. rough 2. rapid.

wham-bam-thank-you-ma'am *n.* or *adj.* a rapid or emotionless act of coitus.

whammo *adj.* energetic; forceful. Also used as an interjection.

whammy *n.* bad luck.

whammy on someone, put the *v.* 1. to wish someone bad luck 2. to cause someone misfortune.

whatchamacallit *n.* any object for which the proper name is not known.

what cooks, what's cooking? *interj.* what is happening?

what do you say? *interj.* a greeting: how are you?

what-for, the *n.* punishment, especially verbal abuse or a thrashing. Often used in the construction "give someone the what-for."

what gives? *interj.* what is happening?

what have you, what not *n.* anything else not mentioned specifically but pertaining to other things in a particular group.

what it takes *n.* the intangible qualities needed for success. Often used in the construction "have what it takes."

what makes someone tick *n.* 1. one's motives 2. one's psychological make-up.

what-not *n.* 1. miscellaneous items 2. small objects with only decorative value.

what say? *See* what do you say?

what's going down? *interj.* what is happening?

whatsisface *n.* any person whose name is not known. Generally, a derogatory term.

whatsisname *n.* any person whose name is not known.

whatsits *n.* any object for which the proper name is not known.

what's the rave? *interj.* what is happening?

what's up? *interj.* what is happening?

what's what *n.* the actual state of affairs.

what's with someone? *interj.* an abbreviated form of "what is the matter with someone?"

what the deuce *interj.* an exclamation of frustration, annoyance, resignation, or disbelief.

what the devil *interj.* an exclamation of disbelief or annoyance.

what the hell *interj.* an expression of disregard for possible consequences of an action.

whatzis *n.* any object for which the

proper name is not known.

wheel *n.* an important person. Often, "big wheel."

wheeler-dealer *n.* [GAMBLING] one who engages in complex, often illegal, business deals. From the spinning of a roulette wheel and the dealing of cards in gambling—*v.* wheel and deal.

wheel horse *n.* [POLITICS] a steady political worker faithful to the party. From the horse in a team who shoulders the greatest work load.

wheelman *n.* [CRIME] the driver of an escape vehicle.

wheels *n.* a motor vehicle, usually an automobile.

wheels, on *adv.* to an extreme degree, usually used with a negative connotation.

wheeze *n.* an old familiar joke or story.

where it's at *n.* 1. the truth; reality 2. the ultimate goal, where happiness and understanding are found.

where one is coming from *n.* one's point of view based on past experiences.

where one's head is at *n.* 1. that which occupies one's thoughts at any given moment 2. one's philosophy of life.

where the action is *n.* the center of activity, especially of the most current popular activity.

whiff *v.i.* [BASEBALL] to strike out, of a batter—*v.t.* to strike someone out, of a baseball pitcher.

whing-ding *See* wing-ding.

whip *n.* [POLITICS] a politician responsible for the presence of party members at a voting session. Often called a "party whip." From "whipper-in," who keeps the dogs on the trail in a fox hunt.

whippersnapper *n.* an impudent person of little importance. Literally, one who snaps a whip to make an impressive show of strength.

whipsaw *v.* [POLITICS] to receive bribes from two opposing sources. From the tool with two blades, able to cut in both directions simultaneously.

whip through something *v.* to accomplish something rapidly.

whip up *v.t.* 1. to imagine 2. to devise 3. of food, to prepare.

whirlybird *n.* a helicopter.

whiskey tenor *n.* one given to singing when drunk.

whispering campaign *n.* 1. [POLITICS] an attempt to undermine a candidate's chances in an election by subtle but persistent references to irregularities in private life or physical or mental health 2. slander.

whistle blower *n.* an informant.

whistle stop *n.* a town too small to merit a regular stop by the train passing through.

whistle stop tour *n.* [POLITICS] a politician's campaign trip across the district—or across the country in the case of national office—with stops in various communities to make speeches and gain local support.

white *adj.* honest; honorable; fair; decent.

white collar *adj.* pertaining to workers not engaged in manual labor—*n.* an ice cream soda made with vanilla ice cream and vanilla syrup.

white elephant *n.* a useless, encumbering possession. In Siam, any captured albino elephant became the property of the emperor. To cause the ruin of any adversary, the emperor could give a white elephant as a gift which the recipient could not use for labor nor destroy, but had to feed at great cost.

white face *n.* a circus clown. From the make-up traditionally worn by clowns completely masking their normal face.

white flight *n.* the emigration of the white population *en masse* from a neighborhood when other racial groups move in.

white-haired boy *See* fair-haired boy.

white hat *n.* a good person. Traditionally, the hero in a cowboy movie wears a white hat.

white hope *n.* [BOXING] a white contender seeking the title held by a black boxer.

white lightning *n*. 1. homemade liquor 2. [DRUG CULTURE] LSD.

white meat *n*. 1. anything easily accomplished 2. a white person considered as a sexual partner.

whiteout *n*. a loss of depth perception and a general disorientation caused by the uniform whiteness of snow and sky under glaring winter sun.

white paper *n*. [POLITICS] a statement of government policy.

white slave *n*. a female abducted and forced into prostitution.

white slavery *n*. prostitution against one's will.

white stuff *n*. [DRUG CULTURE] cocaine.

white trash *n*. poor, uneducated white people. Originally used in the South to describe impoverished rural dwellers.

whitewash *v*. 1. to ignore or cover up misdeeds; thus 2. to restore a reputation. Often used in politics.

whitey *n*. a derogatory term for a white person.

whiz *n*. one exceptionally proficient in any given field—*v*. to speed.

whiz-bang *adj*. exceptional.

whodunit *n*. a work of popular detective literature, cinema, theater, etc.

whole ball of wax *n*. anything in its entirety.

whole hog *adv*. completely; without reservation.

whole shebang *n*. anything in its entirety.

whomp *v*. to defeat conclusively.

whoop-de-do *n*. celebration, excitement, gaiety.

whoopee *interj*. a cry of triumph or delight.

whoopee cushion *n*. an inflatable rubber bladder which, when pressed, emits air causing a loud noise similar to the sound of intestinal gas emission. A whoopee cushion is often hidden under a seat cushion and used as a prank to embarrass one who sits on it.

whoopee water *n*. liquor.

whooper-dooper *n*. a noisy celebration—*adj*. exciting, wonderful, exceptional.

whoop it up *v*. to create a noisy disturbance, as in celebrating.

whop *v.t.* 1. to strike 2. to defeat conclusively.

whopping *adj*. surprisingly large. Also used as an adverb.

whozis *n*. a person or object whose proper name is not known.

wicked *adj*. excellent.

wide open *adj*. 1. without protection 2. [CRIME] without interference by the police 3. unrestricted 4. unprejudiced.

wide open, crack something *v*. to expose something previously hidden from public scrutiny.

widow line *n*. [PRINTING] the last line of a paragraph that is less than a full line and begins the top of the next page in a magazine, book, etc.

wig, flip one's *v*. to become excited, outraged.

wigged out *adj*. 1. crazy 2. [DRUG CULTURE] high on drugs.

wiggle on, get a *v*. to hurry.

wiggy *adj*. wild, exciting, crazy, etc.

wild *adj*. 1. exciting 2. excellent.

wild about (someone or something) *adj*. 1. excited about 2. enamored of.

wildcat *n*. one easily angered.

wild goose chase *n*. the pursuit of a misleading goal.

wild track *n*. [BROADCASTING] sound effects, recordings that can be inserted in part in any broadcast.

willies, the *n*. a state of nervousness, fear, anticipation of fright.

willy-boy *n*. 1. a coward 2. an effeminate male.

willy-nilly *adv*. regardless; in any case; whether one wants to or not.

Willy Weaver *n*. [TRUCKERS' CB] a drunk driver who weaves in and out of lanes.

wimp *n*. a weak, ineffectual, or insipid person.

win *n*. a conquest.

Winchester *n.* a rifle. Originally, one manufactured by the Winchester company; now, any rifle.

wind *n.* 1. the air 2. excessive chatter.

wind, give someone the wind *v.* 1. to reject someone from friendship 2. to dismiss someone from employment.

wind, in the *adj.* 1. faintly detectable 2. imminent.

windbag *n.* a garrulous person.

wind down *v.* to terminate gradually.

winder upper *n.* a conclusion.

windjammer *n.* [CIRCUS SLANG] a member of the circus band.

wind out of someone's sails, take the *v.* to diminish someone's impact.

window, out the *adj.* wasted; futile.

windows *n.* eyeglasses.

window washer *n.* [TRUCKERS' CB] a rainstorm.

wind up *n.* 1. a conclusion 2. [BASEBALL] of a pitcher, rotating the arm while holding the ball before throwing it 3. [BROADCASTING] the last feature on a news broadcast—*v.* 1. to conclude 2. to rotate one's arm before throwing a ball.

wind up, get one's *v.* to become indignant, outraged.

windy *adj.* verbose.

wing *n.* 1. a person's arm 2. [BASEBALL] a pitcher's throwing arm.

wing-ding *n.* 1. a spree 2. a party.

wingdinger *n.* anything exceptional.

wing it *v.* to leave.

wings *n.* [ENTERTAINMENT] the area off to the left and to the right of a stage where actors wait to make their entrances and where scenery and props are kept for use in the production.

wings, earn one's *See* earn one's wings.

wino *n.* one who habitually becomes drunk on wine.

win one's spurs *v.* to attain recognition in any given field.

win out *v.* to eventually overcome obstacles and succeed.

win out over someone *v.* 1. to better another's performance 2. to be preferred.

wipe it off *v.* 1. to forget an affront, an injury 2. to stop smiling, an abbreviated form of "wipe a smile off one's face."

wipeout *n.* 1. [SPORTS] a dangerous fall, usually causing injury. In surfing, a huge wave knocking a surfer off the board 2. a complete defeat 3. a decisive victory—*v.* 1. to kill 2. to defeat definitively.

wired *adj.* known intimately and understood. Often used by surfers in reference to local surfing conditions.

wired up *adj.* 1. elated 2. [DRUG CULTURE] high on drugs.

wire on someone, put the *v.* to calumniate.

wire puller *n.* one who seeks to use personal influence to gain advantages and favors. From the wires used to move marionettes.

wire to wire *n.* [HORSE RACING] from beginning to end. From the starting line to the finish line in a horse race, formerly marked by overhead wire.

wise *adj.* impudent.

-wise *suffix* 1. in the realm of 2. in reference to.

wise, get *v.* to become aware.

wise, put someone *v.* 1. to reveal necessary information to someone 2. to make someone aware of a situation.

wiseacre, wise apple *n.* an impudent person.

wisecrack *n.* 1. a joke 2. a flippant and impertinent remark. Coined by the early twentieth-century comedian Chic Sale.

wisecracker *n.* one who often jokes or teases.

wiseguy *n.* 1. one given to levity 2. [CRIME] a member of the mob.

wise hombre *n.* one who is knowledgeable and alert.

wisenheimer *n.* a wiseacre or wiseguy. *See* wiseacre *and* wiseguy.

wise to something *adj.* in full knowledge of something.

wise up *v.* to become more circumspect, aware.

wishbone *n.* [FOOTBALL] a formation of players with the fullback, quarterback, and two halfbacks so positioned as to resemble a wishbone.

wishy-washy *adj.* 1. feeble 2. mediocre 3. lacking strong emotion 4. without conviction.

witch *n.* an ill-tempered woman.

witch hunt *n.* [POLITICS] a campaign of persecution.

with *adj.* of food, served with all the standard accompaniments for a specific dish.

with a bang *adv.* 1. immediately successful 2. enthusiastically; energetically 3. forcefully.

with a grain (or **pinch**) **of salt** *See* grain of salt, with a.

with bells on *adv.* 1. promptly 2. enthusiastically.

with it *adj.* 1. alert 2. knowledgeable.

with it, get *v.* 1. to begin a task 2. to live up to expectations 3. to become aware and adapt oneself to a changing situation.

with knobs on *adv.* 1. enthusiastically 2. promptly.

with legs *adj.* pertaining to something which sells so rapidly that it seems to walk out of the store on its own power.

with tits on *adv.* 1. enthusiastically 2. promptly.

wizard *n.* one with expertise in any given field.

wobbly *n.* a member of the Industrial Workers of the World.

wolf *n.* a seducer. From the predatory aspect of the wolf.

wolf whistle *n.* a whistle of admiration indicating interest in an attractive woman.

woman-chaser, womanizer *n.* one who pursues women for sexual favors.

womp *v.* to defeat conclusively.

wonk *n.* a student who studies very hard. Also used as a verb.

wonky *adj.* [BRITISH SLANG] shaky, feeble, etc.

wooden-head *n.* a fool.

woofled *adj.* drunk.

wool over someone's eyes, pull the *v.* 1. to deceive 2. to obscure the truth.

woozy *adj.* dizzy; dazed; drunk.

wop *n.* a derogatory term for an Italian. An acronym for "without papers," stamped on the entry forms of immigrants to the United States who traveled without passports during the great Italian immigration at the beginning of the twentieth century.

word processing unit *n.* [BUSINESS] typing pool. *See* typing pool.

workaholic *n.* one addicted to work. A humorous term based on alcoholic. *See* -aholic as a suffix.

working ball *n.* [BOWLING] a forceful spinning ball capable of scattering the pins it hits.

workout *n.* a period of strenuous physical exercise, often in preparation for a competition.

work out *v.* 1. to exercise 2. to train for a physical competition 3. to conclude satisfactorily.

work over *v.t.* to thrash—*n.* working over, workover.

works *n.* [DRUG CULTURE] all the necessary paraphernalia to administer an injection of narcotics.

works, got the *v.* to be the victim of extreme measures.

works, give the *v.* to murder.

works, gum up the *v.* 1. to impede progress 2. to render inoperable.

works, shoot the *v.* to risk everything on one chance or play.

works, the *n.* 1. something in its entirety 2. all available elements.

work up *v.* to bring about or cause (a sweat) by vigorous activity.

world, out of this *adj.* exceptional, exciting, and thrilling.

world class *adj.* [SPORTS] superior in any given field. Literally, fit to compete for the world championship in any given field.

worm *n.* a despicable person.

worm in *v.* to insinuate oneself in an

advantageous situation.

worm out of *v.* to seek to withdraw or to withdraw in a cowardly fashion.

worm something out of someone *v.* to induce someone to reveal secret information or to give something desired.

worry wart *n.* one who frets or worries excessively.

worth one's salt *adj.* meriting one's pay. From the Latin *salarium,* wages paid to a soldier for the purchase of salt.

wow *n.* anything exceptional or admirable—*v.* 1. to startle 2. to please—*interj.* an exclamation of surprise, admiration, etc.

wowser *n.* [CHIEFLY AUSTRALIAN SLANG] a person who is vigorously puritanical, strait-laced, etc.

wrapped up *adj.* 1. occupied 2. assured.

wrap up *n.* 1. a conclusion 2. [BROADCASTING/FILM] the successful conclusion of a recording or filming project—*v.* to conclude. From the process of wrapping purchases for a buyer at the conclusion of a sale.

wreck *n.* 1. a dilapidated vehicle 2. one in a state of anxiety.

wrench *n.* [AUTO RACING] an auto mechanic.

wringer, put someone through the *v.* to cause someone difficulty, thus sapping him of strength. From the wringer on old-fashioned washing machines that squeezed all the water out of clothing.

wrinkle *n.* 1. a new approach to a situation 2. a clever idea.

write-in *n.* [POLITICS] a candidate whose name does not appear on the ballot but is written in by the voter. Also used as an adjective and a verb.

write off *v.* to dismiss someone or something from future consideration. Also used as a noun.

write out *v.t.* [ENTERTAINMENT] to delete dialogue, action, or a character from a script.

write-up *n.* a written account of something, usually favorable to the subject. Also used as a verb.

wrong number *n.* a mistaken notion.

wrong side of the bed, get up on the *v.* to be in a bad mood. From the superstition that rising on the left side of the bed brings a day of misfortune and ill-humor.

wrong side of the tracks *n.* a socially unacceptable background.

wrong with someone, be in *v.* to be in disfavor with someone.

wussy *n.* an effeminate man.

X

X *n.* a signature. From the practice of illiterates signing official documents with an X, witnessed by someone who can read.

X marks the spot an expression indicating the arrival at a goal. From the X on a map, supposedly marking the spot where treasure was buried by pirates.

X on the line, put one's *v.* to sign one's name

X out *v.* to cross out.

X-rated *adj.* suitable for adults only, usually indicating something pornographic.

X-ray machine *n.* [TRUCKERS' CB] a police radar unit.

XYZ *interj.* an admonition to "examine your zipper," indicating that the zipper on a pair of trousers has opened.

Y

yack *n*. 1. a joke 2. anything laughable 3. a laugh—*v*. 1. to prattle 2. to laugh.

yackety-yack *n*. excessive or idle chatter—*interj*. an expression of disdain indicating disbelief in someone's words or annoyance at excessive chatter.

yahoo *n*. a coarse, vicious person. From the race of degraded brutes in Jonathan Swift's *Gulliver's Travels*.

yak *v*. to talk too much or idly; to chatter—*n*. idle or voluble talk.

yammer *v*. 1. to talk excessively 2. to scold 3. to complain.

yank, yankee *n*. an American.

yap *n*. 1. the mouth 2. a noisy person 3. chatter 4. a complaint—*v*. 1. to chatter 2. to complain.

yard *n*. a one-hundred dollar bill—*v*. 1. to commit adultery 2. to be unfaithful to one's current lover.

yardbird *n*. 1. a convict 2. an ex-convict.

yatter *v*. to prattle. Also used as a noun.

yea big *adj*. as big as this, always accompanied by a physical gesture indicating size.

yeah *interj*. yes.

yeah-yeah *interj*. a sarcastic expression of disbelief.

yeah-yeah-yeah *interj*. an expression of disdain for idle talk.

yegg *n*. a criminal.

yellow *adj*. cowardly.

yellow-bellied *adj*. cowardly.

yellow dog contract *n*. [LABOR] a now illegal contract between company management and a new employee in which the employee promises not to join a labor union while employed by the company.

yellow journalism *n*. sensationalism in newspaper stories to startle or influence readers.

yellow streak *n*. a tendency to cowardice.

yellow sunshine *n*. [DRUG CULTURE] LSD.

yen *n*. [CHINESE] a strong desire; a craving. In Chinese, literally "opium smoke."

yenta *n*. [YIDDISH] a gossip.

yep *interj*. yes.

yes-girl *n*. a girl who willingly accords sexual favors.

yes-man *n*. 1. one who always agrees with superiors 2. a flatterer 3. one who never displays personal convictions. Coined by sports cartoonist T. A. Dorgan.

yeye, ye-ye *adj*. fashionable or sophisticated.

yid *n*. a derogatory term for a Jewish person.

yippee *interj*. an exclamation of triumph or pleasure.

yippie *n*. a member of the Youth International Party, a student radical group of the late 1960s that came into particular prominence during the 1968 Democratic Convention in Chicago.

yob *n*. [BRITISH SLANG] a hoodlum.

yock *n*. a loud laugh or something evoking a loud laugh. Also used as a verb.

yoke *v*. [CRIME] to grab a victim with one arm held around the victim's neck and usually holding a knife to the victim's throat.

you bet *interj*. [GAMBLING] an expression of affirmation.

189

you can say that again *interj.* an expression of emphatic agreement with what has just been said.

you-know-what *n.* a purposely unnamed item which is known commonly to all concerned.

young Turk *n.* a dynamic, forceful, usually young person who rejects long established policies for newer ways to attack problems.

yours truly *n.* oneself. From the standard closing of a letter before the signature.

you said it *interj.* an exclamation of affirmation.

yow *interj.* an exclamation of pain or surprise.

yo-yo *n.* a fool.

yuk *n.* a loud laugh of amusement, or something evoking such a laugh. Also used as a verb.

yummy *adj.* delicious.

yum-yums *n.* [BABY TALK] 1. sweets 2. any food.

yup *interj.* yes.

Z

Z *n.* [DRUG CULTURE] one ounce of a narcotic.

zaftig *adj.* [YIDDISH] plump and voluptuous.

zap *n.* 1. a confrontation 2. a humiliation—*v.* 1. to kill 2. to shoot 3. to defeat 4. to impress.

Zelda *n.* a stupid, boring woman.

zero hour *n.* 1. the time of final reckoning 2. a decisive moment. From the military term indicating the proposed moment of an attack.

zero in *v.* to focus activity.

ziggety, hot ziggety *interj.* an exclamation of enthusiasm, delight.

zilch *n.* 1. nothing; zero 2. a person of little consequence, i.e., a nobody. From the name of a character in the *Ballyhoo* magazine of the 1930s.

zillion *n.* a great number.

zing *n.* energy, enthusiasm, liveliness.

zinger *n.* the climactic remark in an argument or speech.

zingy *adj.* lively, energetic, enthusiastic.

zip *n.* 1. energy; verve 2. nothing; zero—*v.* to move quickly or energetically.

zip gun *n.* a homemade gun used especially by teenage gang members.

zip one's lip *v.* to remain silent.

zippy *adj.* lively, energetic.

zit *n.* a pimple, especially one on the face.

zit doctor *n.* a dermatologist.

zombi, zombie *n.* a stupid, boorish, or unemotional person.

zonked, zonked out *adj.* 1. exhausted 2. drunk 3. under the influence of drugs.

zoo *n.* [TRUCKERS' CB] a police station.

zoom in on something *v.* [PHOTOGRAPHY] to focus energy on some project. From the use of the zoom lens in photography that permits a quick change from wide to narrow angle setting and close-up of one specific area.

zot *n.* nothing; zero.

zowie *interj.* an exclamation of surprise or delight.

Z's, cut some *v.* [TRUCKERS' CB] to sleep.

191